HELL
WOULDN'T
STOP

HELL WOULDN'T STOP

AN ORAL HISTORY OF THE BATTLE OF WAKE ISLAND

CHET CUNNINGHAM

CARROLL & GRAF PUBLISHERS
NEW YORK

HELL WOULDN'T STOP
An Oral History of the Battle of Wake Island

Carroll & Graf Publishers
An Imprint of Avalon Publishing Group Incorporated
161 William Street, 16th Floor
New York, NY 10038

Library of Congress Cataloging-in-Publication Data is available.

ISBN: 0-7867-1096-9

Designed by Kathleen Lake, Neuwirth & Associates, Inc.

Printed in the United States of America
Distributed by Publishers Group West

This book is respectfully dedicated
to my brother, Pvt. Kenneth Eugene
Cunningham, USMC, who gave his
youth to the Marine Corps only to
have it snatched away with forty-four
months of slave labor in Japan and China.

I wish to acknowledge the dozens of people who helped me in researching and writing this book: Sergeant Major Ewing E. Laporte, USMC retired, for his help in locating the 120 men who had been on Wake Island; Franklin D. Gross and his WIG-WAG newsletter for helping me spread the word to contact the Wake defenders; James O. King and Laporte for reading the manuscript and offering suggestions and changes. A special thanks to every marine, sailor, and soldier who contributed his experiences to this oral history. There are over seventy of you, and I salute you. An extra thanks to my editor Peter Skutches who helped in organizing the material, and to Claiborne Hancock for guiding the book through the whole process from script to final book. My everlasting thanks to my brother who left me a thirty-page manuscript about his experiences in the Japanese slave labor camps for forty-four months.

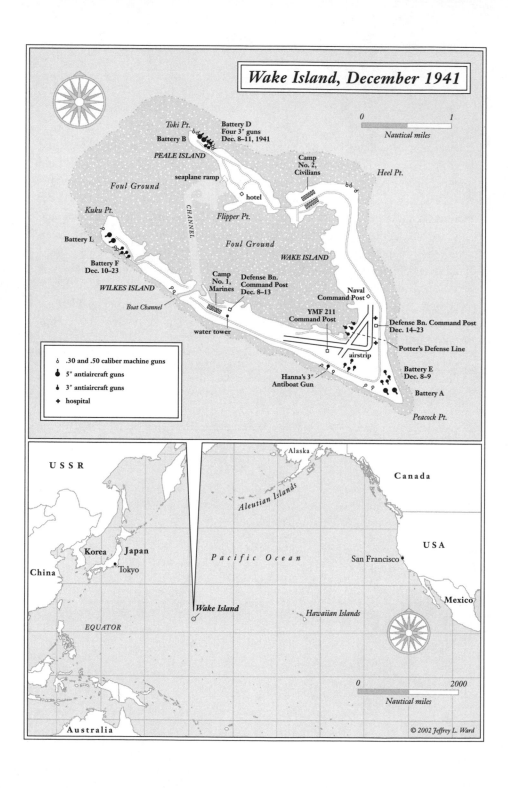

CONTENTS

THE
BEGINNING

M y brother had been gone for over two years before I realized that I knew very little about what happened to him during sixteen horrendous days in December 1941. My brother—Private Kenneth Eugene Cunningham, U.S. Marine Corps—was one of the heroes of Wake Island who fought gallantly from December 8 to December 23 on a tiny speck of an atoll in the middle of the Pacific Ocean at the start of World War II.

Suddenly, after fifty years, I needed to know what he did during those days. I needed to talk to men who had been on Wake Island at the same time he was. Perhaps some of those marines or navy men would remember him.

I knew about my brother's forty-four months in a number of different Japanese prisoner of war camps. He had written a thirty-seven-page manuscript about his POW days shortly after his return. I had read that account years ago and felt a surge of compassion for his suffering and amazement at his strength. I thanked him for writing it. But you didn't hug my brother and blurt out just how much you admired him. Ken wasn't a hugger.

Now, more than sixty years later, I was still wondering about Ken's sixteen days of fighting on Wake Island. What had he done those first few days of the war, that time when, as one marine said, "Hell wouldn't stop"? Could I discover what he did? Could I hope to find men who knew him on Wake Island and in the prison camps?

I'm a writer, so I at once thought about doing a book. But who would want to read an account of a battle that had long ago passed into history? Two generations had been born since then, and most of those individuals don't even know where or what Wake Island is. They have no idea how vital that tiny horseshoe atoll was in the military planning of the Japanese high command and of the U.S. military strategists. Many nations in that era planned and plotted out war games and war contingencies—strategies they would use in the event that a war came. Wake Island played a critical part in the plans of both sides, but would anyone be interested in such historical detail, no matter how vital, today?

I plunged ahead, determined that I would do the research for two reasons: first, to find out what Ken did during the sixteen days of fighting; second, to put it all together into a book honoring both the men who died on Wake Island and those who endured the forty-four months in the Japanese prison camps.

My long search began with a phone call to the Miramar Marine Corps Air Station in San Diego. The public information person there told me that she knew of no groups of Wake Island survivors, but gave me the phone number of *Leatherneck* magazine, the Marine Corps journal. Colonel Walt Ford, the editor, told me about a group called the Defenders of Wake Island. He provided me with the name and phone number of Sergeant Major Ewing E. Laporte (Ret.), a Wake Island survivor and one of the men who helps keep the organization together. Sergeant Major Laporte told me that the group was still functioning and that he would send me a mailing list of the active members and widows of members. I explained to him what I was doing, how I was trying to dig up any information I could about my brother, and to write a book about the sixteen days of fighting on Wake and the forty-four months in Japanese POW camps from the personal memories of the men who were there.

So it began. Franklin D. Gross at the defenders organization publishes a bulletin called *WIG WAG* for its members four times a year. I could hardly believe my good fortune. I now had a gold mine of 140 names of marines, sailors, and army men, or their widows, who had been on the same ground where my brother had fought. I then wrote a carefully worded letter to all the people on the list about my search for any memories they might have of my brother. I asked them to share with me anything they had written or might still remember about the battle on Wake Island at the start of the war and their almost four years as POWs.

Soon I discovered another group called the Survivors of Wake, Guam, and Cavite, headquartered in Boise, Idaho. These were some of the 1,146 civilian construction workers who also had been stationed on Wake Island and captured. I was, however, mainly interested in the military men.

I received many responses, some quickly, some slowly; from many others I heard nothing at all. I had to remember that all these men were near or just past eighty years of age. Memories can fade or in some cases disappear altogether. Many of the men are ill, and a lot of them simply do not want to remember those dangerous days and the prison time that followed.

Material began to mount. None of the men remembered my brother, though. His last name was the same as that of the head naval officer on the island, Commander Winfield Scott Cunningham, but the coincidence didn't help. Still, I kept digging, if without much success, to find out what Ken had done during the fighting.

Before he joined the marines, Ken had a hard time at home. Our family had been blown out of Nebraska in 1937 during the dust bowl. My father was a farmer and had suffered six years without a money crop. He sold his farm equipment, the bank took the farm, and we picked up and moved to Oregon. Our family of five arrived with a bankroll of $120.00.

Things were not any easier in Oregon in the depression years. Our father worked at whatever jobs he could find. He quickly realized that farming in Oregon was tremendously different than in Nebraska. That first winter we ate a lot of oatmeal and grapefruit because both were cheap.

Ken started high school. He had one good shirt and one pair of pants to wear. He wore them every day. Ken had some trouble adapting to the new school. At home, he argued with our folks. Then one day, when he was sixteen, he left home. He hitchhiked from Oregon to California, where he went to work in a garage. After six months he returned home and shortly after that joined the CCC, the Civilian Conservation Corps. There he learned how to operate heavy construction equipment like bulldozers, dump trucks, and graders, as well as how to fight forest fires and to work at forest conservation.

When Ken was seventeen, he and his best friend, Bud Reeher, joined the marines. They entered boot camp together at the Marine Corps Recruit Depot in San Diego, but then were split up. Ken's ability to operate construction equipment got him assigned to the First Marine Defense Battalion that was sent to Wake Island. Later, as the war intensified, Bud Reeher was killed by a Japanese sniper on Bougainville.

I was there when my brother came home in 1945 to a subdued welcome. No brass band, no speech by the mayor, no parade up Main Street of our little town. Not even a promotion to corporal after serving in the Marine Corps for five years; just a quick discharge in Oakland and a flight home. Our mother, who had almost lost her mind with worry during his prison camp years, was relieved and happy that our family was together again. We invited in the uncles, aunts, and cousins and had a "glad you're back" get-together. Ken was embarrassed by all the attention.

For a week he gloried in being free. "Free at last" was not coined in the sixties. It was the immediate cry of thousands of prisoners of war when the U.S. forces liberated them and their Japanese and German guards fled the camps and tried to disappear in the fabric of their homelands.

Once back home, Ken did the things he had missed during his prison camp days. An ardent fisherman, he bought a motorboat to fish in the Columbia River. A talented wood carver, he made and painted dozens of all-wood, full-sized duck decoys for hunters.

Ken married a few months after he returned home. It happened too fast; he wasn't ready yet. A baby came and the marriage ended. Ken struggled to adjust to civilian life. Twice more he married. He had three children. With his third wife, Ken settled happily into marriage for the rest of his life. He accepted the duties and responsibilities of a family man, and he met the pressures of being his own master and guiding his life. He was broken-hearted, though, when his favorite daughter was killed by a wild-eyed gunman in a random shooting.

I watched my brother's return to civilian life in Forest Grove, Oregon, where we grew up. One of his first jobs after the war was with the Washington County Sheriff's Department. There was no formal training for that level of policing in those days. He was an ex-marine and could handle a firearm; he was hired as a deputy sheriff. He didn't stay with the agency long, and he was soon hunting a job again. During this time he took flying lessons and earned his private pilot's license. One day he took our father, who had never flown in any type of plane before, on a ride. They flew into an air pocket, and the small Piper Cub dropped like a bowling ball one hundred gut-wrenching feet. Dad's face turned white. He suggested they get back to the airport fast.

Ken's natural talent for carpentry got him a job building and finishing 88-Cent stores in nearby Portland. He then worked as a carpenter for several firms, one of them the largest construction company in the world. Later he became a contractor in his hometown. He would build a house, move into it, then build another one and sell the first one. He did this several times.

Ken lived on the Oregon coast for a while, back from the beach about four miles, on a thickly wooded ten acres. Every day he went to a small coffee shop nearby and talked with the farmers and fishermen who happened in. I went with him one morning. He knew everyone who came in, called them all by name, and engaged in a lot of good-natured kidding and joking with them. I'd never seen that side of Ken before.

The next day he went salmon fishing in the Pacific Ocean off Pacific City in a dory. These rugged little boats launch through the surf to fish and come home through the breakers. Ken helped the professional fisherman rig the lines and pull them in. Fishing was bad until it was just about time to head back. Then the salmon started to bite. They stayed too long fishing, and when they came back past Haystack Rock, it was dark. A dozen pickups with boats on trailers had waited for them. The pickups' lights lit up the breakers as the little boat hit full throttle and charged into the waves, cutting the power at the last second and sliding up on the wet sand with the load of salmon.

Ken had suffered various injuries while a prisoner. One day he took off his boot and rubbed his right leg. "No feeling below my knee," he said. "It started the last year of prison camp. The doctor said I had some nerve damage. I could cut off my toes with a chain saw and never know it." Later he did lose two and a half fingers on his left hand to a power saw while working as a carpenter on a scaffold in Portland. He had to grab the saw to keep from falling off the third-floor platform.

About ten years before he died, Ken had a brain operation. The problem was due to complications from an attack when a Japanese prison guard hit him on the head with a claw hammer forty-four years before. He never told us anything about the attack—he never talked at all about the war or prison camp—and he doesn't mention it in the thirty-seven pages he wrote about his POW days. Ken recovered from the operation and lived a normal life. He died in 1998 when he was seventy-four. I'm grateful that he survived the prison camps and delighted that he had a good full life.

I'm still trying to discover what role Ken played on Wake during those sixteen days of fighting on the three small atolls in the middle of the Pacific Ocean. So far I haven't found a survivor who knew him. I shall keep hunting, though. One or two men remember him, but not well enough to know what he did in the battle. I hope those days of combat in his life don't remain forever a mystery.

Looking at Ken's manuscript one day gave me the idea to write the Wake Island story—not to recount it from historian's viewpoint or reconstruct it as a military analyst, but to compile it in Ken's own words and those of other survivors. That's when I started to dig into the story.

What I have written and compiled is *Hell Wouldn't Stop: An Oral History of the Battle of Wake Island,* in the words of the men who lived through the sixteen days of bombing and combat, the surrender, and the three years and eight months of captivity by the Japanese. I have talked with sixty-nine of these men, many in personal interviews, some on the telephone. Others have responded to my questions through the mail.

I owe a deep debt of gratitude to all of the men and widows who have contributed to this book. To a man, these marines, sailors, and soldiers will say that they are not heroes, that the heroes are the seventy-one servicemen who gave up their lives defending a speck of coral in the middle of the Pacific Ocean—an island that none of them had ever heard of before they were ordered to go there. Most of them wondered just how they had wound up there, with Japanese bombs and bullets raining down on them. To the survivors of Wake Island, I salute you. May the rest of your days be happy ones, and may all of your memories be of the good times.

This book is unlike any that has ever been written about the heroes of Wake Island: It is told in the survivors' own words. Here you will see, hear, and feel the battle, the capture, and the years in prison camp through the eyes, voices, and souls of the men who experienced it. Some of it is not easy to read, or pleasant, but it is historically true. It comes straight from the lips and pens of the men who struggled through the fighting and suffered years of forced labor in prison camps. While the memories of many of these men have dimmed, others wrote about their experience when it was still vivid and fresh in their minds.

No one knows for sure how many survivors there are today of the Wake Island battle and captivity. We do know there were 1,146 civilian construction workers and supervisors on Wake the day of the attack. There were 388 U.S. Marines, 12 marine pilots, 30 navy sailors sent to maintain the PBYs (flying boats or floatplanes), and 47 Marine aircraft maintenance men to keep the twelve F4F-3 Grumman Wildcats flying. Temporarily stationed at Wake were 6 Army Air Corps men in a radio crew. There were also several naval officers on duty on Wake Island that December 8, 1941.

Many of the men quoted here have never spoken publicly about their ordeal before. This is a "people's report" from the troops in the field, from everyone who can remember what happened and who is willing to talk about it.

PROLOGUE

"Then all hell broke loose. The ass on the guy in front of me disappeared. It was completely blown away. I could hear and see the slugs hitting all around me along with fragmentation bombs. Then the guy behind me yelled and fell. I was scared shitless and knew I would be next. Our fighter planes on the strip were exploding and burning as I ran past them. I looked up at the Japanese bombers and knew I could see the gunners sighting in on me. If only those damn machine gun slugs would stop whining and thudding. How in the hell did I ever get into this mess? Here I was on a spit of an island, in a war I knew nothing about, with death breathing down my neck. My only thought was to run, run, run . . ."

—Dare K. Kibble, USN

WAKE ISLAND:
WHAT, WHERE, WHY

Most Americans today have forgotten or never knew much about Wake Island. It is a small three-island atoll sitting in the Pacific Ocean 600 miles north of the Marshall Islands and 2,300 miles west of Honolulu.

Alvaro de Mendana, a Spanish explorer, first sighted the tiny atolls in 1586. His ships were running low on food and water; however, when he went ashore he found no water and no food—only sand, coral, and some scrubby growth of brush. He took his men back to the boats, named the speck of coral San Francisco, and then sailed on.

The English seafarer Samuel Wake, captain of the trading ship *Prince William Henry,* found the island next in 1796. He fixed its position in the Pacific Ocean by taking exact longitude and latitude measurements, then gave the islands his own name and sailed away. Not long thereafter and unaware of the earlier visits, the captain of the British ship *Halcyon* touched on Wake.

Americans first visited Wake when the USS *Vincennes* stopped there on December 20, 1840. Charles Wilkes, a well-known explorer, surveyed one of the atolls and gave it his own name. On the same ship was a naturalist,

Titian Peale. He collected marine life in the lagoon and named the other atoll Peale, after himself.

The three small atolls were not bothered by humans again until a German ship, the *Libelle,* crashed into one of the many reefs just offshore and foundered. It had been traveling from Honolulu to Hong Kong, and a stormy night had prevented the lookouts from seeing the tiny atolls or the reefs.

The crew and passengers stayed with the ship when it broke up in the storm. After the weather cleared, the survivors made their way to shore. They had saved the most important cargo, $300,000 in cash, but the money couldn't help them as, shipwrecked, they were far from normal shipping lanes and on a speck of sand that offered no food or water. The captain hid the money on the island, and with the survivors he set sail for Guam, 1,400 miles away, in two small boats from the ship that the storm had washed up on the shore.

The twenty-two-foot boat made it to Guam after eighteen days on the sea. The second smaller boat with the ship's captain and seven others was never heard from again. The survivors sent a ship from Guam to Wake and recovered the money.

Nothing was heard of Wake Island again until July 4, 1898, during the Spanish-American War, when ships transporting American soldiers to the Philippines anchored off Wake. Major General Francis V. Greene went ashore and raised a small American flag affixed to a dead branch. A year later another American ship stopped at Wake to claim it formally for the United States. Washington wanted the speck of sand and coral to set up a cable station—an idea that was scrapped when they found there was no water on Wake. In 1906 John J. Pershing, then a young army captain, went ashore and raised a more durable canvas flag. And American scientific expeditions studied the atolls and lagoon in 1922 and 1923.

In the next decade airplane travel swooped down and changed forever the face of Wake Island. Pan American Airways was in the process of expanding its flights across the Pacific using the four-engine "clipper" flying boats that landed on the water. The large lagoon made a perfect landing field, and not a single shovel of dirt had to be turned. Pan Am had made flights from San Francisco to Tokyo and Manila, but now they needed way stations along the route to stop for fuel and to let passengers relax ashore. Wake perfectly matched their needs. In May 1935 ships arrived with materials, and construction began on the seaplane base, the Pan Am office, and a small hotel for passengers. At this time, too, the U.S. Navy made public that it recognized the military value of the island and did a complete survey.

Within three months of intense work, Pan Am built a forty-five-room hotel. The base operations office had also been finished, and a landing "strip" channel had been dredged to eliminate the vicious coral heads that dotted the lagoon. Then the first Pan Am clipper settled down in the lagoon and pulled up to the landing ramp on Peale Island.

The three atolls on Wake Island form a rough U shape with the opening to the northwest. They are in fact the tops of a submerged volcano that shows less than four square miles of land area, and Wake Island makes up over half of that. From Toki Point at the northernmost spot on Peale Island, south to Peacock Point on Wake Island, and then back north up to Kuku Point on Wilkes Island measures a distance of almost ten miles. A dangerous reef close to shore encircles the three atolls. The only entrance into the lagoon is a shallow channel fifty yards wide between the Peale and Wilkes atolls.

Life on Wake from 1935 to 1941 was slow and peaceful. Only two flights a week touched down on Wake, one going east and one going west. Then, in December of 1940, the United States government set out to fortify Wake Island. A contract was awarded to Contractors Pacific Naval Air Bases to build both a navy seaplane facility and a land airfield on Wake. Two thousand tons of equipment were loaded on board the USS *William Ward Burrows,* which was also transporting a construction crew of eighty men. They were hard-working, hard-living men, many of them coming from jobs on the Grand Coulee and Boulder Dams and other big construction jobs, and were ready to take on a new challenge.

The ship was jammed with everything needed to implement the construction job and to sustain the men, including kitchen supplies, food, and personal items. After the ship's holds were filled, more goods and equipment were piled on top of the hold covers. Then a barge forty feet wide and one hundred feet long was loaded with still more equipment—a huge diesel crane, bulldozers, a tractor, two six-thousand-pound anchors—and attached to the freighter by a towline. A fifty-five-foot tugboat, the *Pioneer,* also made the trip. The journey was difficult. The barge broke the towrope twice; twice it had to be recovered. The *William Ward Burrows* traveled thirteen days. Then all of the equipment had to be unloaded and taken ashore before the men could begin their work.

They were late getting started. The three-year contract would not be completed. They would have one year, barely, to get three years' work done.

Back in the 1930s, war planners in Tokyo and Washington D.C. were constantly planning strategies for attacks on and defenses from their real and imagined enemies. Both the Japanese and Americans knew and valued the strategic location Wake Island held in the Pacific. It was the "high ground," and whoever controlled it would find it much easier to be master of the entire western Pacific.

Wake Island figured heavily in war planning on both sides. The Japanese saw Wake as an American dagger aimed at the heart of its mid-Pacific possessions, whereas the U.S. military construed it as an essential early warning station to sniff out any advancing enemy fleet. In 1941 Japan's leading base in the Pacific was at Taongi on the Bokaak Atoll in the Marshall Islands. Kwajalein Atoll, two hundred miles southwest of Bokaak but still in the Marshalls, held the main Japanese air base in the Pacific. It was only six hundred miles from Wake Island, within easy bombing range.

Wake, the closest U.S. base to Japan, presented a threat that could not be tolerated. Japanese war planners had skillfully plotted their capture of Wake Island, Guam, and Midway as the first strokes in the war that they would wage against the United States when the right time came. The Japanese strategy included the surprise attack on Hawaii, but with no plans to capture it. At the same time they intended to attack Wake, take it in one day, and then move on to Guam and Midway.

Vice Admiral Nariyoshi Inouye was given command of the Japanese Fourth Fleet, which included specially trained troops and craft for amphibious landings on beaches. In December 1941, this powerful fleet was positioned in the huge harbor of Truk in the Caroline Islands—now called the Chuuk Islands—positioned to the south and east of Kwajalein, within easy striking distance of Wake. Some historians say that Admiral Inouye had laid out his plans for the capture of Wake and then Guam as early as 1938. In the first few days of November 1941, the Japanese army and navy commanders were given their detailed attack orders.

From observation planes flying over Wake Island in November 1941, the Japanese had determined exactly how undermanned the defenders of Wake were and how incomplete the defensive installations stood. They allotted a small group of ships and only 450 men to assault the beaches of Wake. The Japanese commanders figured it would be a quick victory and that they would then prepare for the thrust against the better-defended Guam.

In December the stage was set. A powerful Japanese fleet had set sail weeks before, heading for the Hawaiian Islands and a date with the U.S. Pacific Fleet tucked into Pearl Harbor along Battleship Row.

Back in the war rooms of the United States, the military leaders knew that war with Japan was inevitable. They had known in the late 1930s that Japan was so aggressive that it soon would look farther west for its conquests. It just depended on when Japan wanted to ignite the fuse. Admirals and generals make war plans during peacetime. On highly detailed maps they chart sequences of actions and counteractions, of deployment and attacks on all sorts of prospective targets and areas.

U.S. military strategists planned to move the Pacific Fleet with its powerful array of battleships out from Hawaii to attack and capture the islands of the Gilbert, Marshall, and Caroline chains. This would put U.S. forces in a good position to support and reinforce the Philippines, which they figured would be attacked quickly by Japan early in any war.

The U.S. planners also wanted a line of island forts in the Pacific to serve as a primary defensive boundary. From these island bases, patrol planes could sweep the skies to the east, watching for any thrust that Japan might try to make against any of the island chains, Hawaii, or even the Pacific Coast. Wake Island was one of these five forward bases, which also included Samoa, Palmyra, Johnson, and Midway.

Wake stood in an exposed position, far in front of most of the U.S. defensive line of bases. Only Guam, just south of the Marianas Islands and just north of the Carolines, faced a tougher situation, as the Japanese occupied islands on three of its sides. The advance planners had written off Guam due to its position. It would be impossible to defend the island against aggressive Japanese military attacks.

The United States' plans and strategies were all good. The only trouble was that Congress dragged its feet in 1938 in granting funding, so it wasn't until January 1941 that the 1,146 civilian workers at Wake began the work timetabled for three years.

In August of 1941 388 U.S. Marines of the First Defense Battalion landed on Wake to serve as a defensive force. They were the only infantry on the island. Work on all phases of the defense of the island proceeded, including the placement of five-inch guns and three-inch antiaircraft guns, as well as the .50- and .30- caliber machine gun nests around the three small atolls.

Commander Winfield Scott Cunningham, forty-one years of age, had been looking forward to returning to the States from assignments in the South Pacific and spending time with his family. Instead, he received new orders. In the middle of November he was ordered to go to Wake Island as officer in charge of all Wake Island activities. He was soon en route.

Cunningham had a feeling the easy days of navy life were almost over. In his journal he writes:

> We had seen the war break out in Europe in 1939, as it had done in 1914, but we were not excited. Congress had passed the Neutrality Act; we wouldn't get involved this time. Surely the Germans wouldn't be so insane as to provoke the United States into war against them. And as for the Japanese, in spite of their saber rattling, they must have known they hadn't the industrial base or the technical know-how required to justify hope for victory in a war against both the United States and Great Britain. They were an inferior people, only capable of imitating the Western man— and not very well at that. They were years behind in the ability to operate naval carriers and other men-of-war. And anyhow, they could never turn out competent airplane pilots. They all had poor eyesight, didn't they?

Pearl Harbor would change that misguided but common outlook in a hurry.

Commander Cunningham's peacetime navy service had been an ideal proving ground for his new duties. He had served on battleships, cruisers, and destroyers. He had held positions there as battery officer, fire control officer, and senior aviator in charge of observation. He was familiar with the five-inch guns that soon would be a major factor in defending Wake Island. The aircraft in his Fighting Five squadron had been the planes the navy flew just prior to the F4F-3 Wildcats on Wake. One navy regulation stated that only officers with navy aviator experience should be in command of Pacific Island bases like Wake.

Commander Cunningham had a briefing before he left for Wake. Captain J. B. Earle, in the office of the Commandant of the Fourteenth Naval District, told Cunningham that the completion of the naval air station on Wake was his top priority. No men, equipment, or material were to be diverted to the defenses then being built on Wake. The captain apparently did not conceive that any immediate danger threatened Wake Island.

When Commander Cunningham arrived on Wake on November 28, he replaced Marine Major James P. S. Devereux, who had been the acting base commander. Devereux, who now would report to Commander Cunningham, would take charge of all marines stationed on the island. The new base commander would be responsible for all of the development and construction on Wake by the workforce as well as for the defense of the island.

On November 27, 1941, Rear Admiral Husband E. Kimmel called a high-level meeting of top navy and army officers in Hawaii. The feeling among the officers was that war with Japan was inevitable. They had realistic and immediate decisions to make about defenses of the Pacific Islands, including Hawaii. One of them was to send twelve Grumman fighters to Wake Island. The same day of the meeting, Admiral Kimmel read a top-priority coded message from Washington: "This dispatch is to be considered to be a war warning. Negotiations with Japan looking toward stabilization of conditions in the Pacific have ceased and an aggressive move by Japan is expected in the next few days."

Secrecy in moving the twelve fighters was absolutely necessary because of the thousands of Japanese living in Hawaii. The military was certain that some of them were spies for Japan. They were right. The twelve planes flew to Ford Island in the center of Pearl Harbor and landed. They were then instructed to fly out to meet the aircraft carrier *Enterprise,* where they observed from the air as some P-40 Army Air Corps planes took off from the carrier. After the army planes successfully made it into the air, the twelve

Grumman pilots were ordered to land on the carrier. It was a surprise to the pilots. They did not yet know that they were on their way to Wake Island to provide air cover and defense. None of the pilots had luggage, spare uniforms, or even a toothbrush and razor.

Shortly after the carrier's own eighty-three planes landed, the public address system passed the word: "Now hear this. This is War Order Number One. The USS *Enterprise* is now under way to Wake Island to deliver fighter squadron VMF-211. Our scouting aircraft will cover our advance. They will be fully armed and prepared to shoot on sight any enemy aircraft; they will sink any enemy surface vessels we meet. More details later in Battle Order Number One."

War had not been declared. No enemy action had been reported. But everyone in the Pacific military knew that war with Japan might be only days away. No one thought, however, that Japan had the capability to launch an attack on the Hawaiian Islands.

On December 4, 1941, twelve Grumman F4F-3 fighters flew off the carrier *Enterprise*. They landed on Wake Island two hours later after meeting a PBY that led them into the airstrip. The planes were the latest in the fleet— so new that some had been flown on the carrier without the machine guns installed in the wings. None of the pilots had ever dropped a bomb or strafed a target from the new planes. It would be learn-as-you-shoot combat operations for the marine pilots.

The Japanese Fourth Fleet had positioned itself near Wake, but the land-based bombers made the first attacks on the morning of December 8 so that they could be coordinated with the strike at Hawaii. Because Wake Island is across the international date line, in real time the attacks on Wake took place only five hours after the bombing of Pearl Harbor. That meant the marines and navy men on Wake had five hours notice that they probably would be hit hard by Japanese aircraft. They knew that the long-anticipated war had started. They also knew that they weren't nearly ready to go into battle.

GETTING READY FOR WAR

Private First Class Merle L. Herron, USMC (deceased)
August 19, 1941
Princeton, Minnesota

I arrived on Wake Island in a navy ship on August 19, 1941. There were 180 of us marines on board as a part of the First Defense Battalion. We were quartered in the old camp, which the civilian contractors had built for their temporary shelter when they first arrived on Wake. It was called Camp One. We lived in tents stretched over wooden frames with screened sides and wooden decks. Five marines were assigned to each tent and we slept on canvas cots. The civilian contractor's men lived in Camp Two. They had wooden barracks, their own hospital, power plant, commissary, refrigeration plant, storehouse, and shops. The food they served in their mess was much better than ours.

First we unloaded the ship we had arrived in. We took off guns, clothing, cooking equipment, and food. We worked for a week, ten hours a day, unloading the ship. Then we went to work setting up our three-inch antiaircraft guns. I didn't know it took so many sandbags just for one gun position. Half of us assigned to the guns hadn't even seen them fire and knew very little about how they operated. That was because we had little time for training. Instead, we were assigned to refuel the big B-17s that landed on Wake on their way to the Philippines. We hand-pumped fuel into fifty-gallon drums, hauled them to the "seventeens" on the airstrip, and then hand-pumped the fuel out of the drum into the tank. It usually took twelve to sixteen hours to get one plane refueled. When a ship came in, we were also assigned to unload it. That left little time for us to find out anything about our three-inch guns.

During this time we were supposed to get three meals a day. Breakfast was fine if you got to chow early. The noon meal was a cold sandwich, which they brought out to us on the job. Our evening meal was pretty good if you were the first to eat. Lots of time they ran out of food and the cooks opened cans of beans, and that was all there was.

In November a two-star general came out to Wake for inspection, and because our uniforms were not pressed and our rifles were not clean enough, he cut our food ration. One Sunday for dinner they served us ox tongue and rice because they had run out of any other kind of food.

Staff Sergeant Earl H. Barnes, USMC
Dunnellon, Florida

On August 19 we landed on Wake Island from the navy transport USS *Regulus*. I had been laid off my job back in California in 1938, and in those days work was hard to find. So in January of 1939 I joined the Marine Corps. I was a member of the 15th Marine Battalion, which later became the First Defense Battalion.

Someone got the bright idea that we needed units to defend U.S. possessions in the Pacific, and we were moved to Pearl Harbor in 1940. I was a corporal working as a transportation mechanic. We were involved in stripping off the wooden decks of warships and getting rid of the fancy items on board, such as pianos. It was August and we were getting the ships ready for battle, but we didn't know when the war would start.

Our job on Wake was to set up defensive positions around the island, preparing for a large force of U.S. Marines that would come and defend Wake. We didn't get the job done before the shooting started.

Private First Class Armand E. Benjamin
October 31, 1941
San Diego, California

I was a PFC when the war started. I had been on Midway doing all the wiring for the five-inch guns. When we got done with that they sent us back to Honolulu. I was there five weeks and then shipped out for Wake. We arrived on October 31, 1941. We went to work doing the wiring to set up the five-inch guns on Wake.

Before the war started we had to refuel B-17s that flew in to Wake. They were on their way to the Philippines to work as tactical aircraft in case of a war. For a while there they seemed to come in every day. It was exhausting work. We got them fueled up during the night and they would take off the next day. Later I learned that all the B-17s were destroyed on the ground in the Japanese attack on the Philippines.

Fireman Second Class Dare D. Kibble, USN
November 1, 1941
Meridian, Idaho

Around November 1, 1941, there was a notice placed on one of the bulletin boards on my ship, saying a few volunteers were needed for expeditionary forces on some of the islands throughout the Pacific, including Palmyra, Johnson, and Wake. A friend of mine and I were planning to buy a couple of motorcycles. The only problem was we didn't have the money saved, and probably wouldn't if we stayed around Hawaii. So we decided to volunteer for some far-out island duty and save our money. After a year, when the island duty was to terminate, we would meet back at Pearl Harbor and take ninety days leave.

I remember how balmy and wonderful Pearl Harbor and the Hawaiian Islands were in those days. There were only about twenty-five thousand people besides servicemen in Hawaii. When the ship was tied up to the dock or at anchor in the harbor, we would sleep on the weather deck under the stars. What a wonderful couple of weeks in my life. I can remember walking along Waikiki Beach with only a few people in sight. The tallest building in town was the Royal Hawaiian Hotel. During those beautiful nights under the starlit skies, I would find myself wishing those days would never end. The wind would blow ever so gently on your face and body, and at that moment you knew this must be what the Lord's heaven will resemble when you enter the promised land. It would be a terrible shock to me, when I returned again to this heavenly land in September 1945, to see how man can totally ruin such a paradise in a short four years.

My friend and I thought about the far-out islands, then put in our requests. After that year was up we'd go to the States, buy a pair of Harley 61s, and zoom through the homeland like a couple of vagabonds. That was when my life took the most bizarre turn any person could ever anticipate.

Corporal Martin Greska, USMC
November 8, 1941
Oceanside, California

I landed on Wake Island from a ship about a month before the war started. We had to climb down rope ladders to a float, where smaller boats came up to take us on to shore. We did a lot of work getting our gun positions into shape, only a call would come and we'd have to help unload ships. I remember during that first month we had to do a lot of stevedore work. We were wrestling fifty-gallon drums of gasoline off the floating dock and into small boats, which we then took to shore and unloaded. It was exhausting work.

★   ★   ★

Chief Warrant Officer Michael A. Benedetto, USMC
November 11, 1941
Highland, California

I arrived on Wake Island on November 11, 1941, after completing a special school in Quantico, Virginia, where I learned how to construct Quonset huts. My part was the electrical wiring, to get them all wired up correctly. When I came to Wake there weren't any Quonset huts to erect, so I was sent to the mess hall to do my duty washing the pots and pans. That was my job until December 8, when I was sent from the kitchen to Peacock Point on the southernmost part of Wake to work on a five-inch gun.

Corporal Carroll E. Trego, USMC
November 20, 1941
San Marcos, California

I left the States on June 16, 1941, on the USS *Altair*. We hit Honolulu on June 26 and left for Wake Island on November 20. We arrived on Wake on November 30, just seven full days before war was to start.

I arrived there with four other radiomen, whose job it was to set up an air-to-ground radio system for the Wildcats and VMF-211. We got the unit up and working; then, on the second day of the new war, the Japs bombed it out of existence. We borrowed a radio from the marine base communications shack and set it up so it would transmit and receive with the Wildcat fighters. We could communicate only with the fighters up to about eighty miles from Wake. We could not talk to Pearl Harbor with this radio the way we could with the one before. We five men were in a headquarters company from Honolulu and not part of the fighter squadron.

Fireman 2nd Class Dare Kibble, USN
November 26, 1941

I arrived on Wake Island on November 26, 1941. You may wonder why the navy assigned a machinist to an island where the only people would be marines, some aircraft personnel, and a construction crew. Our ship, the *Tangier,* was a seaplane tender. It was designed to go to sea for the refueling and support of a squadron of long-range patrol seaplanes, the Consolidated PBYs built in San Diego. We had everything on board to supply the planes or repair them, including fuel, ammo, parts, and bombs. At that time the navy was spying on the Marshall Islands, which were occupied by the Japanese. When the PBYs came out of Pearl Harbor, they had to refuel at Midway, but they still couldn't reach the Marshalls. So the navy decided to send a refueling boat to Wake. We'd do it at night offshore, so not even the Jap subs could spot us. I operated and maintained the engine on our sixty-foot boat, which had a tank amidships holding three thousand gallons of fuel.

I soon learned that Wake was a coral atoll. The highest point is twenty-one feet above sea level, and there is no fresh water. There were thousands of gooney birds and no trees, only shrubs. The three islands together are about ten miles around and so narrow at spots you can almost throw a stone across the land. The three atolls surround a beautiful lagoon. I don't remember how deep it was in the center, but in most places you could see the bottom with no trouble. I used to go swimming every day in the lagoon and watch the beautiful small fish. When you looked down into the lagoon you could see every color imaginable.

We kept our boat tied up at a dock on the lagoon side of Wake Island, next to Camp One, where the marines stayed. The contractors had built a channel to the south side of Wake, so we went out the channel to sea to refuel the planes. We did the work about a mile off the islands.

Several times when we were out at sea, we took along a big hunk of meat, put a large hook in it, attached a heavy line, and fished. Most of the time we hooked sharks. Usually they were so big they straightened out the hook and escaped.

Many times when refueling the PBYs, which took about an hour, we and the plane's crew would go for a swim around the boat and plane.

When I think back to those days, I don't remember wondering or questioning why the PBYs were wandering around down in this part of the South Pacific with bombs on their wings and ammo in their guns. I knew practically nothing about the status of world affairs concerning the Japanese, nor did I realize how close I was to Japan. Wake is four hundred miles closer to Tokyo than to Honolulu. I didn't seem to care.

Herbert J. Horstman, USN
San Diego, California

I had been assigned to a PBY squadron at Ford Field in Honolulu in 1941. They asked for volunteers to go to Wake Island to do the same job there. I'd been to several islands in the Pacific but never to Wake, so I decided that I might as well find out what Wake Island was all about. I was there for only two weeks before the December 8 attack, so I didn't learn much about Wake Island.

Master Sergeant Walter "Tom" Kennedy, USMC
Squaw Valley, California

I went from flying in the rear seat of a SBD-1 Dauntless dive-bomber as the radio operator to digging fox holes in the coral on Wake Island. I was in marine aviation and went to Ewa in the Hawaiian Islands in January of 1941. We did all kinds of flying there—scout missions, dive-bombing and gunnery, night flying, and landing on carriers. We had everything in our squadron—fighters, scout bombers, and dive-bombers. Then they headed us into the South Pacific. They didn't know who to put where, so they took a third of each squadron and put us on Wake. There were fifty-two of us all together, counting the pilots.

I arrived on Wake around the last of November. Wildcats came in on Thursday, December 4, as I remember. The planes didn't have any bomb racks, and some had gunnery sights installed when they were on the carrier. We jerry-rigged the bomb racks there at the field on Wake so they could carry two one-hundred-pound bombs.

Major Robert O. Arthur, USMC (Ret.)
December 4, 1941
Newport Beach, California

I joined the marines May 25, 1938, and took my boot training at the Marine Corps Recruit Depot in San Diego. Then I applied for marine aviation and went to North Island as a mechanic on K2F4 and JRS aircraft. I wanted to be a pilot and radio school was my next step. Soon I was flying in J2F4 as a radioman, but I got lots of stick time as well. I applied for flight school at Pensacola, Florida. I was a corporal, and after only two years in marine aviation I was in flight school.

I had no trouble in flight school and won my wings as a naval aviation pilot designated 8-41. There I was, a sergeant and a pilot, mixing with all those officer pilots. I was a test pilot at the naval air station at Miramar before being assigned to VMF-211 stationed at MCAS [Marine Corps Air Station] in Ewa, Hawaii. I was an excellent pilot and so young that the operations officer, Captain Luther S. Moore, said I wouldn't live to log five hundred hours. I fooled him and retired with more than six thousand hours.

In early December of 1941 we were told we were going to do a weekend of carrier practice on the USS *Enterprise*. We flew to Ford Island and later found the carrier. Major Paul A. Putnam was our lead pilot and officer in charge. We were supposed to observe from the air some army planes taking off from the carrier. After the demonstration we were surprised when an order came by radio that we were to land on the carrier. Then, in the ready room, they told us that we were going to Wake Island. One thing worried me. What about my newly acquired Ford convertible and my redheaded girlfriend? I figured somebody would take care of both of them.

We were briefed before we left the carrier. We were practically at war with Japan. Our orders were to shoot down anything that flew and to sink anything on the sea. On December 4, when we were two hundred miles from Wake, a flying boat met us and we took off and followed the PBY to the tiny speck of sand and coral that was Wake

Island. Then we broke for landing formation, but I had a problem. I hadn't seen the island yet. On my final approach I saw it, a sand and coral runway on a patch of sand and brush. It was long enough but narrow. We wouldn't be able to take off more than one plane at a time. No side-by-side takeoffs. Maybe they could fix that before we really got into the war.

We parked our planes on wooden pallets to keep the props clean. Then we tried to find our quarters. They turned out to be tents, and we ate with the First Defense Battalion up at Camp One.

The Lay of the Land
Wake Atoll, December 8, 1941

The Wake Atoll comprises three small islands. The main one, Wake, is an irregular "V" pointed to the southwest. Most of the buildings are on this island. At the crotch of the land are the airfield and its hangars. Here too are located the hospital, the Defense Battalion Command Post (from December 14–23), and the Naval Command Post. Up the left leg on the "V," near the boat channel that separates Wake from Wilkes Island, is Camp One, where 388 marines were based. This was also the site of the Defense Command Post from December 8 to 13. Across the boat channel is Wilkes Island, home to five- and three-inch guns as well as .50-caliber and .30-caliber machine guns.

No spot on Wake Island stands more than twenty-one feet higher than the surfline, and there are no trees, only some fairly heavy brush. From tip to tip of the three islands the distance is only 4.5 miles in length, and at no place is it more than 1.5 miles wide from one side of the island and across the lagoon to the Pacific Ocean on the other side. The entire land mass is a little more than three square miles.

At the top of the right leg of the "V" of Wake Island, where it curls around to form a small "C," sits Camp Two, where the civilian construction workers were housed and fed. Beyond Camp Two, across the causeway, is the third atoll, Peale. Here is the PBY seaplane ramp, used by both military and Pan American Airways. Here also is the Pan Am headquarters and the company's forty-five-room hotel.

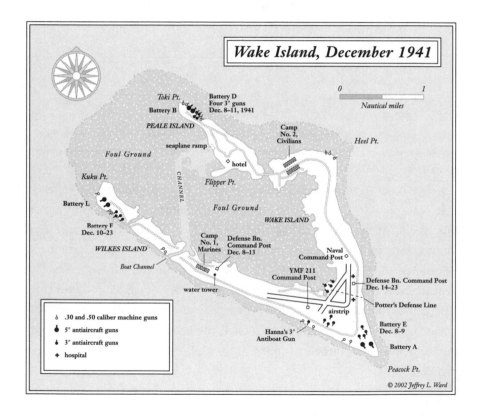

Wake Island, December 1941

0   1
Nautical miles

Toki Pt.
Battery B
Battery D
Four 3″ guns
Dec. 8–11, 1941

PEALE ISLAND

seaplane ramp

Camp No. 2, Civilians   Heel Pt.

Foul Ground   hotel

Kuku Pt.   Flipper Pt.   CHANNEL

Battery L   Foul Ground   WAKE ISLAND

Battery F
Dec. 10–23   Camp No. 1, Marines   Defense Bn. Command Post Dec. 8–13   Naval Command Post

WILKES ISLAND   YMF 211 Command Post   Defense Bn. Command Post Dec. 14–23

Boat Channel   Potter's Defense Line

water tower   airstrip

○ .30 and .50 caliber machine guns
● 5″ antiaircraft guns
◗ 3″ antiaircraft guns
✚ hospital

Hanna's 3″ Antiboat Gun   Battery E Dec. 8–9

Battery A

Peacock Pt.

© 2002 Jeffrey L. Ward

THE
ATTACK

First Bombing and Invasion Attempt
December 8–11

On December 8, 1941, at 0630, Army Staff Sergeant Ernest Rogers was almost through his midnight-to-dawn shift on the Army Air Corps long-range radio that had been set up in a truck and trailer near the Wake Island airstrip. Rogers, part of a five-man Army Air Corps unit and one Army Signal Corps officer working the radio station, was getting ready to go off duty when the radio began receiving an urgent SOS in Morse code. The radio was tuned to the frequency used by the closest United States Army Air Corps base at Hickam Field in Hawaii. The frantic message came through uncoded, violating a dozen military orders. Sergeant Rogers wrote it down and hurried outside. He found a marine on a motorcycle with a sidecar, and they dashed a mile or so north to officer country.

Rogers found his commanding officer, Captain Henry S. Wilson, in his tent and gave him the message. Wilson hurried to a tent nearby.

Major James P. S. Devereux, USMC, had almost finished shaving when Captain Wilson burst into his quarters without knocking and thrust a piece of paper at him. It read: "Hickam Field Hawaii and Pearl Harbor have been attacked by Jap dive-bombers. This is the real thing. This is no drill." Devereux phoned the navy radio station on Wake and asked if they had received any priority messages from Pearl Harbor. There had been a lot of false rumors about war lately and he needed to double-check. The radioman said they had just received an official priority transmission and it was in the process of being decoded. That was enough proof for Devereux, commander of the island defenses. He ordered the bugler to sound the call to arms. The word went out quickly along the line of dark tents at Camp One near the water tower. "This is no drill. This is no drill!" It was December 8, 1941, on Wake Island, which was twenty-two hours ahead of hawaii where it was still that fateful December 7. World War II had started for the Americans on Wake Island. Corporal Carroll Trego from San Marcos, California, had finished setting up a new ground-to-air communications system for the fighter squadron when he heard reports on the radio from Hawaii that the Japanese had attacked Pearl Harbor.

Most of the marines at Camp One had just finished breakfast; now they were dispatched by truck to their combat stations on Wake, Wilkes, and Peale Islands. Marine Gunner Harold C. Borth and Sergeant James W. Hall climbed to the top of the camp's water tower and manned the observation point. Marine Gunner John Hamas, the detachment's munitions officer, unpacked Browning automatic rifles, Springfield .03 rifles, and ammunition for issue to the civilians who had volunteered for combat duty.

The *Philippine Clipper*, Pan Am's big flying boat, had wheeled around when it heard about the war; it returned to the lagoon from which it had taken off just twenty minutes before. Commander Cunningham asked the Pan Am pilot, Captain Hamilton, to do a scouting flight. The plane was unloaded of passengers and refueled with enough gasoline for the search and the flight on to Midway.

As the Wake Island defenders got ready for the expected attack, thirty-four Mitsubishi G3M2 Type 96 land attack planes, called Nells, lifted off the airstrip on Roi in the Marshall Islands at 0710. Shortly before 1200 the Japanese planes arrived at Wake Island. They dropped from thirteen thousand feet down to one thousand five hundred feet. Emerging from a cloud at the south end of the atoll, they initiated the attack on Wake Island. The four antiaircraft guns that made up Battery E stood ready near Peacock Point on Wake. First Lieutenant William W. Lewis spotted the planes and telephoned Major Devereux to warn him.

Fireman 2nd Class Dare Kibble, USN

When the Jap bombers hit the island on December 8, I was in the back of a stake-bed truck at the west end of the airstrip, heading toward Camp Two for lunch. During the morning of the eighth, the boat crew of four men and I had watched the Pan Am clipper take off for the island of Guam. Twenty minutes later we saw the plane coming back. The pilot was dumping lots of his fuel. We wondered exactly what this meant. At that time in my life, I didn't realize a long-haul plane could not land with all its take-off weight. As we watched, the pilot gently set the clipper down in the lagoon. You must remember, Wake Island is only the size of a small ranch, say three square miles, and in some places I could hit a golf ball from one side of the island to the other. When you are at sea, you can easily miss the island from a couple of miles out.

The sky had been stuccoed with cumulus clouds all morning, and we had watched four of our Grumman fighters take off on patrol. At exactly noon, as we were riding along in the stake truck on the airstrip, we looked up and saw all of these bombers coming in from the southwest. All at once we saw the rising sun insignia—they were Japanese planes.

Someone beat on the truck cab and told Mack, the driver, to stop. Incidentally, Mack was the craziest SOB you would ever want as a wartime comrade-in-arms. The truck stopped and we all bailed out, with about five or six of us running single file in an easterly direction. By the time Mack had stopped the truck, we were at the eastern end of the landing strip.

Then all hell broke loose! The ass of the guy in front of me disappeared. It was completely blown away. I could hear and see the slugs hitting all around me along with fragmentation bombs. Then the guy behind me yelled and fell. I was scared shitless and knew I would be next. Our fighter planes on the strip were exploding and burning as I ran past them. I looked up at the bombers and knew I could see the gunners sighting in on me. If only those damn machine gun slugs would stop whining and thudding. How in the hell did I ever get into this mess? Here I was on a spit of an island, in a war I knew nothing about, with death breathing down my neck. My only thought was to run, run, run . . .

I was so damn scared, because I had never tried to adjust my mental tempo to anything as terrifying as this. I was just a twenty-year-old sailor from Idaho who was trained to fight on a ship—not dodge machine gun fire on a desert island.

I had on a pair of moccasins, and I know I was running the one-hundred-yard dash in record time. By the time the first section of bombers had passed me, I had outrun all of the other guys and I sat down to look at my feet because they hurt like the devil. I had run right out of the moccasins—the coral was cutting my now bare feet with every step. They were bleeding quite badly. Eventually, I looked up at the huge tank that was sheltering me from the roaming bombers and their nasty dose of death. Then I realized I was near a huge gasoline storage tank.

Bleeding feet or no bleeding feet, I left there pronto. By then the second wave of bombers was coming in from the northwest, and I started back toward the airstrip, looking for some cover. By this time, I was gaining a little bit of rational judgment. I had to look for any little old thing to hide behind. Remember, there are no trees on Wake, only brush. I found a small ditch by the road and dove into it.

This time the enemy planes were right on top of me, but the bombers' gunners didn't see me. I thought, how could they help but see me? I wished then that I had some kind of weapon to fire at them. I was scared as hell but also mad as hell, not only at the Nips but also at myself for letting such events enter my life. Anyway, I didn't hear any slugs hitting the ground around me. War is the shits! Here I was, sitting right in the middle of one and I still didn't know whether someone was shooting at me. I could hear guns firing every-where. I was lying face up and happened to think, "Do I want to take slugs in my front or back?" I decided to turn over.

After the adjacent fireworks ceased, I watched the bombers fly into the clouds to the south. I then decided to tear my shirt into strips and wrap them around my feet. As I was doing this, I saw our four fighter planes come into the island and turn in the direction the bombers had taken. I was to learn later that the fighters never did find the enemy bombers. Remember, these were the days before much radar. We didn't have any on Wake. The bombers had left the airstrip in a mess. Planes were burning everywhere. Eight had been hit on the ground. There were dead bodies and guys bleed-ing everywhere.

I decided to walk toward Camp Two and see if I could get my seabag, which had all of my earthly belongings in it. I needed to get some clothes, including a pair of shoes, shirts, and a coat. My feet were really bleeding now. When I reached Camp Two, I found my barracks was burned to the ground, along with my seabag."

Pfc. Armand E. Benjamin, USMC

I didn't hear them say that this isn't a drill, when we heard about the alert. I was just coming off the bridge from Peale Island when the bombs started to fall on December 8. I was in a truck that we had used to deliver hot chow to the men on the island. When the bombers came over, I dove out of the truck and tried to find some cover. I crawled into some of the eight- to ten-foot-high brush and waited out the attackers. They didn't hit the truck on that bombing attack. When they were strafing, I could see the bullets come walk-ing up the sand and coral toward me. They missed me. We had been all over the islands before the raid, delivering food.

My job in the marines was a wireman. Most of the time I ran around the three islands mending telephone wires. That's what I did, too, after the bombing started. We did most of our work at night. During the day we slept anyplace we could find a safe spot.

Gunnery Sergeant Robert F. Haidinger, USMC (Ret.)
San Diego, California

I was in the chow line at Camp One just about to get my hotcakes, syrup, and bacon when the General Quarters alarm sounded off. That sent the rest of the marines and me rushing back to our tents to grab our helmets and weapons and then charging to the trucks to haul us down to Peacock Point and our E Battery of four three-inch antiaircraft guns. I was commander of gun number four, but I didn't have a crew, so I moved over to the third gun as second loader. I was still wondering about those hotcakes. Turned out, for the rest of the war and all my POW days I dreamed about those hotcakes.

When I joined the marines in May of 1939, I hadn't counted on getting shot at. Now, as a corporal, I was about to see what it felt like. We got the three guns all set and ready to fire. The first loader is on one side of the gun, and the second loader on the other. The second loader puts the round into the fuse pot, which automatically sets the fuse for height and distance that comes into it from the height finder and the director. I matched the dials with the "bugs" on the box by turning a crank to get the fuse right. Then I pushed the round into the three-incher's chamber; the first gunner slammed it upward into the barrel and the breech closed automatically behind it. Then the first loader yanked the lanyard, the gun fired and spit out the used casing. The three-inch rounds were about twenty-four to twenty-six inches long. We called them three-inch fifty-ones.

Peacock Point is on the southernmost tip of Wake Island, below the airfield, and we had two five-inch guns in A Battery. We were ready and waiting. While there was nothing else to do, I sent three men back to my gun number four and had them move the three-inch rounds into the brush. They scattered them out so that if we got a lucky bomb hit on the gun, it wouldn't set off the rounds in sympathetic explosions. That done, we waited.

When the attack started, we saw them coming in out of the fog bank to the south of the islands. I was on the gun alone, and I got off three rounds all by myself with the earphones on. I got a shell out, put it in the fuse box, shoved it in the breech, and pulled the lanyard, all in rapid order. I got three rounds off at the retreating planes. That's when I realized that I had stuck the shells in without taking the fuse cap off. So they weren't fused to explode and took off into the wild blue yonder. Even though I chewed up the fuse cap in the fuse box, when the rounds went off they didn't hurt the gun any. I have no idea where the rounds landed. There were no bombs dropped near us that first day, as the planes concentrated on the aircraft, the airfield, and the surrounding tents and facilities. They didn't strafe us that first day either.

After the planes left I gathered the men, and we started filling sandbags with beach sand and put protection around about half of the guns. Then the officers decided to take my number four gun and use it down on the beach, like an artillery piece. They called it an antiboat gun, and it was right across from the taxi strip on the airfield, on the beach side of the road.

The next day we were ready for the Jap bombers when they came. We didn't have radar, but the birds told us when the heavy sound was coming, as they took off in large groups. That second day the bombers were at eighteen thousand feet, so we could put our guns to good use. We could fire effectively up to twenty-one thousand feet.

Our guns were moved from Peacock Point north along the airstrip, in the brush between the airfield and the road. From there we moved them to the lagoon side at the middle of the airfield, right across from the concrete bunkers where the hospital and CP were. That was the last time we moved until the end of the fighting. We moved at night so the Japs would target where we had gone from the day before.

I had a small tent with some supplies in it—candy bars, some bottles of whiskey, and other goodies. Every time a gun got credit for a hit and making one of the Nells go away smoking, the crew got a bottle and some candy to celebrate. For a while. One day the Japs scored a direct hit on my little tent and blew it to hell. We never found any of the supplies.

★ ★ ★

Chief Warrant Officer Michael Benedetto, USMC

I'd never even seen a five-incher before. I got sent to Peacock Point the day the Japanese attacked. They were set on a concrete platform and bolted in place so we didn't have to worry about them moving around. I was the rammer. Those guns had to be all hand-loaded with bags of gunpowder after the explosive round was pushed into the barrel. We rammed in the powder bags so they fit tight.

About noon on December 8 we saw the Jap planes come out of the overcast at the south end of the island and head for the airstrip. None of the bombs came near us that first day, but we ducked into any cover we could find. We were bombed again on the ninth and tenth, and then, on the eleventh, we got to fire the gun.

Our gunners did well. We had a hand in sinking one destroyer and hitting some of the other ships. After the Japanese navy gave up on the invasion attempt that morning and steamed away, it was the end of our shooting. We never had any targets to fire at after that, so we became infantrymen, digging holes and trying to set up a line of defense in case the Japs came our way.

On one of the bombing runs a hundred-pound bomb landed almost on our position and killed one of the men I had been in school with at Quantico. I can't remember his name now.

That morning, when we fired our gun, we had good help from several of the civilian construction workers. They hauled around ammo and powder for us from the magazines and helped get the rounds where they were most needed.

I wasn't used to the big gun, never had even seen it fire before. That first round fired out, and the recoil slammed backward as it always does. I was standing too close, and it hit my leg and jolted me down the bank. I thought I'd been shot. The sergeant on the gun yelled at me to get up on the gun and back to business. That knee still gives me trouble today, sixty years later. Some days I can't walk, then some days it doesn't hurt at all.

Lieutenant Commander Glenn E. Tripp, USN (Ret.)
Springfield, Virginia

Myself and most of the sailors arrived on Wake Island 28 November, 1941 with Commander Winfield Scott Cunningham and Commander Campbell Keene on board the old USS *Wright*. The only sailors on Wake before our arrival were Dr. Lieutenant Gustav Mason Kahn, USN, with his staff of seven navy hospital corpsmen and the navy boat crew attached to the First Defense Battalion, U.S. Marine Corps. There were also eight officers under Lieutenant Commander Elmer B. Greey, resident officer in charge and military supervisor of the construction program. He was working with the civilians on constructing the airstrip and the military defense on the island. Dan Teters was the civilian construction boss.

Upon our arrival Commander Cunningham and I set up our office in the construction office building in Camp Two. Commander Keene and his staff and yeoman Richard C. Mayhew established their office in another building nearby. Commander Cunningham was busy meeting with Major James Devereux and Teters planning how to set up the defense of the island. Commander Cunningham turned over the defense to Major James P. S. Devereux, as it was his men who would defend any attack on the island. He also gave Major Paul Putnam, USMC, a free hand in how to use his air group.

The radio alerted us about the raid on Pearl Harbor, and the defenders went on full alert. As the noon hour approached, I went to my barracks to get ready for the noon meal. As I headed to the mess hall, I heard planes overhead. Looking up, I saw several planes coming out of a low bank of clouds at the south end of the island. They began to drop bombs and fire machine guns as they passed overhead. As I had been trained to do in boot camp, I lay down facing the planes, and after they roared past I dug up spent bullets close by. The raid did not last long, and when the bombers were gone I went to my office. Commander Cunningham was there. After a time he told me that I could do little to help him at this time and I should make myself available to the marines.

Cpl. Martin Greska, USMC

I was with the artillery, manning the five-inch guns on the north end of the island that first day of combat. We had two guns. My job was to sight in on the target. The very first day, one of our guys was out in the open, and when the bombers came over, just after noon, a fragmentation bomb hit right in front of him and blew him to pieces. His name was [Private John] Katchak, as I remember. He was the only man in my battery who was killed on Wake. That first day none of the Japanese bombs scored a direct hit on either of our five-inch gun emplacements. We were well dug in and that protected us from the flying shrapnel and most of the strafing.

Senior Master Sergeant Ernest Rogers, U.S. Army (Ret.)
Aurora, Colorado

Shortly after I took the message to Captain [Henry S.] Wilson, I went back to the radio for any further instructions. Our radio unit was on Wake to communicate with the B-17s that were flying to the island for refueling before they went the rest of the way to the Philippines. Our long-range radio kept in contact with Hickam Field in Hawaii and with the planes as they moved on farther east.

The first Japanese attack, about noon that same day, did not damage our radio station. It was mobile, and we had positioned the trailer and truck near the airstrip runway. Fortunately, none of the bombs or strafing runs hit our equipment that noon.

As soon as the attack was over, we moved our radio receivers and transmitter into a concrete bunker just south of the runways.

Later on, the navy's radio station was destroyed in the Japanese attacks. The navy used our equipment to keep in contact with their headquarters in Pearl Harbor. Our men took care of the transmitters, and the navy radiomen handled the receivers.

We had no close bomb hits to our position. We didn't put up a high antenna to advertise our location. We had an antenna on a pole that we raised just outside the bunker when we transmitted and received, then pulled down when we were through. We knew when the bombers would be coming over, so we didn't use it during the raids.

When we knew the end of the fighting was near, we destroyed the transmitter and the receiver. We burned them out and wrecked them so the Japs wouldn't be able to use them.

Sergeant Max J. Dana, USMC
Washington, Utah

On December 8 (we were across the international date line and practically on the doorsteps of the Japanese empire) Wake Island was not a healthy place to be, as we were attacked the same as Pearl Harbor. We did not know that even as we were hearing the news from Pearl many Japanese ships and planes were on their way. It was around noon when the first wave of bombers, twenty-seven in all, sneaked in under heavy clouds. Lacking radar, we had no way of knowing until they were right on top of us. The Japanese came in so low we could make out the expressions on the aviators' faces. As they dropped their bombs, machine guns mounted on the sides of their bombers strafed the island.

The attack that first day lasted less than ten minutes, but in that time seven of our twelve fighters were totally wiped out and two severely damaged. Most of our gasoline reserves were destroyed, plus the machine shop—a devastating blow, as we were not well equipped and most of our weapons were of World War I vintage. Thirty-four men were killed or wounded in the first attack.

I was in a four-foot-deep machine gun nest on Wilkes Island during the battle, manning a .50-caliber machine gun with two other men. We escaped any injury on the first raid but were at the mercy of bombs dropping all around us, some just a few feet away. The planes swung around and made another pass down the main stretch on the island. Another wave showed up shortly after the first.

The bombers came almost every day, flying high with clear skies and well within reach of our three-inch antiaircraft guns. Wilkes

Island is barely one-eighth of a mile wide and a little less than one mile long at the most. A flight of bombers, usually twenty-seven, could cover the entire stretch with one pass if their aim was good, which it usually was. They generally came in two and three waves, one right after the other. Everyone crouched in terror under the best cover they could find and did a little praying. When the Japanese released the bombs, it looked like they were letting down a Jacob's ladder. They were hundred-pounders and you could hear them march up the island as they exploded. Talk about a hair-raising experience!

The bombs landed close but miraculously didn't hit in our small machine gun nest, although we did have a very close call one day. A new channel was proposed for Wilkes, and right behind us the civilian contractors had a warehouse with twenty-two hundred cases of dynamite stored in it. It took a direct hit—what an explosion! Even though I was in our machine gun nest below ground level, the concussion was so great it felt like my skin raised an inch from my entire body.

The third day they came in with heavy cruisers and shelled the island from a distance offshore. The shells whistled over our heads, which was more terrorizing than the bombing. You didn't know when or where they would hit, but as long as you could hear them, you knew that you were still alive.

Chief Boson's Mate William H. Manning, USN (Ret.)
Cottonwood, Arizona

We'd been picking up and relocating marker buoys in the seaplane channel in the lagoon the morning of December 8, then we went for chow at Camp One. I'd just collected our mail when the planes came over. A guy named Julian Sandvold and I were running across the airstrip and we both got shot up.

I got nailed with a .27-caliber machine gun bullet in the lower left part of my back. It's still in there. The medics said it was too close to my spine to be fooling with out there on Wake. They told me the body would build a kind of protective sheath around the bullet, like an oyster does with a pearl, so it couldn't move. It didn't hurt much or slow me down, so they patched me up and I went back to duty. Even now it does hurt a little on damp days, and I don't understand why.

The next day I got hit again. This time it was in my right arm, where a machine gun bullet ripped into me. About the same time, I had a grazing shot to my head. I was over by Camp Two at the new hospital they had set up. I had gone to fill up the canteens for the men I was with, because I couldn't do any shoveling work. Then the bombers came in. For five years I couldn't bend my thumb and two fingers. Then stateside they did an operation on me, so I can use my thumb and one finger, but I still can't bend the other one. Only good thing about it was I got two Purple Heart medals.

When I got hit with the machine rounds, it turned out to be the better of two evils. I had been running, and I made a sharp turn to the left and was hit by the machine gun. Almost at the same time a bomb hit in front of me. It landed almost exactly where I would have been if I had kept running straight ahead.

A civilian doctor, Dr. Shank, sewed up my arm. For a while they thought they might have to cut it off because it was so damaged and had turned cold from lack of circulation. But Dr. Shank saved it. He was one of those left on the island when most of the last group of prisoners and civilians were shipped off. They left ninety-eight civilians there to do construction work. I heard that later on they beheaded Dr. Shank, before they machine-gunned the ninety-eight civilian workers when they thought the American invasion was coming.

I went to the hospital when I had the second wound, and stayed there until the big invasion and the surrender. When the Japs said to hold up my hands, I could lift only one of them.

Sergeant Elwood M. Smith, USMC
Encinitas, California

I was a sergeant when the war started in 1941. When the bombs started falling that first day, we all dove for whatever cover we could find. We were in the open, and we tried to get into a ditch to protect ourselves. That's about all I remember about those days. I don't want to remember any more. I've had too many nightmares about Wake Island and the POW days.

Corporal Jack R. Skaggs, USMC
Edmond, Oklahoma

I joined the marines in June 1940 and wound up on Wake Island in a five-inch artillery battery. Our two guns were on Wilkes Island in Battery L with Second Lieutenant John A. McAlister as my battery commander.

That Monday morning we got the command for General Quarters, and everyone raced to their posts for combat. I was over at Camp One getting supplies for the battery so we could lay landlines in to the guns. We hurried back to our gun on the north end of Wilkes Island, which lies just north of the main Wake Island. About noon the first eighteen Japanese bombers came out of the cloud bank at the south end of the three-atoll group at only fifteen hundred feet and headed straight for the airstrip, the parked planes, and the buildings around the field. It looked like bushels of apples falling as the planes released their bombs. They ripped up the field and destroyed seven planes.

That first day, no bombs fell on Wilkes and our guns were spared. They came over in waves, and the destruction took only ten to twelve minutes. The second day, the Japanese bombers started coming down our side of the island and laid the bombs on us. One of our guns was hit. The hundred-pound bomb landed right in the battery and we had two men killed, Corporal Paul Tokryman and a civilian who was helping us with our ammunition. A warrant officer and I took Tokryman down to the dock to get across the channel to Wake Island and the hospital. There was a boat there but nobody to run it. After a while the two of us started the boat and took the wounded man across the channel and beached it on the other side. Tokryman died before we could get him to the hospital.

The engineers were cutting a new channel through the coral in the lagoon, and they used lots of dynamite. The project stopped with the attack, but there was lots of dynamite stored in a shed near the end of the island. The captain decided the powder should be moved, and so we dug a pit and lined it with the cases of dynamite. A few days later a bomb made a direct hit on the pit. All of the explosives went off in one thundering roar. The blast scalped that end of the island of all leaves on the brush and left a huge new crater.

Radioman Chief Petty Officer Marvin W. Balhorn, USN (Ret.)
Marion, Iowa

I was a Radioman Third Class when the war started on Wake Island. That morning of December 8, 1941, I was in the radio shack up near the civilian Camp Two, standing watch on the navy radio station. I took the coded message that came in from Pearl telling about the bombing attack by the Japanese. I decoded the message and passed it around as fast as I could.

When the bombers came over that noon, we were in the small radio shack, but the bombers concentrated on the airfield and the aircraft on the ground and didn't bother with us. After the raid our CO told us to dig a bunker to put ourselves and the radio gear in. There were eight of us navy radiomen manning the station around the clock. We all dug with shovels. We dug out a hole ten by twelve feet and about six feet deep, then we got heavy timbers and put them over the top for a roof. On top of them we put layers of sandbags. It took us until 2:00 A.M. to get it done and moved in.

So the second day of bombing we were safely tucked away in the bunker. Good thing. Our old radio shack took a direct hit and got demolished. Later the bombing wiped out our radio equipment. We had no assignment then. Our CO told us to take care of ourselves and not to get killed. I didn't have a weapon of any kind. I came through the fighting without a scratch. Later on in the bombing, the radio guys moved to one of the concrete bunkers down by the CP [command post] in back of the airfield.

Corporal Dennis C. Connor, USMC
Ellisville, Missouri

I was sitting in my tent in Camp One cleaning my rifle a little after 0600 on December 8, 1941, getting ready for our inspection at 0800. We had rifle inspection every Monday morning. That was about the only thing military that we did. Some army sergeant came past our tent. He had a kind of wild look in his eye and said the Japs had just bombed Pearl Harbor. He was from the Army Air Corps radio trailer that was guiding B-17s to Wake Island and to the Dutch East Indies and the Philippines. They had a long-range radio. He was on the way to tell his CO, Captain Wellman, who would tell Devereux about it.

The tents were right there close together. We went to chow. When we started out the mess hall door after breakfast, the general alarm or call to arms sounded. I went back to my tent, and "Benny" Benjamin, Jimmy King, and another guy were in the tent. We had a box of rifle ammunition, so we split it up and grabbed our rifles and helmets and then ran out to the trucks that were waiting to take us to our positions. I was assigned to a .50-caliber machine gun. We waited there until about noon and the first bombing raid. It was a good thing they never came over that low again, about fifteen hundred feet, because they would have caught a lot of our rounds.

I was between the airport and the south shore, and I got off a rifle round or two at the planes. After the raid I went to the airstrip and saw all the dead bodies and the fires and the burned up and smashed Wildcat fighter planes.

Then I was assigned to wire duty, and I worked at establishing communications where the bombs had ripped them out. We'd go out and splice the lines back together, both day and night, whenever we found they had been cut. I did that the next three days.

First Sergeant Charles H. Camp, USMC (deceased)
Poteau, Oklahoma
(from Wanda Camp)

My late husband joined the marines in 1938 and retired in 1962, after twenty-four years of service to his country. When he was on Wake Island, he said, he fought until they told him to stop. He said that most of the time he was scared to death. Charles could be contrary. If someone told him to turn right, he usually turned left. If they said sit down, he would stand up. He said that got him into a lot of trouble in prison camp. He told me that sometimes they beat the hell out of him because he was so stubborn.

First Sergeant Franklin D. Gross, USMC (Ret.)
Independence, Missouri

That first day the war started, I had just come out of the chow hall at Camp One when the bugle blew what we thought was fire call, and we were a bit confused. Turned out it was General Quarters. Then we learned what was going on, and we grabbed our rifles and World War I helmets and got in our truck and rushed down to our guns at Peacock Point. I was a corporal, in charge of three .50-caliber machine guns on the southern point of Wake Island. We got ready for action, then waited.

About noon I was standing on top of a shelter and talking to our battery commander, Second Lieutenant Robert M. Hanna. We saw some planes come out of a hole in the clouds to the south; we figured they were some more B-17s to refuel and send on to the Philippines. But they weren't. A minute later they had plastered the airfield with pattern bombing and destroyed everything in their path.

One of our fifties got off eight rounds at the planes, then fouled. The head space was wrong. We got that fixed but never had another chance to fire at the Jap planes. It wasn't until December 23, when the Jap dive-bombers came in low, that we had a chance to fire our .50-caliber guns at them again.

Our job was to protect the five-inch guns down near us and to fire on any landings made in our area. No Japs ever came in over our beaches. We had three men on each of our guns, and three civilians who helped us out wherever they could. We were on the tail end of the food delivery system. We sent a man up to a distribution point to pick up our rations, but by the time the trucks got to us, usually the food was all gone or down to the scrapings. One day we got four sandwiches for the eight of us.

We knew that there had been food and supplies hidden all over the island, so if we were captured the Japs wouldn't get it. But Major Devereux had warned us that it would be damned near a capital offense if any marine looted those food caches. One of our civilian helpers, Sonny Kaiser, volunteered to go find some food.

He took a walk the next morning and came back loaded with cans of beans, cans of fish, shredded coconuts, candy, and cigars. He apologized for not bringing more. We were grateful for his help. We would have starved to death without Kaiser. He never would tell us where he got the loot, but he kept furnishing us with food, candy, and cigars as long as we needed them.

Our gun positions didn't get hit the first two days of the war. On the third and the abortive Japanese invasion, we couldn't see much. We were around the point and the action was across from South Beach. I climbed up on a rock and did see the close-in Jap destroyer get hit and sink. Then Jap shells started whistling over and I got down and found a hole.

We got bombed every day but one after that. Our battery didn't get any direct hits. One close miss blew in the side of one of our dugouts and scratched up three men on the crew, but nobody was killed. Nearly fifty years later I put the three up for Purple Hearts, and they got them awarded in the year 2000.

Sergeant Major Robert E. Winslow, USMC (Ret.)
Eugene, Oregon

I was eating breakfast at Camp One when we heard the General Quarters call. They told us that Pearl Harbor had been bombed and for sure we would be next. We got the word from Platoon Sergeant Johnalson E. "Big" Wright that this was no drill, and I believed him. Wright was the three-hundred-pound marine who was later killed by a direct hit of a hundred-pound bomb.

As soon as we heard General Quarters we all went out to our gun positions. I was in the three-inch antiaircraft guns in Battery D. We were on Toki Point up on the north end of Peale Island. We only had three of our four guns operating at first, and Sergeant Orville J. Cain was our gun captain. I was second loader on the firing team. I took the shell out of the fuse box and gave it to the first loader, who shoved it into the breach.

Our fourth gun was operated by a crew of civilians. Walter A. Bowsher Jr. led the crew. He was a corporal at the time, I think. The civilians' gun did pretty well considering the guys were trained on the spot.

On that first bombing run by the Japanese we didn't get much firing in. We weren't ready for them. We did get in a few shots just as they were disappearing over the horizon. They were so low and fast. They hit mostly the airfield that first time, so we didn't get touched by the bombs or strafing.

Staff Sergeant Ralph J. Holewinski, USMC
Gaylord, Michigan

I enlisted in the marines in May of 1939 and made corporal before the war started. My duty station on Wake Island was part of the south shore in back of the airport, where I had a mile and a half of beach to defend. They gave me two thirty-caliber heavy machine guns and seven men. After the first landing attempt, the brass wondered why a mere corporal had two guns and that much beach under his command. So 2nd Lt. Robert M. Hanna was put in charge of the area.

That first day of the war, I was just leaving the mess hall at Camp One when the alert was sounded, and we all scrambled to get to our guns. Our two were dug into the sand with just the muzzle of the gun showing over a few rows of sandbags to protect us from rifle fire and shell shrapnel. We manned our guns and waited.

Brigadier General John F. Kinney, USMC (Ret.)
Cupertino, California
(*From his book* Wake Island Pilot, *Brassey's, 1995. Used by permission.*)

The destruction that greeted me at Wake when I returned from morning patrol that December 8th was more than I was prepared for. The enemy bombers had come in low, the constant roar of the surf masking the noise of their engines, and caught most of the men on the atoll by surprise. Our total lack of radar further prevented their detection until they were already over the island and beginning to release their bombs. None of our aircraft revetments were complete. Our planes on the ground were like targets in a carnival shooting galley, stationary targets that could not shoot back.

The Japanese pilots began that day to disprove the stereotypes we had of them as being only mediocre aviators and so nearsighted they could not hit their targets. Japanese machine gun fire and bomb fragments hit every one of our planes still on the ground. Seven of them were so badly burned as to be completely unsalvageable. The eighth one, number 8, looked like it might be able to fly again, although it had received hits in both wings, the tail fin, stabilizer, fuselage, elevators, hood, fuse box, radio cables, left flap, and auxiliary gas tank. (The seven wrecks certainly provided a likely source for spare parts over the next two weeks.) To make matters worse, Captain Elrod's number 9 had hit some debris on the airstrip that bent the prop on his plane when he landed after his patrol. Thick black smoke boiled skyward from the two above-ground fuel tanks as 25,000 gallons of gasoline burned fiercely, and many of the individual drums of gas stored at various points were also hit.

Our tents were shredded or burned, some of our oxygen bottles were destroyed, and our air compressor and virtually all of our meager supply of spare parts were gone. Major Walter J. Bayler's ground-to-air radio gear was reduced to so much scrap metal.

My decision to stay aloft as long as I did after the raiders departed saved me from actually witnessing all the human carnage on the first day of the war. By the time I landed, the military and civilian medical staffs had begun to treat the wounded at the hospital at Camp

Two, and able-bodied survivors had taken all the dead to the refrigerated storage facility until proper burials could be arranged.

Hardest hit the first day were the men of my VMF-211 squadron. Out of the fifty-five personnel on the ground when the attack struck, we lost twenty-three killed and eleven wounded. A casualty rate of almost 62 percent. That in the course of ten or twelve minutes. Three of my fellow pilots, Major Paul A. Putnam, Captain Frank C. Tharin, and Staff Sergeant Robert O. Arthur, suffered minor wounds but continued to perform their duties.

Second Lieutenant Henry G. Webb, my golfing partner from Hawaii, was in much more serious condition. Japanese bullets had taken three toes off his left foot and another bullet had lodged in his abdomen. Three other pilots died. When the enemy bombers first appeared, First Lieutenant George A. Graves, and Second Lieutenants Robert J. Conderman and Frank J. Holden were together discussing the upcoming escort mission for the Pan Am clipper. Frank Holden scrambled toward the relative safety of some nearby brush, but was killed before he reached it. George Graves and redheaded "Strawberry" Conderman both sprinted for their Wildcats, hoping to get into the air, where they could have a chance to inflict some damage on the attackers.

Graves made it into the cockpit, but before he could get under way, a Japanese bomb scored a direct hit on his plane. Machine gun fire cut down Conderman before he could get to his plane, the bullets tearing into his neck and both legs. Corporal Robert E. L. Page did not wait for the attack to subside but immediately tried to help Conderman and other wounded marines nearby. Conderman may have realized that his wounds were so serious that there would be little Page could do for him, because he told the corporal to attend to the other wounded first. He really had guts. He remained conscious all day, but died that night in our little hospital.

★ ★ ★

Gunnery Sergeant Ed M. Bogdonovitch, USMC
Greenwood, Wisconsin

Yeah, it irritated me a little that I didn't get breakfast that December 8 back in '41 when the big war started. They told us Pearl Harbor had been bombed by the Japanese and we probably would be next. It was about 0730, and they issued ammunition and told us to get to our General Quarters positions. I had been a quartermaster, delivering goods, food, powder, and shells to the five-inch gun sites. When General Quarters sounded, I jumped in a truck that ran our Battery D team up to Toki Point at the north end of Peale Island. That was about four and a half miles away. We got the three-inch antiaircraft guns ready to fire and sat there waiting.

My duty assignment at General Quarters was first loader on a three-inch gun. I'm the one who pushes the round into the gun after the round has been fused and is all set to go. The planes came in too low that morning for us to get off any shots at them, but we were ready. The first planes came out of the south at ten minutes to twelve. We could see the bombs falling and the airfield getting hit real hard. We did get some strafing that first day, but they never hurt us with the strafing and they didn't get any bombs up near us.

We had seen the big Pan Am clipper take off early that morning, but when it got the word about Pearl Harbor, it turned and came back. It was sitting in the lagoon next to the loading dock. Still, it got hit only a few times by machine gun bullets from the strafing planes, and none of the hits were serious.

My issue weapon on Wake was a Browning automatic rifle, the old BAR. It was the big weapon in a rifle squad and had been developed for World War I. It had a twenty-round magazine and could fire five hundred rounds a minute. It shot the same round the Springfield rifle did, the 30.06, and had a bipod near the muzzle that could be folded down. It was, in effect, a handheld machine gun.

We kept our antiaircraft guns ready. There were four of them in our battery, and we had a height finder to help us fire at the right altitude to hit the Jap planes when they came in at twelve thousand or fourteen thousand feet or even higher. We almost for sure shot down two of them. We saw the hit and smoking and, I think, watched them drop into the ocean. We had bombing raids every day. About halfway through the attacks, we took a direct hit on our position and the bomb ruined our height finder. After that we had to rely on the altitude phoned in from another finder.

Corporal Robert B. Murphy, USMC
Thermopolis, Wyoming

I was on a three-inch antiaircraft gun, in E Battery, just north of the middle of the airstrip, when the war started that Monday morning. We got off some rounds when the first planes came over, but I don't remember if we hit any of them. We moved our gun several times; it was a lot of work. We wound up north of the airstrip in the brush. I didn't get wounded during the fighting.

Gunnery Sergeant Martin A. Gatewood, USMC (Ret.)
Norfolk, Virginia

That first morning of the war, when the bombs started falling, I was promoted quickly from second loader to first loader on my three-inch antiaircraft gun in Battery D on Toki Point. The first gunner was supposed to ram the round home after I took it from the fuse box and pushed it into the tube. This guy was watching the Jap planes come over instead of doing his job, and we lost the shot. The gun captain promoted me at once to first loader. He said he had to have a man who was watching what he was doing.

We got off quite a few shots that morning during the twelve minutes of the Jap raid. I'm not sure exactly how many. They were bombing the airfield down on Wake. Toki Point is at the top of Peale Island, the atoll north of Wake Island. We saw the planes come over slightly to the side of us at about fifteen hundred feet, and we kept firing. No bombs hit near us that first day, and we weren't strafed either.

After the raid we went back to filling sandbags on the beach and building up the protection around our gun. Some of the bags we had in place were old and leaking out sand, so we replaced them. We also sandbagged around our ammo dump.

The second day, the bombers came over high, at least fourteen thousand feet. Lots of their bombs landed in the lagoon, while the wind kept blowing others over the other side of the atoll into the ocean.

On the third day, when the Japs tried their first landing, all the men on the three-inch guns were told to stay in their holes. We had no targets to fire at. After the first raid, we had dug a hole near the gun position and covered it over with wood and then sandbags on top of that. We'd be safe in there except for a direct artillery shell hit. We crawled into the dugout when the Jap cruiser began lobbing shells onto the islands. None of them hit our immediate area. We couldn't see the Jap ships, but we heard that at least one had been sunk.

Corporal Richard L. Gilbert, USMC
Ashville, Alabama

The war started for me like it did for most of the men. I was having breakfast at Camp One. General Quarters sounded and we ran to a formation. There they told us about the attack on Pearl Harbor. I grabbed my combat gear and personal weapons and went down to our five-inch artillery piece on Peacock Point, the southernmost part of the Wake atoll group. I was in Battery A. We had two guns, and there were four antiaircraft three-inchers near us and two .50-caliber machine guns in place.

We couldn't fire at the bombers, so the first two days we just had to put up with them. The second day, a bomb came close to our guns. It hit one of the dugouts where we took cover from the bombers. It was a direct hit, on the spot where Private John Katchak had been waiting. He was the first man killed in the marine defense battalion. We buried him right there in his dugout.

Maj. Robert O. Arthur, USMC (Ret.)

We'd been trying to get the Wildcats into combat readiness for the three days we'd been on Wake. On December 8 I was working on a direction finder for the F4F. I had it all wired in when someone shouted, "Here comes the air force." I climbed out of the belly of the F4F and looked, and lo and behold, it was the Japanese air force. We had heard of the Pearl Harbor attack and realized we were at war with Japan, but who would want this island?

I shouted, "Air force, my ass, take cover!" I took off running ninety degrees to the plane's path and almost made it. Just as I dove behind a rock, a bomb landed just behind us, showering us with rocks and dirt and shrapnel. Some hit my back, and a piece of the shrapnel caught my left hand and cut the tendons and nerves. I took a truck around the island to sick bay to get my hand cleaned out and taped up. While I was there, we had another bombing raid. I was in a concrete bunker. After it was over, I went back to the squadron to see how bad we were hit.

My Wildcat had the reserve gas tank shot out. Some pilots had tried to start their engines and were killed with their crew chiefs. Four planes on combat patrol never saw any of the attacking Japanese planes. Seven of our Wildcats were totally destroyed on the ground. Most of the mechanics were killed running toward the planes, and the administration tents were demolished and more people killed. We were in a fix. We had only four planes that would fly, we had no mechanics, and our planes were left sitting out in the open. We called on the civilians to help us. They dug holes in the sand to help hide the remaining planes and to build a big hangar out of a sand dune.

I went on telephone watch. We covered the phone twenty-four hours a day. I was also a pilot. I shared a dugout with Major Putnam. Whoever heard the planes got on the phone and notified everyone. For my weapon I carried a Thompson submachine gun.

Gunnery Sergeant Artie J. Stocks, USMC (Ret.)
Layton, Utah

I joined the marines when I was eighteen, and after basic I took training as a machine gunner. I arrived on Wake Island December 2, 1941, and was assigned to a machine gun position on Kuku Point on

Wilkes Island, just north of the main Wake Island. During the attack that first day our communication telephone lines were blasted apart by bombs, so we had no direct orders. After that, it was bombers overhead once or twice almost every day.

Then, early morning on December 23, the Japs came with their big invasion. They came in on the south island, and our boys couldn't hold off the twenty-five hundred men in the landing party.

First Sergeant James O. King, USMC (Ret.)
San Rafael, California

My post was on the blinker tower, which was only twenty-one feet high. ("Blinker" was Morse code being sent with lights.) At approximately 1000 I saw a "recognition signal" being flashed by a submarine. I immediately called our commanding officer, Major James P. S. Devereux, and informed him of the signal. He asked, "Did you acknowledge their signal?" I replied, "No, sir, I am awaiting your orders." He then instructed me to send the following message: "Stand clear of gun range: War declared," which I did immediately. The sub flashed an abbreviated form that "message was received" and immediately disappeared.

A short time later, Sergeant Donald R. Malleck, Radio Chief, came up and asked if I had noticed anything yet. I told him about the sub and the major's order. We talked for a while, and all of a sudden we saw planes dropping out of the low, dark clouds right over the beach less than a hundred yards from where we were, but not coming in our direction. The planes dropped their bomb loads, and we felt helpless with only a loaded 03 rifle, which held only five rounds. We did not fire at them, as they were already out of range. But it was frustrating not to be able to do anything.

I spent almost all of my time on Wake Island working the BD-72 telephone switchboard in the command post. First we were on the beach up by Camp One. The CP was so small that I had to set one of the switchboards on top of the other one. There was room for only four or five men in the CP at one time.

Day two or three of the fight, I remember being in the beach command post and hearing the bombs falling, with the sound of them coming closer and closer. Finally one of them hit near us and dust and dirt rained down. I had to hold up the switchboards so they wouldn't fall over. The blast blew dirt and coral all over us. Standing in the doorway Major Devereux said, "That was close." Then he went outside to inspect the damage.

Later on we moved the CP down behind the airstrip, where there were concrete bunkers. There we had more room and a lot more protection.

I worked closely with Major Devereux, and I thought he was one of the best marine officers I ever knew. I say that even though he did court-martial me one time. I was in the front seat of a truck going up to camp one day when Sergeant Johnalson E. Wright came along and told me to get in the backseat. There was a jump seat in the back, where two men sat. I told him I was the assistant driver and I was supposed to sit in the front seat. Sergeant Wright told me to get in back again; he said it was a direct order. Again I refused. One man in back got out and the sergeant got in. The next day I had to go see the major. He gave me a deck court-martial, the lowest level possible. I explained to him what had happened and he said I should have moved. He gave me a probationary reduction in rank from PFC. Which meant I got to keep my stripes and my pay grade, unless I messed up again. I didn't. He was very fair about the whole thing.

Sergeant Norman Kaz-Fritzshall, USMC
Buffalo Grove, Illinois

I never did get breakfast on that first day of the war. I was coming off guard duty on the water tower near Camp One when General Quarters sounded. I hurried to my tent, got my helmet and some ammo, and jumped in the truck that took us around the airstrip, up the other side of Wake Island, across the bridge, and onto Peale Island. I was a .50-caliber machine gunner situated out on the end of Peale at Toki Point. I was in Battery B and we had two fifties.

We saw the Jap planes coming over about noon and got some shots at some of them. Not sure we hit any, but one of the guys said he saw one of the planes smoking. I was busy with the gun, firing it, getting ammo, and making sure the pump pushed water up into the water-cooling jacket on the weapon.

We didn't get hit with any bombs that day, but later I did get some nicks and scratches in the shoulder from shrapnel. Good enough to get me a Purple Heart medal.

Cpl. Carroll Trego, USMC

I had been a corporal in the marine reserves and was called to active duty in 1940. They sent me to the Marine Corps Recruit Depot in San Diego, and since I was a corporal, I was made a drill instructor. I'd never even been through marine basic training, and now I was one of the tough marine D.I.s. I put two platoons through the training and only had to wash out one man. That one couldn't keep cadence when he marched and always had his feet out of time with the rest of the platoon.

The day the war started, I was walking from the west end of the airstrip on Wake Island south toward the truck that would take us to noon chow at Camp Two up the right-hand wing of the island. I heard the Japanese planes coming. There were twenty-seven twin-tailed Japanese bombers flying right toward the airstrip; I knew what they were at once. We all scattered. I ran to a small tree about three inches in diameter and hugged it for protection. The bombs started falling, mostly on the airstrip. But after the bombers had roared past, my ten-foot-tall tree had been cut down to a five-foot stub. I didn't get any wounds in the process.

Later I learned that the bombers were from the Japanese Air Attack Force Number 1 of the Twenty-Fourth Air Flotilla based at the island of Roi, 720 miles south of Wake. Three flights of the nine planes dropped down and attacked us that first day.

Corporal Willis Tate, USMC
Perry, Louisiana

That first day the bombs started falling I was on a truck. I leapt off and tried to take cover, but a bomb hit close to me and covered me up with dirt and coral. I wasn't wounded. After I got uncovered I went on down to Peacock Point, where I was a loader on A battery of the five-inch long guns.

Machinist's Mate Third Class William O. Plate, USN
Wasilla, Arkansas

I was attached to the Wake Island Naval Air Station when the war started. I was on the airfield that first day that they hit us with the bombers. Bomb fragments wounded me, but the medics patched me up and I was assigned as gun captain on a .30-caliber machine gun down on the beach. I stayed on the gun until we surrendered on the twenty-third.

From there on I did what most of the other guys did. The hell ship *Nitta Maru* to Shanghai, Woosung prison camp, and then Kiangwan. We moved to Osaka, Japan, in 1943 and were burned out by B-29 bombers. They moved us to Niigata, there on Honshu Island, until the end of the war.

I spent some time in a hospital on Guam, and then Oak Knoll Hospital in Oakland. After that I went to Long Beach Naval Hospital. I was discharged from Terminal Island in San Pedro, California, on February 17, 1946.

Ed Hassig, Chief Warrant Officer, USMC (Ret.)
Minneapolis, Minnesota

I joined the marines in 1929 and put in twenty-seven years before I retired in 1956. On Wake Island I was a tech sergeant assigned to the three big arc searchlights. I arrived in September of 1941, and we put in the three lights in various spots around the three atolls. The lights burn carbon shafts about an inch thick. In those days one carbon would last for about forty-five minutes. We had gasoline-fueled generators to power the big lights and other generators to provide power for other uses. The big lights used direct current; the other equipment, alternating current. We had converters to change the type of current when needed.

That first morning of the war, on December 8, I was in Camp One having breakfast. Just after we ate, somebody sounded General Quarters, so we went out to the lights as we were supposed to do. My station was the light up on Peale Island. We used the lights a little bit during the Nips' landing on the twenty-third, but they were soon hit by shells and put out of commission.

I don't remember much about the surrender or the trip on the boat to China. I was in the same prison camps most of the other men were. When I got back to the States in 1945, I already had sixteen years in, so I decided to go for twenty. I got my Warrant Officer rating in 1951 and retired as a chief warrant officer. I'm ninety years old and looking toward ninety-one. Semper Fi."

Sergeant LeRoy N. Schneider, USMC
Barrington, Illinois

It was just after noon chow, and I was walking up to my gun on Toki Point on Peale Island when the first Japanese bombers came blasting over us on December 8, 1941. They were strafing the airfield and we got in the line of fire, but they missed us as we ran for cover— the little cover that was there.

I had been a truck driver, but when General Quarters sounded I went to duty on one of the three-inch antiaircraft guns up on Toki Point. I was an ammo carrier. My job was to be sure the gun had all the rounds it needed so the crew could fire as fast as possible while the targets were in our range. Captain Bryghte D. Godbold was commander of the four guns in Battery D.

Almost every day after December 8 we were firing our three-inchers at the Japanese bombers. They came at different times, so we stayed on the guns all day. Then, at night, we moved our guns so the Japs wouldn't know where we would be the next day.

The guns had to be jacked up, their legs folded, and a carrier put under them. Then a truck hauled the guns to a new spot. It was usually some place in the brush, where we would have partial concealment. There were quite a few civilians who helped us every time we moved the guns. It would have been a lot harder to do without them. We moved almost every night and then had to be ready to fire the gun the next day. Usually we didn't get much sleep.

Captain James J. Davis, USN (Ret.)
Huntington Beach, California.

Monday morning, December 8, we heard rumors about the war starting, but nothing definite. Then the Pan Am clipper took off, so I figured they must be just more rumors. A short time later the clipper returned and began dumping fuel so it could land. Something unusual had happened. At our command headquarters in Camp Two, I heard that the Japs had attacked Pearl Harbor.

I was an ROTC ensign at the time, and my duty assignment was supply and accounting officer. I went to a conference with Commander Cunningham and the skipper of the Pan Am clipper. He agreed to fly a big circle around the island and see if he could see any ships or enemy planes. A pair of Wildcats would fly cover for him.

Two of the fighters were getting ready to go when the twenty-seven Japanese bombers came out of the rain squall just south of the Island and swung in, making their bombing runs. The revetments were not finished to protect the planes on the ground. The runway itself was made of coral that had been rolled down hard by big steamrollers. The Japanese bombers and strafers caught the eight planes on the ground and destroyed all but one. They did some damage to Camp Two as well before they pulled away without taking a single bullet in response.

The attack was over in ten to twelve minutes. The Pan Am clipper had survived, miraculously getting only a few bullet holes in her from the strafing planes, but they had hit nothing vital. The crew threw off all the mail and freight they had picked up and took on board all of the Pam Am personnel at the base except one employee who had driven some wounded Chamarros to the hospital and another man from the Bureau of the Budget. Pan Am didn't take any of the Chamarro natives aboard, and they ended up in the POW camps along with the military and civilians.

The second day, the bombers burned down my quarters at Camp One and smashed the whole area; not much was left. They bombed the hospital, and many of the men inside died. The next night, I was sleeping when the Japs tried their first invasion attempt. They woke us up so we'd be ready, but there wasn't anything we could do. None of the navy personnel had weapons or helmets. We weren't prepared to fight a battle. But when the Japanese ships got close enough to be well within range of the five-inch guns and Major Devereux gave the order to fire, the gunners sank one destroyer and damaged two more ships, and the Japanese fleet pulled back and sailed away. The Wildcat pilots sank another Japanese man-of-war and damaged two more before they got out of range.

Sergeant William F. Buehler, USMC
Joliet, Illinois

That first morning, I had just finished breakfast—hotcakes as I remember—and we were told to grab a ride and get up to our guns on Wilkes Island. I was assigned to Battery L, the two five-inch naval guns up on the end of Wilkes. We got the guns ready to fire, then Sergeant Henry A. Bedell told me to go out near the beach and keep a sharp lookout for ships. I wasn't taking this threat of the Japs seriously, and Bedell chewed me out good and told me to walk out almost to the beach, where I could see anything that moved out at sea. So I did. I didn't see anything.

First thing unusual came almost at noon, when I saw that formation of planes coming out of the clouds from the south toward Wake Island and the airfield. At first I thought they were ours, then I saw the rising sun on them and I knew they had to be Japs. *Good God,* I thought, *those bastards up there are trying to kill us.* But no bombs came anywhere near us that first day. After that we got busy digging foxholes and trenches to dive into if the bombs did come our way.

Then, on the eleventh, we had our turn. The major held the five-inchers from firing until the Japs were suckered in real close, maybe four thousand yards. Our gun fired and the other five-inchers fired, and we sunk one destroyer that had ventured in close. A round hit either the powder magazine or some depth charges it had stored on deck, because it went up in one big explosion, broke in half, and sank. We fired at the other ships, but too soon it was over and the Japs turned and ran out of range.

That was the shooting war for us, the only time we got to use our five-inchers.

Staff Sergeant John Doyle, USMC (Ret.)
Blackwell, Oklahoma

When the General Quarters call came about 0730, I was in my tent in Camp One. Most of us figured it was a fire drill, so we grabbed our fire buckets and ran out to fall in. The sergeant yelled at us that this was no drill, the Japs had just bombed Pearl Harbor. We were at war. We rushed back and got our web belts on, picked up our weapons, and fell in again. We were quickly sent to our duty stations.

I had been a company clerk, but had told them I wanted to get out of the office and go into the five-inch guns. I had been promoted to sergeant in October, but the order never got to me, so I was a corporal during the fighting and the POW days. I was assigned to sight in the gun for elevation on the L Battery, near Kuku Point on the far end of Wilkes Island. Lieutenant McAlister was our battery commander.

We were in our gun emplacement all morning, then four of us piled into a truck and headed up to Camp Two for lunch. We were just beside the airstrip when we saw the planes coming from the south, three flights of nine each. They merged and bombed and strafed the Wildcat fighters and the runway and some tents nearby.

The driver said we should bail out of the truck, that we were being bombed. We surged out of the truck and ran. But we were too close to the runway, and the bombs and machine gun bullets from their wing guns got us. We dove to the ground. I didn't really feel anything, but I had taken a .27-caliber machine gun round in the middle of my back. It lodged there. After the attack I went to the civilian hospital, where we had navy corpsmen. They patched up the surface wound, but couldn't do anything about getting the Jap slug out of me. It didn't bother me that much, so I went back to duty. We had dead and wounded all over the airstrip. And we lost seven Wildcats.

The second day, the bombers found our gun. Even though we were in the brush and camouflaged, they hit close enough to us to ruin half of our aiming sight. We lost the azimuth scope, and had only the height scope left. All of us had dug shallow slit trenches to drop into during the air raids. When the strafing got fatal, we found out we could dig our holes quite a bit deeper, even in the rocklike coral.

Sergeant Fenton Quinn, USMC
Tucson, Arizona

That first morning when the war started, I heard the General Quarters call and loaded up my three-inch gun crew and took them down to their gun position on Peacock Point at the southernmost part of the atolls. After that I was stringing telephone wire. Had two guys in the back of my two-ton six truck with one of those big reels of telephone wire. We were somewhere between Peacock Point and Camp Two on Wake when I saw the Jap planes coming in. I knew we didn't have that many planes. We all bailed out of the truck and hit the ground. I got my Springfield rifle up in time to get off seven shots at them. I'd follow them and lead them a little and fire. Don't know if I hit any of them.

We were off to the side of the bombers and didn't get strafed or bombed. We had one bomb come close to us later.

It hit about twenty feet from us, but by the time it went off, three of us were flat on the ground. Nobody got hurt. All of the shrapnel went over our heads.

Private William B. Buckie, USMC
Hickory Hills, Illinois

I turned 21 years old when I was on Wake Island, and there, on December 8, 1941, I wasn't sure I was going to make it to twenty-two. I was in my two-ton truck near the airport on Wake Island when I saw the Japanese planes come in and the bombs falling. I stayed in the truck, and luckily it wasn't targeted by the planes. None of the bombs hit closer than fifty yards from me. As soon as the planes left, I drove to the airport and picked up wounded and took them to the hospital up at the civilian Camp Two. There were a lot of wounded.

Strange how it started. When they called General Quarters about 0730 we thought it was another drill. We'd had one the day before and everything had got fouled up. My truck wouldn't start, because the plugs were wet from the fog and dew—I was right on the coast no matter where I drove—and that meant I couldn't take the gun crews up to Battery B on Peale Island, about eight miles away. So, on Sunday, when they blew General Quarters, I figured it was just another test run. Only it was the real thing. I got my gun crews to Toki Point on Peale Island, which is way up on the far end of the little island.

My main job was driving for Battery B up on Toki Point. The battery consisted of two five-inch guns. I took the crews up there from mess and in the mornings, and made sure they had enough ammunition and powder. With the truck I was all over the three islands.

When the first Japanese invasion try came on December 11, I was on the beach digging a hole as fast as I could. My battery was firing at the ships once they came in close enough. I had a shovel on my truck, and that made digging easier. Surprising how fast you can dig when the naval artillery shells are coming over.

Then for the next twelve days we had almost daily bombings. I never got scratched during the entire battle on Wake. I had a couple of close calls as the Nips tried to hit the truck, but luckily for me, they missed.

Seaman First Class Cassius Smith, USN
Arcata, California

That first morning when the war started, I was in the navy warehouse on Peale Island, up by the Pan Am facility, uncrating a new motorcycle with a sidecar. We only had it partly out of the box when the Japanese bombers came over. I hugged the outside of the warehouse for the only cover I could find. I was working with James Monroe Mullins from Oklahoma. No bombs came anywhere near us that first day.

Fifteen minutes after the last Jap plane left, I was assigned to go work with the marines. Twelve of us sailors were given our first job—to help pick up the wounded and take care of the dead. There were a lot of them. Then we helped clean up the airstrip so the planes we had left could land and take off.

After that, the other sailors and I reported to Marine Second Lieutenant Arthur A. Poindexter. He was in charge of a group of machine guns. He sent four of us up the beach by the water tower to man a .30-caliber machine gun. I'd never much fired the .30-caliber, but I did do some work on one at Ford Island in Hawaii. I could tear it down and put it back together again. So we were a machine gun crew right out on the beach a short way from Camp One and the water tower.

The bombers that came over the second day were far too high for us to shoot at, so we lay on mattresses and watched them.

We were sailors, we didn't have a shovel to dig a slit trench. We didn't even have side arms or rifles. Just our machine gun. The second day, a civilian with a bulldozer came and built a dugout for us with beams over the top and dirt and coral on top of that. It gave us a place to hide when the bombers came over.

Corporal Jack Hearn, USMC
Boerne, Texas

I and about half the other marines on the islands were having breakfast at Camp One when we heard the General Quarters call. I grabbed my gear out of our tent and our truck ran us down around the airport, then north past the civilians in Camp Two and on up to Toki Point on Peale Island.

Most of the bombs that fell that first day, and most of the strafing, took place on the airstrip, where the eight Grumman Wildcat fighter aircraft had been dispersed. One of the three-inch antiaircraft guns on Toki near us did sustain some damage.

Gunnery Sergeant Thomas W. Johnson, USMC
St. Joseph, Missouri

I was a corporal in the Corps on December 8 when the war started. We'd had early chow and were on our way to take more sandbags over to our three-inch gun on Wilkes Island when the general alarm sounded. We didn't take it seriously. We'd had these dry runs before, lots of them. John Hamas came running across the area yelling at us, "This is not a drill, this is for real. Get your rifles, helmets and ammo."

We thought he was kidding. We went back to our tents and got our rifles and helmets but no ammo. When we got to the truck, they sent us back to get the big green cans of rifle ammo. Then they took us over to Peale Island in the truck to our D Battery of three-inch guns. We were positioned up on the north end of it along with two five-inch guns, our four three-inchers, and two .50-caliber machine guns.

At the gun position we checked our height and range finders and had live ammo ready. We unpacked the rounds from the wooden cases, which held four each, and stacked them in safe little bunkers near the gun. We checked our electrical for the height and range finders and everything was working well, so we turned it off and waited for the need to use the gun.

Not long after that, Captain Godbold told us on the phone that it was all for real, that Pearl Harbor had been savagely attacked without warning and we were at war. He expected that we would be hit soon.

About noon we heard the planes and then the bombs going off. We couldn't see them down at the airstrip. Then the planes appeared overhead as they circled around to bomb the airport again. We didn't get bombed at all that first day. We tried to get our guns up and firing, but the juice went off. Evidently the generator wasn't working, because we couldn't fire. I was number one loader on the gun, but by the time we got it all working the Japs had flown away.

Master Sgt. Walter T. Kennedy, USMC (Ret.)

Monday morning three other guys and I were at Camp One putting up another tent when I heard the siren. I looked at the other guys, and they wondered if we should get over to the airfield. I said "It's just another fire drill, we'll stay here."

The gun crews fell out at Camp One, the marine's base, and then broke ranks and grabbed their combat gear. The men came out with machine guns and their belts. So I stuck my head in a tent and asked what was going on. A kid said the Japs had just hit Pearl Harbor and we'd probably be next. I didn't believe him, because there had been a lot of false rumors about war starting and even more realistic war exercises.

Then Major Walter L. J. Bayler came up to us. He was an expert in laying out and building military airfields. We had a truck, and he asked if I'd take him down to the airfield about a mile away. He told me the Japs had really hit Pearl Harbor. At the airfield I let him off and then went over to Sergeant Bob Barker, who was building a loop antenna. I helped him on the antenna, and after a while he said, "Let's go to chow." We'd go up to Camp Two, the civilian camp, because the civilians had better sandwiches than the marine camp served.

We went over to the operations tent on the airstrip, and a minute later somebody opened up the back of the tent and said, "Hey, look at the airplanes." They weren't ours. There were three flights of Japanese bombers coming directly for us out of a cloud bank. We scattered. We didn't have helmets, weapons, or anything.

I looked up and saw three formations of nine planes each as they hit the airfield. They weren't more than fifteen hundred feet in the air. The bombs had two-foot-long pins on them that evidently set off the bomb, so they went off before they hit the ground, making them almost like an airburst. We were running like hell; all I could do was dive for a bush. A bomb went off near me, covering me with dirt and coral, and I heard the bullets hitting from the strafing runs. When the planes passed after the first run, I tried to get up, but I couldn't bring my arm around. I moved so I could swing my arm around with my body; I grabbed my wrist. Then I started to get up but couldn't move my left leg. I saw the shrapnel wound below my kneecap. I sat there awhile and I didn't feel too good, so I took this little cap and leaned back on it. Then somebody came and gave me a tetanus shot. A while later they came and picked me up in a truck and took me to the hospital.

The bone was broken in my right arm, and it was chopped up bad from the .27-caliber machine gun round from the strafing Jap plane. My leg wasn't so bad. A few days later the piece of iron worked up my leg, past my knee, and just above my knee the medics cut it out.

They set my arm and then put it in a straight splint, then in an airplane splint so I couldn't move it. They had me in the hospital at Camp One, but most of it was blasted apart.

I was in the hospital for the next two weeks and during the battle of the twenty-third. During that time, they moved us out of the trashed old hospital to the new emergency hospital bunker down near the airstrip.

In less than ten minutes the Japanese bombs and bullets totally demolished Pan Am's facilities on Peale Island. The Pam Am hotel was set on fire and five Chamarro employees died in the blaze. The raid also destroyed a stock room, fuel tanks, several other surrounding buildings, and ruined the firm's radio transmitter. Nine of the Pan America's sixty-six-man staff were dead. Two of the clipper's crew were wounded. The twenty-six-ton aircraft, now empty of passengers and cargo but fully refueled, had not been seriously damaged. It rode easily at its moorings at the end of the dock. One bomb had exploded a hundred feet ahead but hadn't damaged the plane. Strafing runs had produced twenty-three bullet holes, but none of the rounds had hit the large fuel tanks.

The scouting mission was forgotten. Pan Am Captain Hamilton suggested evacuating the passengers, and the Pan Am staff and Commander Cunningham agreed. Everyone got on board except one staff man, who was driving an ambulance and didn't hear the evac order. The last plane to leave Wake Island before the surrender took off for Midway Island at 1330.

At 1145 on December 9 twenty-seven Nells planes struck at Wake. Second Lieutenant David Kliewer and Technical Sergeant William J. Hamilton met them at about eleven thousand feet and shot down one of them. The rest hit hard at Camp Two, where the civilians were housed. The hospital there was burned to the ground, and all the barracks were blown apart or burned. All but three patients were evacuated from the hospital. Those three were killed in their beds by machine gun fire. Commanders said three marines were reported missing: Robert W. Mitwalski, William M. Tucker, and Quince A. Hunt. All three were later found KIA.

Dr. Lieutenant Gustav Kahn, USN, and the civilian doctor, Lawton Shank, and their helpers evacuated the wounded and saved as much equipment as was possible. Dr. Shank carried wounded men from the hospital. The medical staff moved the wounded to magazines ten and thirteen, below the airstrip. There the medical personnel set up two twenty-one–bed wards.

Fireman 2nd Class Dare Kibble, USN

About dusk on the ninth some marine officer came along and ordered me and another sailor to climb up the water tower. We were to keep a lookout for anything we might see concerning enemy presence, either on land or at sea. They had strung a field telephone line up to the tower for communications. Where it went to, I was never told. I only knew that when I cranked the handle, someone answered on the other end. It may have been the Japanese, for all I knew.

There was no fresh water on the islands. All of the water was made with evaporators like the ones on the seagoing ships. It was then pumped up to the water tower to give some water pressure to users.

The first night, I covered half of the horizon and the other guy took the other half. About midnight I went around to see how he was doing. He was asleep. I swung my pair of night binoculars at him and hit him in the head. They didn't hit hard enough to knock him out. He wanted to know why I hit him. I told him this wasn't a game anymore, this was for real. I hinted strongly that I wasn't going to give my ass to the Japs just so he could have his beauty nap. If I caught him asleep on watch again, I'd throw him off the tower. I didn't have a gun with me or I would have shot him. At the time, I couldn't remember when I'd been so mad. I actually believe this swabby didn't realize what serious trouble he was in. He didn't sleep the rest of our time on the water tower.

Lt. Cmdr. Glenn E. Tripp, USN (Ret.)

The second day, I was assigned to the water tower in Camp Two. The job was to notify anyone if we saw or heard bombers coming. The surf was always loud and it was impossible to hear any planes. The second day—again, about noon—Japanese planes arrived out of the clouds to the south. This day the marine gunners were ready for them, and several planes were damaged or shot down.

After the second day most of the sailors left Camp Two and moved closer to Camp One, where most of the marines were stationed. I found myself assigned to a five-inch gun on Wilkes Island; Sergeant Wiley E. Tipton, USMC, was the gun captain. Here I served until after December 11.

Corporal Joe M. Tusa, USMC
Vista, California

I was a crane operator on Wake Island on December 9. I helped build bunkers and used the big crane to move materials around. Sorry, I just don't want to remember those things anymore.

Battery E of the three-inch antiaircraft guns on Peacock Point had opened fire on the attacking Japanese planes both days of their bombing. When Major Devereux analyzed the pattern of the bombing, he realized that one of the main targets had been the battery at Peacock Point. Certain that the Japanese had the battery pinpointed and would try to wipe it out the next day, Devereux ordered the battery to be moved six hundred yards northeast. The relocation proved to be a tremendous job. For one thing, work couldn't start until nightfall in case a Japanese spotter plane came over; for another, it was too large an undertaking for the marine gunners alone, so the major asked the head of the civilian construction men, Dan Teters, for some help. Teters brought a hundred men and trucks, and they went to work.

The large legs of the gun were folded and jacked up and set on a dolly, then jacked down and secured. A truck towed the gun to the new position. There it was reset, secured with the hundreds of sandbags set around it, and camouflaged. Hundreds of three-inch rounds were trucked and stacked near each gun. Then they made wooden guns and put them in the old location so it looked like they hadn't been moved. It was exhausting, time-consuming work, and the men had it done just when it turned light. The crews for the five batteries would make these gun position moves more than a dozen times during the course of the fighting.

Ken L. Marvin, USMC
Gig Harbor, Washington

I was in D-Battery AA three-inch guns. We were short-handed, with only enough men to handle three of the four guns we had. The second day there were ten civilians who volunteered to man the remaining gun. They stayed at their post throughout the battle and became very proficient. Many of the civilian construction workers toiled day and night building shelters, filling sand bags, and bringing us food and water. Many of them died for us by exposing themselves to gunfire even when they had no protection. They built bunkers, helped as mechanics, worked at the airport and at the hospital. They helped us move our guns at night. Without the help of hundreds of civilians we would not have lasted as long as we did.

Gunnery Sergeant John S. Johnson, USMC (Ret.)
West Plains, Missouri

When I arrived on Wake Island on August 6, 1941, I never thought I'd be in charge of two .30-caliber heavy machine guns manned by six civilians and two marines. The first two days there, I was assigned to a .50-caliber machine gun, then we came up short on personnel and long on the heavies. I'm not sure how they found the volunteers, but sixteen of them showed up and Lieutenant [Arthur R.] Poindexter told me to set up the two guns and teach the new crew how to shoot and supply them. We were placed out on Kuku Point on Wilkes Island, way up north.

Sunday, the seventh, the day before the war started for us, we had the whole day off. Lots of us wrote letters home, did our laundry, and cleaned our guns. Major Devereux must have known that a war was coming. He told us to get a fresh canteen of water every morning. He had sent a box of 30.06 ammo to each tent, so we all had fresh rounds.

We had that General Quarters call Monday morning about 0730 when I was headed to the mess hall to get breakfast. No such luck. We ran to our tents and grabbed our personal weapons and charged to our GQ stations. Mine was with the .50-caliber the first two days. I saw the pilots running for their planes with their parachutes. We didn't have Jeeps in those days. We had Ford pickups without the metal cab. They had canvas-covered front seats and benches in back so we could carry nine men with their gear. When the first Jap bombers came out of that cloudbank south of the airfield, we had a chance at them with the .50-caliber. The attackers came in low, maybe fifteen hundred feet, so I fired at the planes when they came over Peale. Some of them dropped their bombs, made a turn, and came back for more strafing runs. I fired at those guys, too, with my fifty. Then they were gone, and on December 10 I had a new assignment with my green crew of civilians on the two thirties. I trained them the best I could in the time we had.

General Quarters bugle call came at 0500, rousing the sleepy-eyed marines and sailors out of their air shelters and foxholes. The third day of the war came bright and clear. Breakfast was taken to the men in their gun positions and foxholes, and a Condition One alert was proclaimed by Major Devereux. That meant all lookouts were posted, and all weapons, phones, and fire-control equipment were manned. A dugout blackout shelter was built for the Wildcats; there a plane could be worked on all night.

Second Lieutenant Kliewer and enlisted pilot Technical Sergeant Hamilton took off in Wildcats to serve as CAP, Combat Air Patrol, flying close by over the island to watch for enemy bombers and, if they came, to attack them.

The expected bombing raid arrived at 1130. The two fighter pilots spotted them and ripped into them with their .50-caliber machine guns blazing. They shot down one of the attackers; it crashed into the sea. The bombers did heavy damage at the airfield, Peacock Point, and Camp Two. Then they attacked Peale Island and destroyed the under-construction naval air station, the aerological building, a hangar, radio station, and a warehouse filled with a million dollars' worth of supplies.

The three-inch gunners claimed their first kill—one of the bombers, smoking heavily, was seen plummeting into the sea. Four other bombers were smoking as they flew away.

Cpl. Carroll Trego, USMC

The third day of the war, December 10, Major Paul A. Putnam, commanding officer of the air group, asked me if I could drive a semi truck. I said sure, though I was not quite positive that I could. They sent another man and me down to the tanker truck that was used to haul gasoline out to the Wildcats and refuel them. We got it started and figured out the gear shifting. Then we had to pick up gasoline from the PBY underground fuel tanks that had not been touched by the bombers. There the fuel was pumped up into the big tanker with hand cranks. It took two men to crank the fuel out of the ground. During the fueling of the Wildcats, I had to stay in the truck with the motor running in case of an air attack—so that I could pull the tanker away from the plane and not let it become a two-thousand-gallon gasoline bomb.

After filling the tanker, we drove up to the airfield and out to the Wildcats that were still able to fly. Using another hand crank, we filled up the tanks of the fighters. Each one took six to seven hundred gallons of fuel. It was tough work. My partner and I kept up the work fueling the planes until there were no more Wildcats that could fly. Each day, when we were done fueling the planes, I drove the tanker back down by the lagoon, away from everything else, where it would make less of a target for the bombers. It was never hit.

That underground gasoline tank got me into trouble. On the prison ship to Japan the soldier guards found out I had driven the gas tanker, and they kept asking me where the hidden fuel storage tanks were. I told them I forgot, and they worked me over with their batons, which were about an inch in diameter and eighteen inches long. They called me up on deck and questioned me six times, each time by a different interrogator. After each session they beat me again. I was lucky not to get any broken bones out of it. I had a lot of bruises but no broken bones.

Lieutenant Colonel Charles Harrison, USMC (Ret.)
Grass Valley, California

I arrived at Wake on board the USS *Regulus* in August of 1941. It was a lot of work unloading the ship's goods onto flat barges for transfer to shore, since there were no docking facilities. Our first commanding officer didn't understand the urgency of our situation at the time. He was replaced by Major Devereux, who worked us from dawn to dark fortifying the gun locations on all three of the islands.

I was trained as a range rates operator with Captain Godbold's D Battery of the three-inch antiaircraft guns situated on Toki Point on Peale Island on the far north part of the three atolls. My job was to visually track incoming enemy aircraft with a twenty-four-power scope, part of the Sperry M-7 director. It took a lot of practice and training to be able to keep the scope steady on the incoming planes, but the readings enabled the director to transmit information directly to the three guns of the battery. We had expert gun crews, and we were successful as a battery in shooting down a number of

Japanese planes. When our fire-control capability was bombed out of existence, our guns were used with height and range from other units.

Most of the details of my Wake Island and prisoner of war experiences have faded. I played an insignificant role in the fighting that December. I do remember seeing our pilots in their little Wildcats, with their machine guns blazing, dive right through the center of large formations of Jap bombers. They were magnificent.

After days and nights of constant bombing, we took a direct hit on the director itself. Platoon Sgt. Johnalson Wright was killed in that raid. I was five feet from the point of detonation and was most fortunate to escape with no more than a concussion.

In the final days our gun was out of commission, so we took our personal weapons and participated in the ground defense. I lay no claim to personal heroics. I just did my job as the Marine Corps had trained me to do. I stayed in the marines after being freed from the Japanese. I fought in three wars and was captured by the Chinese in Korea, then later served in Vietnam. I put in thirty years in various officer billets from company commander to battalion commander. I retired in 1969.

The three wars I fought, two of them with assignments carrying awesome responsibility, took a heavy toll on both my mind and body. I am eternally grateful to the VA for teaching me how to blot out of my mind most of the worst of the experiences and to help do away with nightmares and awful memories. I am now eighty years of age and in remarkably good health, considering my long career of wartime experiences. I cherish the good memories, and am especially proud to have been among the survivors of the battle for Wake Island and of the POW experiences that followed it.

Cpl. Jack Skaggs, USMC

Early the third morning, the Nips tried an invasion. My job on the five-inch gun was to work the range finder. Since the first alert, we had been on four-hour shifts—four on and four off, then four on again. I'd had my shift and was trying to catch some sleep down on the beach when I heard ships shelling us from the ocean. I ran back to the gun and went up the ladder and looked out and saw a destroyer get hit right in front of us. One or two rounds from our battery must have hit the destroyer's powder magazine. There was a huge explosion, and the ship broke in half and sank in two or three minutes. We never saw any survivors. The ship was no more than four thousand yards offshore. The water was three thousand feet deep, as there were no coral reefs on that side of the islands, and that's why the Japanese made their amphibious landings over there.

Gunnery Sgt. Thomas Johnson, USMC

On December 9 and 10 the Jap bombers came over at about fifteen thousand feet. This was right in our good range, and we fired a lot of rounds and sent some of the planes toward home smoking. We worked hard when the bombers were there. When they were gone we had to get more ammo, beef up our sandbagging, and get ready for the next day.

On the first invasion try, all we could do was sit there and watch. After that we fired at the bombers every day except one until the end. We moved the guns to foil the Jap photo recon planes. It was a load of work getting them moved to a new spot and all sandbagged in again. Some civilians helped us on the move, and we appreciated it. I don't remember sleeping, but we must have, sometime. We moved the guns at night, so the Japs wouldn't know. Before long we were tired and scared.

We kept firing at the bombers right up to the last day they came over, the twenty-second. I can't say we shot down any of the bombers. A lot of guns were firing at them, but the group of three-inch weapons smoked a lot of their planes. Six or eight of them must have dropped in the ocean before they got home.

Master Sergeant Walter A. Bowsher, USMC (Ret.)
Bull Shoals, Arkansas

My first duties on Wake Island in August of 1941 were as postmaster. Then I was in the hospital with a knee swollen up so bad that I couldn't walk. When the war started, the swelling went down and I was sent to Captain Godbold's Battery D of three-inch antiaircraft guns on Peale Island.

He only had three complete crews, so he told me to go get some civilian volunteers and train them how to fire the fourth three-incher. I had sixteen volunteers, including one man who was seventy-two years old. It took me a few days to get them trained. At first they would fire a shot and look up and wait for it to go off in the air. They got over that. After three or four days of firing they did fine. Our height finder was out of commission, so Captain Henry T. Elrod radioed down from his Wildcat the height of the enemy planes and we'd set our fuses for that height.

Cpl. Jack Hearn, USMC

I was a second shell man on Wake Island. It was my job to throw the fifty-pound explosive five-inch projectile into the big gun before the powder man pushed in the required powder charges and the breach was closed and the weapon fired. You have to literally throw the shell into the gun's chamber, and it has to hit the center so you don't damage the breach. Pick up fifty pounds sometime. Some sacks of ready-concrete mix weigh fifty pounds. After throwing in eight or ten rounds, you get bone tired. That early morning of the eleventh of December I bet we fired twenty to thirty rounds.

I was in the five-inch battery on Toki Point on Peale Island. That morning the Japs tried to invade us the first time we had the ships at point-blank range. The five-inch weapon can fire out almost ten miles, 17,600 yards. Major Devereux ordered the gun captains to hold fire until the Japanese warships were within 4,000 yards.

Japanese Rear Admiral Sadamichi Kajioka had left Kwajalein in the Marshall Islands on December 8 to move on Wake Island. His force included his flagship *Yubari*, a light cruiser; six destroyers, *Mutsuki*, *Kisaragi*, *Yayoi*, *Mochizuki*, *Oite*, and *Hayate*; and Patrol Boats No. 32 and No. 33. These two boats were ex-destroyers reconfigured to launch landing craft over a stern ramp. Two armed merchantmen, *Kongo Maru* and the *Kinryu Maru,* also accompanied them, and *Tatsuta* and *Tenryu,* two light cruisers, were added to give more gunfire support.

Weather conditions were not favorable. Planners had decided that the northeast coastline was not suitable for a landing that required the converted destroyers to put 150 men on Wilkes Island and 300 on Wake. If more men were needed, they would be pulled from the supporting destroyers. The weather had moderated, so the fleet positioned itself toward the atoll's south, or lee, in the predawn hours. The admiral was confident that two days of land-based planes bombing the tiny atoll had knocked out most of the island's defenses.

Two marines patrolling South Beach at Wake on December 11 stared hard to sea. They thought they saw something. They looked again, talked about it, then looked intently into the night sky and the dark water. It was nearly 0100, and they didn't want to wake up Major Devereux with a false alarm. They watched another minute or two and were convinced they saw movement. One of them cranked the field telephone that rang in the major's quarters.

The commander of marine forces on the islands took the phone from his corporal aid and asked what kind of movement the men saw. They said something seemed to be moving, then to vanish, and then come back. They said they thought they saw some blinking lights as well.

The major asked the other sentries if they had seen anything. He didn't want to roust the troops for a false alarm. Then a report came in from the end of Wake near the boat channel. Yes, a lookout had reported that he had seen some sort of movement off the south coast.

Fireman 2nd Class Dare Kibble, USN

On the eleventh I was sent down to Camp One to man a machine gun. It was a .30-caliber, Browning water-cooled and shot about six hundred rounds a minute. The gunnery sergeant, who gave a sailor called Moon [Carl Moon] and me our five-minute course in gunnery, said we were to shoot in bursts and to take the breech apart if we had a jam while firing. He forgot to tell us how you did this operation. They gave us our gun, two boxes of ammo, and five empty burlap sandbags. The marine sergeant then told us to go back in the bush toward the lagoon and set up facing the beach.

We had only the gun, ammo, and sacks. No bedding, no clothes, no food or water, and no shovel. I told Moon he could be the gunner and I would carry the ammo. He said, "Bullshit," and let me know he had never fired a gun before except to qualify in boot camp on a .30-caliber Springfield rifle.

When I was a youngster—I was all of twenty now—I had done a great deal of hunting with all different kinds of guns. So I decided I would feel better relying on myself facing the enemy than trusting Moon.

Moon and I sat down about two hundred feet off the lagoon side of the road, which ran from Camp One to the airstrip. We decided we needed a few necessities in order to survive, such as a few tools, a couple of mattresses, some water, and one hell of a lot more ammo. The boxes only held 250 rounds. Less than a minute's worth of firing. Moon took off and was gone a while. He returned with two mattresses, which later probably saved our lives. Then Moon found some water and hardtack and some tools. Moon learned where the marines had a big cache of ammo. He purloined ten thousand rounds of .30-caliber ammo for us, which we hid in the bush. I'm not sure, but Moon may have been a second-story man in civilian life.

The next day, we were able to get some shovels and fill the sandbags. We stood the sandbags in a stack and placed the machine gun on top so we could fire at low-flying aircraft. Those same sandbags were, later on, to save our lives.

Why the mattresses? The highest point on Wake Island was twenty-one feet above sea level. If we dug down two feet, we could be standing in water, so no real foxholes could be dug. The land area of the three atolls is about the size of a small dairy farm, and you always had twenty to thirty bombers looking for you. Those bombs are the most disheartening weapon in any arsenal; they scared the living daylights out of me every time I heard those engines droning overhead. Moon and I calculated we could dig a hole until we hit seawater and then lie down in the shallow hole and pull a mattress over the top of us. The bomb would have to be a direct hit to get us. The mattress would protect us from shrapnel. Most of the men killed by bombs are killed by perimeter blasts and shrapnel, not by the bomb blast itself.

Over the fifteen days of bombing, there must have been four hundred sorties by planes dropping bombs. We were a short distance from a favorite target, Camp One. We had bomb craters everywhere you could glance. Did you know that you can hear the bomb coming that's going to kill you?

Cpl. Willis Tate, USMC

Lieutenant Clarence A. Barninger was our battery commander, and he was anxious to return fire at the Japanese ships on December 11, when they tried to invade our islands. Once the ships were close enough, Major Devereux finally gave the order to fire. Our gun traded shots with the cruiser *Yubari,* and we hit her at least three times. We couldn't tell if she sank or not.

I don't remember most of it. We surrendered and then were on the ship and then in prison camps. I remember the coal mine up at Hokkaido. After the war was over, the Japanese people were much kinder to us.

1st Sgt. James O. King, USMC (Ret.)

The morning of the eleventh of December, I was on the switchboard when lookouts sighted the Japanese ships coming in to attack us. Second Lt. John A. McAlister, of one of the five-inch guns, was asked what the range was to the ships. He kept giving the changing numbers to the major, who kept telling him to hold fire. McAlister kept asking for permission to fire. The ships were at seven thousand yards, then at six thousand, then at five thousand. McAlister kept asking for permission to fire his five-inch battery. The ships were well within range.

Major Devereux kept telling him to hold fire. Finally, when the ships were under five thousand yards, the major gave the word to open fire. The rounds went out immediately, and the Japanese destroyer *Hayate,* which had been taunting the defenders, was hit on the first salvo. It must have taken a round in the powder magazine, because it blew up, broke in half, and sank within two or three minutes. The major had held fire until he had sucked the Japanese fleet in close enough to make most of the ships good targets. He'd also kept the Mustang fighters on the ground until after the artillery opened fire to make the surprise total. Soon the rest of the fleet turned and steamed away, failing to make a landing.

There were two or three of us operating the switchboard around the clock. One of the men was Johnson P. Holt. We were concerned about him because he had a heart murmur.

Sgt. Max J. Dana, USMC

We spotted lights in the early morning sky and movement on the water well before daylight on December 11. As it became lighter, we used our night binoculars to see if they really were ships. Soon we could see the vague shape of the Japanese ships, and they were coming closer. I was one of the first to see them, and I reported it to the officers immediately. As dawn broke, several ships appeared, and they were moving toward the islands.

One troop ship should be enough to take the island. We braced ourselves for a landing. Our orders were to hold fire in order to lure the Japanese in close enough so our artillery would be effective—the five-inch guns were the biggest we had. It worked. When our guns opened fire, one destroyer, the *Hayate,* right in front of us received a direct hit, broke in half, and the bow rose straight up in the air like a monument and sank. It was a sight I would never forget. We expected survivors to drift ashore later, but none ever showed up. Probably because the waters were well infested with sharks. Other ships were damaged as they turned tail and steamed away from us. Our Wildcat fighters chased them and damaged one ship they think sank later. We heard one report that the abortive landing cost the Japanese 725 men dead and three ships sunk. Maybe so. It's hard to believe, but we had only four men dead and three slightly wounded during the attempted landing. Our morale rose, which we badly needed.

Gunnery Sgt. John S. Johnson, USMC (Ret.)

On the early hours of the eleventh we could see the lights from the Jap ships. Probably message blinkers, so we knew they were out there. It was daylight before they sent their destroyers in close. Major Devereux was smart to hold off the five-inch gun captains, who wanted to open fire when the ships were at twelve thousand yards. We kept watching for something to come floating ashore after our guns had sunk the destroyer. No bodies, just one canvas bag. We cut it open and inside we found a piece of heavy rope about eighteen feet long. There were no survivors of the 167-man crew on the destroyer.

The bombers kept coming, but they never did any damage to my two guns or my crews. We were on the far side of Kuku Point, maybe fifty yards back from the beach. Our job was to stop any Jap ships from trying to get across the coral reefs and into the lagoon. We didn't know what kind of boats they might have. As it turned out, they didn't try to come in that way.

So we watched the bombers come over almost every day. After that first day of low-level bombing and strafing, they were way too high to fire at, even with a fifty. The three-inch antiaircraft guns did the work on those days.

Our daily routine included cleaning the guns and test firing them. Then we checked the ammunition to be sure none of it was corroded, because we were right there on the beach. Usually we worked seven days a week there, but we did get December 7 off just before our war started.

I wrote these notes starting the day of the war, since I decided I might as well keep a record. Then on Wake I ran out of paper.

Pfc. Armand E. Benjamin, USMC

When the first invasion try came on December 11, I was trying to get to sleep on the beach. We had just come in from working on the wires. We worked at night with blacked-out flashlights; they didn't want us working on the wires in the daytime, because we made too good a target for the bombers. Then we heard about the ships coming. We were on the south side of Wake when the shells started whispering over us from the Japanese navy ship gunners out at sea. Most of the rounds were short into the surf or long and went over our heads into the lagoon. I sat there with my Springfield rifle and the five-round clip, waiting for somebody to try to get on shore.

Our gunners on the six old five-inch guns were ordered to hold fire until the Japs came within easy range. These were old guns, having come off destroyers after World War I. But they worked well. At last the word was given and all six of our five-inchers fired. Two on Peacock Point, two up on the end of Peale at Toki Point, and two on the end of Wilkes Island at Kuku Point. The ones on Peale fired right over the lagoon and over Wilkes to get at the Japanese ships.

Cpl. Martin Greske, USMC

The morning of the eleventh, the Japanese tried to invade us with a small fleet. Our officer was told to hold fire until Commander Cunningham gave the word.

When we began to fire, we hit two of the ships. One blew up and sank while we watched. Our guns and the Wildcat fighters sank another ship before one of the guns hit the flagship. After the cruiser was hit by a five-incher, the Japs turned around and steamed out of range in what the Japanese called one of the worst defeats in Japanese naval history.

Sgt. Maj. Robert Winslow, USMC (Ret.)

During the first invasion attempt on the eleventh, we didn't have anything to shoot at. The officers wouldn't let us lower our guns so we could shoot at the Japanese fleet. We could have fired our three-inchers like artillery. But the officers somewhere said no. All we could do was sit in our gun position and hope for the best. The Jap ships were firing at us, and our five-inchers were firing at them. We had one Japanese round hit in the ocean in front of us. Then the next one hit behind us in the bay, so the Jap gunners had us bracketed. The next one would have been right on us. Only before they fired the next round, one of our five-inch rounds must have hit them.

Cpl. Richard S. Gilbert, USMC

On the eleventh, we got back at the Japs when we fired at and hit a destroyer that had moved up within four thousand yards of our muzzle. We fired and the closest destroyer took a direct hit. It went down in what some said was less than three minutes. There were no survivors picked up by other boats or who came ashore.

The marines could only sit by their best offensive weapons and wait as they watched the ghostly shapes of the Japanese fleet steal closer and closer.

The time crawled to 0400, then to 0500, and the invasion fleet steamed closer. Then the cruiser *Yubari* sailed parallel to Wake's south shore and from 8,000 yards began firing at the beach. The rounds from the big six-inch guns slammed into the beach but missed the men and guns. The cruiser moved in to 6,000 yards and fired again. More rounds jolted into the Wake south shore but did no damage. By then it was 0600 and the marines still hadn't been able to fire back. Moments later the big cruiser moved in to 4,500 yards, and the command came for the marine's five-inch guns to open fire.

The gunners had been following the big ship in their sights and fired at once. The first rounds went over the cruiser, and it turned and raced way. The marines kept firing. At 5,700 yards two rounds hit the cruiser. Then there was another direct hit.

Another battery of five-inchers on Wilkes had plenty of targets. Directly in front of it were three destroyers, two transports, and two light cruisers. The battery fired at the lead destroyer at 4,000 yards. The third salvo from the guns hit the destroyer. There was a huge explosion, then a screen of smoke and water. In two minutes the destroyer sank.

The marine's five-inchers kept firing, hitting another destroyer, a transport, and another cruiser. By then the task force had scattered, its ships zigzagging in all directions to avoid the marine's deadly fire. A short time later the task force pulled away out of range and the gunners stopped firing.

Gen. John F. Kinney, USMC (Ret.)

The mere fact that the defense battalion's artillery could no longer reach the fleet did not mean that the battle was finished, because this was not to be entirely a duel between enemy ships and land batteries. Major Putnam and Captains Elrod, [Herbert C.] Freuler, and Tharin took to the air as soon as it was light. Even parked in their revetments, our planes would not have been completely safe from the big Japanese naval guns, and we did not want them on the ground in case enemy planes had accompanied the fleet. After convincing themselves that the invasion attempt was not supported by enemy aircraft, and after waiting for the defense battalion's five-inch guns to open up, the Wildcats attacked the ships. Again and again they dove through fierce defensive fire to try to land their hundred-pound bombs where they would do the most good. Then it was back again to the landing strip for more bombs and more .50-caliber machine gun ammunition.

As the planes continued ferrying back and forth between the fleet and the island, they began to show increasing amounts of battle damage. Captain Freuler, flying number 11, took two heavy-caliber slugs in his engine and just barely made it back to the airfield. Captain Elrod's plane had so many holes in its oil system that the engine froze up due to lack of lubrication. He coaxed his Wildcat back to the island, but he could not get it all the way to the landing strip and crashed on the island.

In the meantime Sergeant Hamilton and I relieved Putnam and Tharin and continued to attack the ships, many of which showed the effects of the earlier sorties. This would be my first chance to practice dropping bombs from our new planes. As Hamilton and I hurried to overtake the retiring enemy fleet I spotted the wounded destroyer *Kisaragi* limping along beneath me. It was on fire, the result of someone else's earlier bomb run, and I was anxious to finish it off. The flames aboard must have reached an ordnance storage area just as I began my attack, because a huge explosion engulfed the ship and she rapidly began to sink. From a purely detached point of view, this was a welcome sight, but on a personal level, I had a brief feeling of having been cheated out of a chance to sink this ship myself. The feeling soon passed, and I looked around for another target upon which to practice my bombing skills before returning to the island.

Flying west, I soon located another destroyer trying to escape. I regretted the fact that there had been no opportunity for us to practice our bombing skills with the Wildcats before the war began, but there was no point fretting over that now. I lined up for my bomb run, hoping that my on-the-job training would suffice. I released both bombs at what I calculated to be the most opportune moment, but instead of seeing another Japanese ship go up in smoke and flames, I saw two near misses. With no more bombs on board, I headed back to the island.

After Hamilton and I landed following our final sortie, I began to hear the battle reports from the other parts of the atoll. The First Defense Battalion's five-inch guns, useless against airplanes, had done great work against the Japanese ships. Damage due to enemy gunfire had been negligible. We had lost more of our fuel, but human casualties were limited to three wounded, and four dead. Japanese losses, on the other hand, were staggering. We sank at least three ships, damaged seven others, and probably caused the loss of between five hundred and seven hundred lives. We all felt justifiably proud of our performance. This was to be the first instance in the war of a defender successfully turning back an invasion.

Gunnery Sergeant Mackie L. Wheeler, USMC (Ret.)
Flagstaff, Arizona

I was in our five-inch gun position on Toki Point on the far end of Peale Island in Battery B with First Lieutenant Woodrow M. Kessler, the battery commander, when the first bombs fell that Monday morning. We couldn't fire at the bombers, so we just huddled in our gun positions and hoped they didn't get us with a direct hit.

Then, on Wednesday morning, they tried to invade us. The ships came in close and the guns down on Peacock Point got in some good hits. At last a group of three destroyers came up our way and out about ten thousand yards. We fired at them and they returned fire. They blew out our communications with the command post. Then the recoil cylinder plug on gun number two blew out, putting the gun out of action. We kept firing the other gun, and after ten salvos we hit the lead destroyer. One of the ships spewed out a smoke screen, and the ships sailed out of range.

We were on the far side of the lagoon from the ships, so we had to fire over the lagoon to hit our targets. That was the last time we had any ships to shoot at. We put up with the daily bombing, crawled into our shelters, and waited. One big bomb hit near one of our dugouts, but nobody got hurt.

Cpl. Carroll Trego, USMC

During the first invasion attempt, I was sleeping down by the lagoon near the truck. Gunfire woke us up, but there was nothing we could do. There was some shelling by the destroyers, which were trying to get our guns to open up so that they could find out what our range was. Then the Japanese ships got in close enough, and the five-inchers exploded; the planes took off, and two destroyers got sunk. The rest of the Imperial Japanese Navy turned and ran.

Just after dark, the marines gathered for a solemn ceremony. It was the first chance they had to bury those killed since the December 8 attack. Defense for the living had to come first. Now the whole island paused as a civilian with a dragline scooped out a long trench that served as a common grave. There could be no individual graves, since that would tell the enemy how many men had died.

Trucks brought the dead from the refrigeration plant where they had been held. They were wrapped in sheets and laid side by side in the trench. More than seventy men, both military and civilians, were buried together.

There was a four-man firing squad. A civilian Mormon lay preacher said a short prayer, the four marines fired their rifles, and a bulldozer quickly filled in the trench. Only a few men were at the funeral. No more could be spared from their battle-ready positions.

Daily Bomber Raids
December 12–22

HONOLULU, HAWAII

The commander in chief of the Pacific's staff had completed its overall estimate of the Pacific situation and gave the word to go ahead with the plans to reinforce Wake Island. Plans had been made days before, specifying the equipment needed and troops that would be sent. Now the work began.

It was early dawn when the troops began loading equipment and supplies on board the *Tangier*, berthed at Navy Yard Pier 10 in Honolulu. They put on the following items:

* ☆ Replacements and needed spare items for all five-inch seacoast fire control, ordnance tools, and gear previously damaged.
* ☆ Three complete sets of fire-control instruments and data-transmission systems for three-inch antiaircraft batteries. Also additional electrical data-transmission cables and ordnance tools and spares.
* ☆ Three million rounds of belted .50-caliber and .30-caliber machine gun ammunition, plus ample rifle and pistol ammunition and grenades. Barbed wire, antipersonnel mines, and additional engineer tools.

☆ Nine thousand rounds of five-inch shells and twelve thousand rounds of three-inch shells—the three-inchers equipped with the new thirty-second mechanical time fuses, which would give the Wake antiaircraft batteries a higher ceiling and far more dependable performance.

☆ Several radar devices (something most marines had never heard of), including one early warning set, an SCR-270, and a primitive fire-control radar, the SCR-268. These were carefully stowed aft on the flight deck of the ship.

Once the supplies had been loaded on board, the men followed. They included Battery F of the Fourth Defense Battalion, FMF, three-inch antiaircraft; Battery B of the Fourth Defense Battalion, FMF five-inch guns; the machine gun detachment from Batteries H and I, Fourth Defense; and the Headquarters and Service detachment of the Fourth Defense Battalion.

Loaded on board the carrier *Saratoga* was VMF-221, the marine fighter squadron. The planes—the older and temperamental Brewster F2A-3 Buffalo fighters—had never operated off a carrier, so landings would be a problem if they had to take off and return. It was tough to maintain the Brewster even at a stateside air base with all of the facilities and conveniences. Trying to operate them at an advance base like Wake, which had also been bombed and cut to ribbons, would be exceptionally difficult, the officers aboard the ship had warned.

So the *Tangier* and *Saratoga* were ready, but could not sail yet.

Gunnery Sgt. Robert F. Haidinger, USMC (Ret.)

From the twelfth to the twenty-second, it was mostly the bombing runs. We never got hit and none of our people were wounded. One night a big flying boat came over and bombed, and then the next day was the only day we didn't have a bombing raid.

The day we hurt the Japs the most was when we had one of the Wildcats up and the pilot radioed in the height and direction from which the bombers were coming. We threw up a barrage of flak right in front of them and they had to fly through it. I'm not sure how many we shot down or hurt that day, but that was our best shooting.

Gen. John F. Kinney, USMC (Ret.)

On Friday there was a break in the pattern of midday bombing raids. At about dawn only two Kawanishi Japanese four-engine flying boats attacked. Their bombing accuracy was not very good, perhaps hampered by the defense battalion's antiaircraft fire. Captains Tharin and Freuler both got into the air, and Tharin chased one of the intruders out to sea, where he shot it down. This early morning attack was the only one we had that day.

About four o'clock in the afternoon, Dave Kliewer was patrolling about twenty-five miles southwest of Wake when something on the surface of the ocean caught his eye. There, ten thousand feet beneath him, was a dull gray submarine seemingly unaware that there could be any hostile aircraft in the area. Kliewer knew that the American submarines *Triton* and *Tambor* were operating in the waters around Wake and certainly did not want to fire on one of them by mistake. Still, this was the type of target that presented itself only on rare occasions. If it was a Japanese sub and the crew learned of his presence, they would take the boat down as quickly as they could.

As all these thoughts raced through his mind, Kliewer flew to a position west of his target and started his approach directly out of the sun. As he dove closer he looked for any markings that would identify the nationality of the boat, but the only thing he saw was an unfamiliar mark on the conning tower that he decided must be Japanese. He might have only enough time for one pass, so it had to be a good one. As soon as he was close enough to be sure of his aim, he began firing his wing-mounted .50-caliber machine guns but waited until the last possible moment to release his bombs. When he did, both bombs exploded almost on top of the sub—and in fact, the blast damaged the underside of his plane as he pulled out of his dive. By the time he gained altitude and came around again, the sub had disappeared, leaving only an oil slick to indicate that it had ever been there.

When Kliewer landed and told the rest of us about his most recent victory, we all shared in his elation.

First Lieutenant David D. Kliewer, USMC
Corvallis, Oregon

I do not think of that time much anymore, but every December 8 memories do come back. It is now sixty years ago that the battle began. I was a fighter pilot with VMF-211, and we arrived on Wake just four days before the war began. After the surrender I was one of the twelve or so marines who were dropped off in Yokohama. I am sorry, but I did not write about those difficult days. I have since become a peace activist and am dedicated to working in the development of a world in which conflicts are resolved without violence.

A break in the routine came December 13, the first day since the war started that there were no air raids. The officers thought this was due to the sinking of the Japanese submarine the day before. The theory was that the sub had been broadcasting a homing signal for the Japanese planes to follow on their 720-mile flight across the trackless ocean to the tiny atolls of Wake.

The marines and civilians spent the day working on the defenses and trying to snatch a little sleep. The days had begun to merge together, as the men had little to do but dig foxholes and wait for the bombers to come.

On this day, though, the marines lost one of their planes—but not in battle. Captain Herbert Freuler had just started to take off when his plane suddenly veered toward a group of civilians and a large crane parked on the edge of the runway. To avoid hitting the men and crashing into the crane, at the last moment he swerved away from them and ground-looped the plane off the runway into the dense undergrowth. The plane was a total loss. They dragged it back to the edge of the runway, where it served as a dummy target for the Japanese bombs.

Pfc. Armand E. Benjamin, USMC

We had about fifteen guys in our communications section. Randolph June was our sergeant. We had wiremen from the three-inch guns and from the five-inchers. Most of our time was spent splicing together telephone wires that were ripped up by the bombing and strafing. That kept us busy.

We didn't have any radios between units back then. Telephone was the only communications. Commander Cunningham had the base radio, and then there was the Army Air Force long-range radio with its six operators in a truck out near the landing field. I don't know if that truck lived through the bombings or not.

The three-inch guns had one range finder for all the batteries. The operator would get the height and distance on the incoming planes and then telephone the information to the other guns so they could set their weapons. We made sure those lines were kept working.

If we had only had the radar equipment that was sitting on the dock back in Honolulu, we could have shot down more planes. They had the equipment but didn't know how to run it. There were men taking classes at Pearl to learn how to run the radar on December 8. We should have had it out there on Wake.

There were explosive charges set every so many feet down along the runway, so we could blow up the landing strip if it looked like we were going to be defeated. The charges were never set off. I don't know if the wires to them got cut or if somebody just forgot to push a switch somewhere.

Lt. Cmdr. Glenn E. Tripp, USN (Ret.)

On December 13 I left Wilkes Island and returned to Wake Island, where I helped repair airplanes and move the three-inch antiaircraft guns around after each air attack so the Japanese plane pilots would not know where they were from the pictures they took on each bombing raid. It was work all day and most of the night to keep ahead of the raids, which were almost daily. This went on all the time until December 23.

Cpl. Martin Greska, USMC

The bombers came on December 14 and almost every day. They arrived at different times and bombed and strafed everything that moved or was still standing. They didn't hit any of our five-inch guns. We had the bushes for some natural camouflage, and we were well dug in for further protection.

Sergeant William E. McFall, USMC
Des Moines, Iowa

I was just getting ready to go on duty as corporal of the guard on that first day of the war. We heard the general alarm and got down to our guns. I was on a three-incher at Peacock Point. They started bringing live ammo up to us, so we knew it was for real. We put the ammo in our ready boxes and stood by.

The first hit by the Japs was too low for us to get off any shots with the three-inch guns. We had to wait until the next day. They bombed mostly the airport that first day, and no bombs came near us. It was a good omen, I guess, because I never was wounded during the rest of the sixteen-day war.

We fired a lot of rounds on December 14. I was first loader on the gun. I rammed the round into the breach and pulled the lanyard firing the gun. When the Japs came over, bombing us at twelve thousand to fifteen thousand feet, they were just about where we wanted them. We sent a lot of the bombers away smoking, so I bet some of them dropped into the ocean.

Sgt. Max J. Dana, USMC

Today (Sunday, December 14) we had the usual air raid about noon. It was becoming routine. We had dugouts near our three-inch gun, but the nearest one to me was always full by the time I'd raced there, when the bombs had begun to fall. There was a huge rock that jutted out on the beach and under it a cave facing the ocean. It looked like a perfect shelter. It was quite a distance away, and I couldn't leave my battle station until the alarm sounded. Today when the alarm sounded, the planes were far enough away that I made a dash for it. When I reached the rock, my perfect hideout was nearly submerged by the sea. I hadn't figured on the tide, so with no time to turn back, I jumped in. Every wave slammed me against the back side of the cave, and I had to hold my breath until the wave rolled out. My helmet saved my head from getting bashed in.

I have no idea how long I was in there, but it was scary. Raid or no raid, I at last scrambled out, but when I dragged myself onto the beach, another problem faced me. Half-dazed, I looked down the barrels of eight rifles from the squad. We had been told to keep a sharp lookout for survivors from the destroyer, but I didn't think I would be mistaken for a Jap. The eight men were far enough away that they didn't recognize me. It was my red hair that saved me. In desperation I threw off my helmet and pointed at my hair. When I finally got back to the gun, the squad told me the bombs hadn't even been close.

Each gun position had a party line phone. We listened in to see what was happening. Today our commander, Captain Wesley M. Platt was talking with Major Devereux. The major told him about a radio show they had picked up from the states, the Kay Kaiser show. The bandleader had dedicated a song to the Wake Island marines. Captain Platt asked: "What did they play, taps?"

At 0330 Sunday morning, three big four-engine Japanese flying boats roared over Wake rousting everyone from their sleep and dropping bombs that fell with little damage around the airfield. The biggest loss was the sleep by the weary marines, sailors, and civilians.

Then at 1100 thirty bombers raced over the atolls. It was one of the heaviest raids so far. They concentrated on Camp One and the shelters built close to the shore. Major Devereux and some of his staff were in the command post nearby. It was built underground with heavy timbers overhead and covered with three feet of sandbags and coral.

As Devereux and his staff waited, they heard the bombs stepping closer and closer to them. Then a nearby blast shook the eight-foot-deep shelter, and sand and dirt sifted down through the spaces between the timbers.

A moment later a tremendous blast seemed to lift the whole shelter. Flames roared across the entrance and the whole command post filled with smoke and swirling sand. The blast knocked every man there off his feet. Later, Major Devereux wrote that when the men lifted themselves up, they looked at each other as though they could not quite comprehend what had happened to them Then Devereux felt a great weight lifting from his chest. "You men won't die today, not this morning anyhow," he told his staff.

Outside, the men saw to their horror that the Japanese hundred-pound bomb had hit directly on the corner of the dugout. Three feet more and it would have turned the command post into a grave for every man who was inside.

PEARL HARBOR, HAWAII

Task Force 14 at last left Pearl Harbor for its relief and resupply mission to Wake Island on December 15. The group consisted of one carrier, the *Saratoga*, with Marine Fighter Squadron VMF-221 on board; three heavy cruisers—the *Astoria*, *Minneapolis*, and *San Francisco*; nine destroyers; the *Tangier*, a seaplane tender good for transporting troops and equipment; and a fleet oiler, the *Neches*. The projected date for arrival at Wake Island was December 24.

The plan was to launch the marine fighters when nearing Wake and to fly them into the airfield. The seaplane tender would moor offshore and begin the process of landing the reinforcements, ammunition, and provisions by small boat. After unloading, the *Tangier* would take on 650 civilians and all of the wounded men and return to Pearl Harbor. The staff estimated that the offloading would take two days and the loading process only one day more; the ship was scheduled to head back to Pearl on December 27.

On Peale Island Captain Bryghte Godbold put his men on full alert around their artillery pieces on December 15, and they went through the usual routine of replacing the natural camouflage around the guns. The men went off alert at 0700. Then they worked on shelters near the guns and began a bunker near the height-finder position. At 1700 they returned to full alert. A half hour later the observers reported an aircraft flying in and out of low clouds to the east.

At 1800 four Japanese flying boats came in at one thousand feet and dropped bombs on the northern part of Peale Island—near the barracks at Camp One, the men thought. Then the Japanese strafed Batteries B and D. The bombs did little damage but killed one civilian. Marine Gunner Clarence B. McKinstry at Battery E reported that almost all of the bombs landed in the water.

Private Michael Olenowski manned his .50-caliber machine gun on the beach near Peacock Point. He aimed his gun at the strafing planes and fired. Enemy rounds tore into the coral around him but missed, and Olenowski stayed on his gun and kept firing.

As the planes roared overhead, he swiveled the gun and fired at them as they flew away. Quickly the big planes were gone over the lagoon and out of range. Still Olenowski kept firing. Someone yelled at him to stop firing, but he didn't. At last he used his left hand to pull his right hand off the trigger. He told his sergeant that he never thought that a man could be as tired as he was.

Sgt. Maj. Robert Winslow, USMC (Ret.)

About the fifteenth, our three-inchers got a hit on one of the high-flying planes. We saw the smoke coming out of it, but it just kept going and we never saw it splash down, so we're not sure if we shot it down or not. We had our director and height finder working to let us know how to set the fuses. The fuses on each round were set by hand, with a turn and click for a certain altitude. When it hit that height, it went off in an air burst. On one bombing raid we usually fired from ten to twenty rounds. The rounds were supposed to be good up to twenty-one thousand feet.

Almost every night we moved our three-inchers so the Japs wouldn't know where we were. They bombed some of the spots where we had been. Moving them took a lot of work. We had civilians helping us. We'd work most of the night moving them and getting set up to fire. Then by noon the next day we were hard at work getting the rounds in the air during the next bombing run. Sometimes, after the gun was in place, we would catch a few catnaps. But we had to be ready to fire at any time. The Japs didn't come at the same time every day. They did send some night bombers over—PBYs of some kind—but we didn't fire at them at night. We didn't know if the moves fooled the bombers or not. They were at eighteen thousand to twenty thousand feet, so a hundred yards on the ground didn't make much difference.

We set up our gun in the heavy brush for protection. The brush was six to eight feet tall and so thick you almost couldn't walk through it. Then we had camouflage over the gun until we fired.

Between the twelfth and the twenty-second, we fired at the bombers every day when they came over. We saw a couple Jap planes smoking, but we didn't know if we shot any down.

Robert W. Greeley, USMC
Ocean Springs, Mississippi

On Wake Island I was in Battery D on Peale Island, up by Toki Point. During the attack on December 16, we moved the guns so the Jap pilots wouldn't know where we would be the next day. I spent time in Woosung prison and in Kiangwan prison. Sorry I can't remember anything more.

December 16 produced another air raid, but it was different. Pilots Kinney and Kliewer were on patrol high over Wake and spotted thirty-three Nells bombers heading for the atolls. They were at eighteen thousand feet and ten minutes away from the target. Kinney and Kliewer radioed the approach of the enemy planes and their altitude to the antiaircraft batteries. The data was entered into the M-4 director and the settings sent on to Captain Godbold at Battery D. The shooters sent up ninety-five rounds, many exploding directly in front of the formation of Nells.

Observers reported that one of the lead planes in the formation began smoking and dropped out of formation. Captain Godbold said that four more planes were hit and smoking by the time they finished their bombing run and that one bomber fell into the sea.

Master Sergeant Randolph E. June, USMC (deceased)
Palatka, Florida
(*In February 1947, Master Sergeant June wrote this report to the Director of the Division of Public Information, Marine Historical Section at Quantico, Virginia.*)

The communication system of the First Defense Battalion Wake Island Detachment consisted of two BD-72 switchboards located at Battalion Command Post and serving the units. Due to the short distances involved and the shortage of personnel, it was decided that this system could best serve the needs for wire communication on Wake. I believe this system gave quicker and better service, while also releasing personnel to repair and replace damaged lines. Sound-powered telephones were used for interbattery communication in the five- and three-inch gun emplacements.

Our First Battalion CP was located on the beach near Camp One. On December 14, the command post was moved to one of the new concrete ammunition dumps, where it remained until the end.

On December 10, a warning net system was installed. This consisted of a single line connecting to all units and manned twenty-four hours a day. This made it simple to warn units to take cover or man the guns when planes were spotted. The line, being used for warning only, was not connected through the switchboard and required no ringing.

Since we were short one height finder for the three-inch batteries, we had to maintain a direct line between Batteries D and E for the purpose of transmitting data to the battery not having a height finder.

Repairing and installing new circuits was quite a problem, since the majority of this work had to be done at night with little or no light at all. This made it necessary to lay lines close to the roads and the edge of the underbrush on the beach. Lines near the road were a disadvantage, because the enemy would drop bombs on the roads and beaches, thereby knocking out all lines in that vicinity. That problem was almost unavoidable, since the lines were laid at night, making it almost impossible to go through the thick underbrush.

Our biggest maintenance problems arose when the lines were bombed out, which happened during virtually every bombing raid and usually required that complete new sections of wire be laid. We also had quite a bit of trouble with tractors running over the wire, especially around the airfield.

Heavy rains pelted the atolls during the night of the seventeenth. At 0200 lookouts on Wilkes Island reported that there were ships not far offshore. Major Devereux was awakened and went on top his command post to scan the area but saw nothing. By then more reports from other lookouts had come in. The messages were the same: twelve enemy ships close in to shore. The defenders had been expecting a night landing by the Japanese. This could be it.

Major Devereux alerted all units, and every weapon was loaded and manned. Even the marines at the airfield were alerted to stand by and be ready to repel invaders.

The lookouts strained to see through the mists, rain, and darkness. The minutes slowly ticked away. Fingers hovering over triggers on weapons grew tight and strained.

An hour passed and nothing happened. At 0330 the ocean was still out there, but no ships were charging the beaches. Then the lookouts reported they no longer could spot any ships.

Major Devereux took half the troops off alert and ordered the rest of them to sleep beside their guns.

Another hour passed with no action.

When dawn crept over the horizon, it illuminated a flat, empty ocean where the landing force was supposed to be. The night became a mystery. Had there been Japanese ships there, and had they turned around and left? Or had it been a stray U.S. Navy ship that they didn't know about? The mystery remains today.

Fireman 2nd Class Dare Kibble, USN

Around noon today (December 18) Moon and I heard the bombers coming in on their daily milk run, so we laid down in the little trench that we had dug and pulled both mattresses on top of us. Then we heard this whistling sound coming right for us, and we both knew we were going to die. When the bomb hit, the concussion threw us both four feet into the air, and when we dropped back down, Moon started yelling that his back was on fire. The blast had sent a red-hot piece of shrapnel under Moon while we were up in the air. After Moon's initial yell, we felt a tremendous weight on top of us. I believe we were both unconscious for a while, how long I don't know.

After a while we started talking. I was on my side facing Moon's rear end. We could not lift the mattresses off us, nor could we see daylight. We could breathe from the air pocket made between the mattresses and our bodies. Then, after what seemed like an eternity, we decided we were buried at the edge of the crater created by the blast of the bomb in the earth. We thought we'd been buried alive by the blast of a hundred-pound bomb. We were sure that in a few minutes we would suffocate.

What we didn't know was that a few marines under a gunnery sergeant had happened upon our gun position. They were walking up the road after the planes left and checking out the devastation the bombing had caused in Camp One. They decided to come see if the bombs had hit any guns or troops. When they arrived they found the gun wasn't touched by the blast, but they couldn't find us. They started looking around. We could hear the gunner yelling at the marines, and saying he knew there were some sailors around this gun somewhere. He was a Dane or a Norwegian. He also was one good marine, and I really grew to like him in the next four years.

When the marines came close enough for Moon and me to hear them, we started yelling as loud as we could with the little air left in our temporary tomb. The gunner heard us and started digging as fast as he and the other marines could even though there were no shovels. They finally pulled us out of our nest and then they bandaged Moon's back. He had an ugly burn from the shrapnel. So, you might say that those two mattresses really saved our lives.

The air war continued. Every day the Japanese sent over their bombers. Every day the marine pilots staggered into the air with their small defenders. For a few days they would have four planes in the air. Then one would be shot up or not quite make it back to the runway and they would be down to three. Sometimes they could only fly two planes.

The damaged planes that could no longer fly became parts bins for those that could. Lieutenant Kinney, Sergeant Hamilton, Aviation Machinist's Mate 1st Class James F. Hesson, and a few civilian volunteers worked day and night cannibalizing parts from one defunct plane to make another one function.

They had almost no tools, no spare parts other than those from the other planes, and none of the usual equipment used to service and repair airplanes; yet they managed to do everything that needed doing. They replaced engines, rebuilt engines, patched the body and wings, salvaged propellers from other aircraft, replaced different assemblies and parts, and repaired the fuselages, landing gear, wings, and tail surfaces.

Furthermore, Kinney, Hamilton, and Hesson were working on aircraft they had never seen before, and without benefit of repair manuals or instruction books. These few men created fighter aircraft where there should have been none that would fly. They produced many minor miracles to get the machines into the air. Not only did Lieutenant Kinney and Sergeant Hamilton repair and reconstruct the planes, they then jumped into the cockpits and flew the newly created Grummans into combat.

Major Robert M. Brown, USMC (Ret.)
Sun Lakes, Arizona

I was taking a much overdue nap in the brush near our beach dugout on December 19, when the bombers came over. The bombs "walked" up the beach toward where I slept. A young Chinese boy who had joined us from the contractor's camp missed me. He dashed out to find me, woke me up, and we sprinted for cover with only seconds to spare. When the raid was over, I returned to recover my gear and found only a crater and a few bits of charred blanket where I had been sleeping.

Another time I was in the command post bunker when we took a hit on the very edge of it. The blast of flame flew across the entrance, and with the stunning force of the concussion, the place was filled with choking clouds of coral sand falling from the shaken roof. It is of such memories that today's nightmares are made.

Fireman 2nd Class Dare Kibble, USN

It must have been about December 18 or 19 when I was working at some job at Camp Two and a navy officer came along in a truck. He stopped. He called another guy and me over to the rig and gave us a job to do. He had several boxes of greenbacks, good old U.S. bank notes, that he said we were to destroy because he didn't want to take any chance of the Japanese grabbing the money. We took the boxes down toward South Beach and found a pile of ammo boxes, which were supposed to be waterproof. We decided we wouldn't destroy the money and proceeded to stuff thousands of dollars into the ammo boxes. We didn't take time to count it. We thought someday, if the war ever ended and we were still alive, we'd come back and retrieve the money.

Anyway, we buried it all by a big rock and by a big piling for a marker. I also had four paychecks from the navy in Honolulu that I had been saving and carrying in my wallet. I tore them up, for I determined I could always ask the navy to reissue the checks—provided

I would ever again see the United States in this lifetime. Boy, what a miscalculation, if there ever was one. After the war ended and I once again returned to the States, I did ask the Department of the Navy to pay me the wages they owed. I swear it almost took an act of Congress to get the monies that the great white father owed me.

The routine air raid on the nineteenth came at 1135. Twenty-seven Nells arrived and dumped their bombs on what was left of the Pan Am facility on Peale and on Camp One on Wake. Seventy rounds of antiaircraft fire peppered the sky. Captain Godbold and marine gunner McKinstry reported one of the aircraft trailed a large plume of smoke as it vanished over the ocean. That day Wake's gunners had scored hits on twelve of the twenty-seven Nells, for their best shooting ever.

The same day, Admiral Frank Jack Fletcher's Task Force 14 plowed through the Pacific toward Wake. The aircraft carrier *Saratoga* and her escorts were 1,020 miles east of Wake. They had determined that they would sight the islands on December 24. The gun squads had been practicing on the ships' five-inch guns and had their equipment all ready. There were two hundred marines on board, all of them eager to get on land and help defend Wake Island.

Light moments were few and far between on Wake during those days of continual bombing raids. One was occasioned by Gunnery Sergeant Raymond Gregg. He was wearing his earphones during a raid in which he kept his men firing until the last possible second, before ordering them into their shelters and foxholes. He then raced for his own hole, but he had forgotten to take off his headset. When the twenty-foot cord played out, it jerked him unceremoniously to the ground. By then the bombs were falling and the machine gun bullets zapping into the ground all around the gun. He rolled over and put his arms over his head to protect it; he wasn't injured. When Gregg's men came out of the shelters they were grinning at him. One brave young marine smiled at Gregg. "Hey, did the Sergeant hurt him little self?" he asked.

A lot of marines remember December 20. They had been through twelve days of bombing and strafing raids; now maybe there was some help on the way. Word raced around the islands. A PBY was coming in and would land. The day was dark and a constant rain pelted down. That in itself was good news, since it would hamper, and might even prevent, the Japs from staging their usual bombing run.

The men wondered why the PBY was coming. Was it bringing in reinforcements? Or new equipment? Maybe radar so they would know when the enemy planes were coming. Maybe some much-needed supplies. The radio message about the arrival came at 0700, so the marines had all day to speculate. It wasn't until 1550 that the PBY eased down, landed on the lagoon, and taxied up to the Pan Am dock. Some dirty, war-weary marines stood near the dock when a young ensign in clean, starched whites stepped down from the plane and asked the marines: "Where is the Pam Am hotel?"

At first the marines were so surprised they couldn't talk, then one pointed to a pile of rubble and told the officer that was all that was left of the hotel.

The plane brought official mail for the commander and word that the task force would arrive on December 24. It spelled out exactly what they were bringing, including a squadron of fighters to beef up the island's air force.

Orders also indicated that all but the most essential 350 of the civilian construction men would leave the island with the convoy. The head of construction, Dan Teters, began working out his list of which men would go and which would stay. Major Walter L. J. Bayler, who had finished his temporary work at Wake, was ordered to return on the PBY. He would be the only one evacuated on the big plane.

For the rest of the day, marines by the hundreds wrote letters that would be taken back on the PBY. They were the last letters sent from Wake Island.

Cpl. Carroll Trego, USMC

I did odd jobs around the island after my main duty was over with the radio. One of my jobs the first day was picking up the dead bodies and taking them to the morgue. Later I cleaned up after the bombings. The five-man team and I were scheduled to return to Hawaii on December 21. We didn't get to go. After the officers on

Wake loaded their personal luggage on the two-engine PBY, there was no room for us five radiomen who were scheduled to leave. Another case of officers dumping on the EM.

The PBY took off on schedule, and the marines went back to watching the skies for Japanese bombers.

That same morning, Japanese Rear Admiral Kajioka left the Marshall Islands on his second attempt to capture Wake. The attacking force included most of the ships that had sailed on earlier missions, with the addition of the destroyers *Ssanagi* and *Yunagi*; the four additional heavy cruisers *Kako, Aoba, Furutaka*; and *Kimugasa,* and the seaplane carrier *Kiyokawa Maru.* Each destroyer held 250 infantrymen, instead of the 225 on the prior run. Landing exercises had been conducted at Kwajalein. Also on hand were the aircraft carriers *Hiryu* and *Soryu*.

At 0700 on December 21, the carriers turned into the wind and launched their planes. They sent out twenty-nine dive-bombers and eighteen fighters. They arrived over Wake at 0900 and began attacking shore installations. The early morning raid caught the defenders by surprise, as Wake felt the effects of their first attack by dive-bombers. The planes included Zeros, Mitsubishis, and Aichis. They left the area about 1020. Only one of the Grummans was able to fly. It was not damaged in the attack, but Major Putnam, who was in Camp Two when the Japanese attacked, couldn't get back to the plane before the enemy fighters and dive-bombers flew away. He took off and tried to follow them, but he lost them and had to return to the airfield.

The attacks weren't over. In the afternoon thirty-three Nells bombers came over at eighteen thousand feet. Some of the bombs fell around Captain Godbold's Battery D, including a direct hit on the director emplacement that killed platoon Sgt. Johnalson E. Wright and wounded three others. While the heavy M-4 director took a direct hit, in doing so it deflected much of the killing power of the bomb and saved the lives of many other men.

Through the early morning hours of December 22, the men on Wake were making revetments to protect the new squadron of planes that would soon be flying in. In the blacked-out hangar, Lieutenant Kinney and Sergeant Hamilton patched together a second Grumman so it could be flown the following morning. Both men were so tired they could hardly stand up, and Kinney had diarrhea, which had been charging through half the men on the islands.

All that night the relief convoy sailed westward, but at the restricted speed of twelve knots due to the slow-moving oiler. The other ships could have sailed at twice the speed. At midnight the navigator on board the *Astoria* figured they were a little over six hundred miles from Wake.

Admiral Fletcher knew what was going on at Wake. Commander Cunningham's frequent reports to Pearl by radio were at once transmitted to Fletcher. He knew that Japanese navy planes were now dive-bombing the islands. That meant there had to be at least one carrier in the area. He was also worried about his destroyers running out of fuel if they had to engage in battle with any Japanese ships. On the morning of the twenty-second, Fletcher decided to refuel the destroyers from the oiler. Bad weather slowed the process, and by the end of light they had refueled only four of the eight destroyers.

Back on Wake, both remaining airworthy planes took off in the morning to patrol. They soon ran into thirty-three dive-bombers and six Zeros. They attacked. Each American pilot shot down two of the planes, but Captain Freuler's Grumman was badly damaged. He dove for the waves to shake off the Zero and barely made it back to the runway, where he landed with wheels up and little control. The plane was smashed beyond repair.

The crews waited for 2nd Lt. Carl Davidson's Grumman to return to the base, but it never came back and Davidson was reported as missing in action. It was the end of the air war by the marines over Wake Island. What was left of the marine air crew went with Putnam to the command to report for duty as infantry.

The relief task force was still five hundred miles east of Wake Island by the afternoon of the twenty-second. They had several conflicting orders that were quickly canceled. The new commander in CincPac (Commander in Chief, Pacific Fleet) was in Washington. An acting commander was named and he had trouble deciding what to do. The aircraft carrier was too valuable an asset for the navy to risk. Still, by dusk no firm orders had been given the task force, and it kept moving toward Wake.

By that time Admiral Kajioka's force of amphibious attackers were within ten miles of the three tiny atolls.

The night of the December twenty-second was dark and moonless, and rain squalls peppered the island. Before midnight several reports came from lookouts that a lot of lights were showing to the northwest. One lookout reported it looked like gunfire from naval vessels, as if an extended gun battle was being waged. The flashing lights were never explained.

The Final Battle
December 23

After midnight on December 23, the lights continued, then faded. There was no attack at that time. The invading force was facing trouble. The squalls and heavy seas were making the loading of the landing craft extremely difficult. Some of the small boats capsized. At last the small craft were loaded. Two destroyers angled for the reefs off Wake's South Beach and built up speed to twelve knots to ram into the landmass.

By now Devereux had reports of sightings all along South Beach and Peacock Point. Barges were moving toward the atoll. Devereux figured he had about two hundred marines, sailors, and civilians to defend the south shore. Half of those had to remain on their artillery pieces. That left forty marines and sailors manning the machine guns, and about forty-five riflemen. He figured there could be up to two thousand men coming ashore.

The two destroyers rammed into the coral reefs across from the airstrip. Landing craft hit the beaches and the fight was on.

The first shots were fired at 0235 in the last battle on Wake Island.

Shortly after that, Commander Cunningham sent a message to Pearl asking if any help was coming. The answer was that no friendly ships were within twenty-four hours of the island. The task force had been turned around and headed back for Pearl.

Gunnery Sgt. John S. Johnson (Ret.)

The morning of the invasion on the twenty-third, we had no direct targets, because they didn't come across near us. But I could hear firing beyond us and then behind us. I got so I could tell the different sound of the Jap rifles firing from our Springfields. I couldn't do anything until daylight. I wondered what I should be doing. Our people knew where we were. If we moved, we could be mistaken for the Japs and hit with friendly fire.

I had communications. It was a mouthpiece that slung around your neck, like the telephone operators used back in the twenties, and earphones.

Our men had done a good job with the Japs who landed on Wilkes. The .50-caliber got a lot of them. We had taken two prisoners for interrogation, and somebody said there was another Jap playing dead. I got word to move my guns. I had to decide if I needed to break down the guns and take them off the tripods. I didn't know where the Japs were, so I decided to carry, them set up and ready to fire. I had two men carrying the gun, and the other man packing all the belts of ammo he could carry as well as the men's rifles. I went into the brush with them. We went up the beach past guns twelve through ten. Number nine was pointing into the woods, so that's where we went in. Somebody said it was the only time in history that there had been a machine gun attack. We set down and fired on a thirty-three-degree arc. Then the other gun set up and fired while the first one advanced. And we leapfrogged, one gun after the other, the way riflemen do.

We couldn't see the Japanese in the heavy brush. We heard some screams, but somebody in there kept firing. Farther into the brush we found some dead Japs. They were masters of camouflage. They even had sticks and leaves tied to their uniforms and their weapons. Their shoes were canvas and had a seam between the first two toes.

Before long the last of the Jap forces on Wilkes were dead and we had the two prisoners, so we were feeling good. We started down toward the channel to cross to Wake Island, thinking we could help with the fighting there. We didn't know that Commander Cunningham had made the decision to surrender the island. Then, near the channel, we met Major Devereux, who told us to drop our arms, we had been surrendered.

Pvt. William B. Buckie, USMC

That last morning of our fight on December 23, I was down at the command post, between the airfield and the ocean, where Major Devereux was. There was nothing more I could do with the truck. Soon I became part of the line of men forming a defensive perimeter around the back of the command post. We watched for any Japs who might be coming in from the beach. None ever came that way. They had landed on South Beach and moved on the airport.

We knew things were going badly. Most of our communications were out. I never saw Major Devereux go out with his white flag, but he did. Pretty soon they told us to lay down our rifles, we were surrendering. I never did get to fire my Springfield. The Japs came and stripped us naked and tied our hands behind our backs. Later they herded us up to the airfield, where we sat in front of the machine guns. There was one about three feet from me.

Not all of our men had surrendered by that time. A strafing plane came over; one of our .50-caliber machine guns jolted bullets into the plane, and it soon trailed a plume of smoke. The Japanese machine gunner right beside me jerked the lever backward, slamming a round into his machine gun. I figured I was dead. But he never fired. Less than two weeks later we were on the luxury cruise ship, *Nitta Maru*, heading for Japan.

Gunnery Sgt. Robert F. Haidinger, USMC (Ret.)

The night of the twenty-third, we were sitting and waiting. We heard the firing and the two ships that had grounded themselves. Nobody assaulted up our beach in back of the CP. The big invasion was on the South Beach, across from the airport. We sent out patrols from our guns, but we didn't learn much. We had no wire communications, so we didn't know what was going on. Our guns were of no value in this fight.

After a while my gun was taking some rounds from Japs, and so was the director. It was some Jap lying in a drain pipe the construction guys had been installing along the road. I used my Springfield and fired some shots at the position, but I don't know if I hit the guy. That was the only time I fired my rifle during the whole battle.

Fireman 2nd Class Dare Kibble, USN

On December 21 the marine command decided it would put our machine gun crew (along with two other gun crews like ours, including two sailors per .30-caliber) down on the beach. Our mission was to frustrate and impede the Japanese landing parties as long as we could stay alive. We were to stop the first wave of the enemy to land at this point on the island.

We were directly opposite Camp One on the ocean side, or southern beach, of the island. The other .30-caliber gun crew on our left was about three hundred yards down the beach, and another one was on our right at the same distance.

The civilians took a dozer and built a bomb shelter for us on the beach with beams and coral stacked on top. You had to crawl in and lie on your belly, but it would hold all of the navy gunners who were on the beach.

We set up our gun on five sandbags with the muzzle pointed out to sea and waited. My loader was Carl Moon from Los Angeles. I was thinking what a wonderful episode this could have been in my life. The air here in the South Pacific was so balmy and soft it actually caressed your skin, and when the moon was shining its beams of light, they made the ocean glitter with a million star flecks. No matter where you were on Wake Island, you could hear the gentle crash of the surf on the coral reefs and the shore.

I loaded the gun and waited. About midnight on the twenty-third, we began to see flashes of light on the horizon. We figured the

Nips were signaling from ship to ship. I can remember how utterly depressed I was while watching those lights on the horizon. I knew the war and my world were coming to a sudden climax, and I was ill-prepared to face the enemy.

Our gun was about fifteen yards from the surf, and we had no side arms. You can't use hand grenades in hand-to-hand combat. I knew one thing for certain—this little machine gun hadn't better fail me. I walked over and talked to First Class Bos'n Binny about the lights. He was over in the bomb shelter. I could tell by his face that none of his thoughts on the subject were encouraging.

I thought again how capricious life was for leading a twenty-year-old boy from the little old Rocky Mountain State of Idaho along a path that would place him in jeopardy such as this.

I had found a pair of leather gloves to wear when firing the gun. The machine gun would get hot as the devil after firing a lot.

Along about 0200, even though it was still dark, we could see some of the ships coming over the horizon, and there were plenty of them—ships of all kinds, except we could see no carriers. We knew they would be lying farther off the island. We counted thirty or forty ships and then stopped.

To bolster our faith in the U.S. Navy, I ran over to the bomb shelter and asked Binny if he recognized any of the silhouettes as being our ships. All I had to do was look at his face to know his negative answer.

A couple of hours before daylight we saw two destroyers run full speed to the beach and ground themselves about half a mile to our east. A three-inch gun position was situated directly between the two Japanese tin cans. I thought the Japanese used beautiful military strategy in their battle plan. The airstrip was just across the beach. The Nips had planned on running landing craft in between the two beached destroyers, using the ships' guns for protection against the defending forces. The three-incher didn't have a height finder, so it couldn't be used against the aircraft. So it was used against the landing craft and bore-sighted against naval ships.

We started exerting extreme vigilance in surveying the surf that lay in front of us. It seemed to get darker as the dawn awakened. The clouds moved in and covered the moon, which had shone when we had first glimpsed the ships on the horizon.

It must have been about 0230 when I heard something in the surf that sounded a little different. I asked Moon if he heard it; he said he did. We decided it was an engine running, a one- or two-cylinder diesel. In a few seconds we could see the front end of a gray landing boat. It came directly at us.

I told Moon I wasn't going to let it get to the beach before I opened fire, because if we could get them running scared before they beached, they might back the barge down and leave us alone. So much for wishful thinking. I told Moon to get some more belts of ammo, and I turned the gun to fire on the landing barge and pulled the trigger.

What happened next is difficult to explain. I became mesmerized. I believe for a person to know what it's like to fire a machine gun at another human, the person would have to experience it.

The old World War I water-cooled .30-caliber Browning kind of gave you the feeling you were operating a trip-hammer. It made a sound resembling a "slam-slam-slam" in your hand. I held on to the gun with both hands and used the tracers for sighting. I remembered the marine instructor saying you should fire the gun in bursts, but I wasn't very sociable with the Nips at the time and didn't care to get in any hand-to-hand combat. We could see the barge fairly well from the trails given off by the ricocheting slugs and the tracers. I just kept firing and moving the stream of tracers like a water hose over the upper part of the barge.

The Jap landing barge was built a lot like the design of our landing craft used later in the war. I can't remember ever seeing a landing craft in the U.S. Navy up to the time of the Pearl Harbor attack. The Nip craft had a ramp in the front and an armored housing around the pilothouse to protect the sailor while running the barge in under fire. I could see my slugs going right through the armor there. It wasn't doing much in the way of protecting the man driving. By then I could see my slugs ripping through the bow of the barge.

I kept firing a steady stream of slugs, and Moon would have a new belt ready the instant I ran out of ammo. He and I were a pretty good team. We liked each other and got along fine.

The belt of ammo on a Browning .30-caliber machine gun has a metal leader attached to the front of the belt. The ammo man can push the leader through the slide of the breech opening, and the gunner grabs the leader and pulls on it while working the breech. You can hear the lead round enter the firing chamber and you are ready to fire again. I did a lot of firing that early morning.

Seaman 1st Class Cassius Smith, USN

Being right there on the beach, we had had front-row seats as our five-inch guns took on the Jap fleet in the first invasion. We saw the ships go down and the one break in half. After that, during the bombing raids, we didn't have any action. We ducked into our bunker and waited. Sometimes I stood watch up on the water tower, looking for any approaching Jap ships—it was the highest place on the island—but I never saw anything. I was up there without a weapon of any kind.

On the night of the twenty-third, we were up and on our gun there near the water tower. While it was still dark we heard the shelling and the fighting to the south near the airport. Then we spotted what we figured were two patrol boats or landing craft coming right at us. We opened fire, and we could see the tracer rounds bouncing off the craft and ricocheting all over the place. We could see the dim outline of the two boats, and we fired at both. Most of our rounds slanted off the protective shielding around the coxswains driving the boats. Mullins and Cecil Doke were also on our gun.

Partway through the firing, Lieutenant Poindexter came down to our gun and asked us what we were shooting at. The two boats came over the coral reef and ran right up on the beach in front of us. They were no more than thirty yards away. We stopped firing the machine gun and took hand grenades and ran down the beach and threw them into the boats. It was the first and last hand grenade I ever threw.

James E. Barnes, Lieutenant Poindexter, and I all ran down and threw grenades into the ships. We only saw one Jap come out of the two craft. But it was dark, so we couldn't be sure. Later, Barnes was killed in action.

About 0800 I took a rifle round in my leg from somewhere. I was hit while I was bringing more ammo to the gun. That was the only wound I had during the fighting.

Cpl. Dennis C. Connor, USMC

On the morning of the eleventh, I was at the CP up by Camp One on the coast. Jimmy King was on the switchboard and Armand "Benny" Benjamin was there. We went outside the bunker and saw the first salvos from our five-inchers hit that Jap destroyer; it went down in maybe two minutes.

After that it was endure the air raids and then go out and splice back together any lines that had been torn up. There were a lot of them. We did that all through to the twenty-third, when the big invasion try came. I was up on the north end of the island that night working lines when I started seeing flashes out to sea. They looked like signal blinkers. I went back to the CP, which had been moved from the beach near Camp One to one of the secure bunkers down below the airfield.

Later on we heard a lot of shelling, and then the two Japanese destroyers rammed into the sand on the south shore across from the airport and we had been invaded. Gunner John Hamas told us to fix bayonets, and we established a perimeter around the CP. There were only four of us out there that I know of. There may have been others. Bill Cash, a civilian, came in beside me and he had a rifle. He said he'd never used a rifle except to hunt deer. I told him that was just fine. A few more men showed up with weapons. Only one Jap made it up to our perimeter, and he was dispatched in a hurry. We kept the perimeter until the surrender.

We saw two men coming through the brush, but we couldn't make them out well. They came closer, and we saw that one held a white flag. It was Major Devereux and Sergeant Malleck, and the Major said we were surrendering. I buried the bolt from my rifle and threw my ammunition into the brush.

Sgt. LeRoy N. Schneider, USMC

Sometime in the morning on December 23, Captain Godbold said there was nothing more we could do with our guns at Battery D, so we destroyed them. There had been no Japanese landing on Peale. We went down to Wake Island, and they put us in a defensive line that Major [George H.] Potter had set up. But then word came that we were surrendering. Our line was the last one fighting. We pulled the bolts out of our rifles and threw them into the brush.

Master Sgt. Walter A. Bowsher, USMC (Ret.)

On the twenty-third of December the big invasion came, and Battery D didn't have any more high-flying targets. Around nine o'clock they pulled us off the guns. We took out the oil plug in our gun and blew it up. Then they put us in Major Potter's defense line down near the airfield.

Private First Class Jack E. Davis, USMC
Hereford, Arizona

It didn't take long for us marines to kill off all Japanese resistance on Wilkes Island. Captain Wesley Platt, the island commander, asked some of his men to take a couple of prisoners for interrogation purposes. We spared the lives of two wounded Japs and brought them to the captain. The rest of the enemy, including some more wounded men and a few sulkers trying to play dead, were quickly disposed of with gunshots or bayonet thrusts.

Inspecting the corpse-strewn clearing, Captain Platt remarked in a matter-of-fact tone: "Well, we've secured the island." The rest of us, too dazed by the recent fighting to celebrate, stood around the searchlight truck exchanging terse comments and smoking cigarettes. Among that bedraggled crowd, Captain Platt recognized me from his own Battery G. It was my searchlight that had highlighted the Japanese landing craft some four hours earlier. Captain Platt remembered that my birthday was 23 December.

"So, Davis, happy birthday. Now that you're twenty-one and an adult, how does it feel? I just hope you enjoyed the birthday fireworks I arranged for you."

"Yes, sir," I responded with a grin, "And to think these people came all the way out here to Wake Island from Japan just to help me celebrate."

Master Sgt. Randolph E. June, USMC (deceased)

During our last night, communication failures were due entirely to our lines being cut by the enemy.

All lines on the beach opposite the airport were out around 1:00 A.M. December 23, soon after the enemy landings. This cut communication to motor transport and to the reserves who were stationed near Camp One. Switchboard circuits to Wilkes Island were also cut; however, communications were maintained to these units for an hour or more through the warning net. This line was cut when the enemy reached the other side of the airfield and located the line. Since all our communication men were on the firing line, no attempt was made to restore these units. We still had contact north of the battalion CP when we surrendered, but everything west had been cut.

Only some of the .50-caliber machine gun positions had telephones. The other weapons were so located that they were within hailing distance of a position with a telephone.

1st Sgt. Franklin D. Gross, USMC (Ret.)

About 0200 on the twenty-third of December, the big invasion started. We had no part in it down on Peacock Point. No troops came through the surf near us. Most were up on South Beach and points north. All we could do was sit and watch and wait. My phone line was still intact with the CP. About nine o'clock the major told me to go over to the five-inch guns and tell them that the island had been surrendered and that we should destroy the guns and stand by to be taken prisoner.

I sent a man over to the five-inchers, but he couldn't find them. They had moved farther along on the point. When he came back we got out a white T-shirt and tied it on a stick and held it up, surrendering. We walked down a brushy path toward the CP, but we couldn't see anything. We heard shots fired, and then there was a Japanese squad of soldiers right on top of us. They stripped us and tied us up and pushed us into the brush. They had a machine gun set up and I knew they were going to kill us. From reports of other Japanese invasions, we all had heard that the Japs didn't take prisoners of enemy soldiers. I knew I was going to die.

But we were all calm and quiet. Later I learned that this was a defense mechanism we use when all hope is gone and all is lost.

After an hour or so they pushed us out to the road and to the hospital bunker behind the airfield. They jammed us in around the sick and wounded patients. We stayed there several hours before they took us up to the airport, where we sat on the coral for a night and a day before they marched us up to Camp Two on Christmas Eve. On January 12 they loaded us on board the *Nitta Maru,* heading for Japan.

Fireman 2nd Class Dare Kibble, USN

At our machine gun emplacement at the surf, Moon and I could hear voices coming out of a beached barge not forty yards away. Once in a while there was a scream or a yell. Then the most dreaded incident any machine gunner can experience happened: I had a jam in the breech. I thought I would freeze up, but much to my astonishment, I was deadly calm. Moon asked me what I was going to do. I told him to grab a couple of hand grenades and keep a watch on the beach.

I had a screwdriver in my pocket, and I flipped the breech open, reached down under the jammed cartridge with the point, and flipped the offending shell out slick as a whistle. I closed the breech and pulled the activator to load another shell, and tripped the trigger. The machine gun fired again.

After we had completely riddled the barge and the people inside quit making any noises, we slacked off the continuous firing and started watching for any signs of life coming out of the barge. All the time there was a terrific battle going on up the beach between the two grounded destroyers. We could see explosions aboard the ships and an abundance of muzzle blasting from the beach. There was another navy-manned .30-caliber machine gun between us and the destroyers, but we never saw them firing their gun.

About 0500, it started to get light and was a rather cloudy day. Moon and I had fired about eight thousand rounds through the gun, and we decided to try some hand grenades on the barge. Moon took a couple and walked down about a hundred feet toward the barge, pulled the pins, and threw the grenades. I kept the gun ready in case any Nip showed himself as a threat to Moon.

Later on I took two grenades and threw them in the barge for some practice, or maybe because I was sure that someone in the barge had a slug with my name on it. Then we settled down to watching the armada of ships cruising on the horizon and closing in on Wake. During this whole battle Moon had been watching our backside, because we knew we couldn't depend on the marines.

I kept wondering why the Nips had not tried to drop off the back side of the barge and go up or down the beach in the protection of the water. While I watched for some movement, I saw a Jap soldier coming out of the water. From where I was I could see he must have been gut shot. He crawled across the beach and dropped behind a good-sized boulder. While he was trying to make it from the water to the boulder, I didn't have the stomach to shoot him.

The only thoughts going through my mind were how I hated the bastards who had inaugurated this fracas and how it was changing my life, and here I was having to decide whether I was going to kill a man I had never met.

Moon and I talked about what to do. We knew if we took him prisoner, we ran the risk of being killed if he was booby-trapped. We had no side arms to use to guard him. If he had a hidden side arm, he could easily kill us both before I could cut him down with the machine gun.

After a short period the man climbed up on a rock and sat down. He was close enough that I could see he was sick, probably from his wounds. Then Moon and I decided he had to be killed. I can remember now as if it were yesterday what horrible, gut-wrenching pain I had felt when we finally made the decision. I asked Moon if he would shoot the man. "Hell no," Moon said. "You're the gunner, you do it." The only solace I felt was having considered every possible alternative. It came down to his living or our living.

I put the gun on him and pulled the trigger. I saw the slugs tear into his torso, bouncing him off the boulder. I turned away and vomited. Why in hell couldn't he have been a healthy Nip marine charging me with his bayonet fixed? In that event I wouldn't have blinked twice at cutting him down. I still to this day dream about the man.

Shortly after that, the Nips sent in waves of dive-bombers. Moon and I decided if we stayed on the gun position, we would be sitting ducks. It was a snow-white beach with no cover or concealment. We could run two hundred feet to the bomb shelter, which was well camouflaged. It was then light enough that we could see out to sea plainly and would have plenty of time to run back to our gun if a landing party threatened our section of the perimeter.

Private First Class Wiley W. Sloman, USMC
Hondo, Texas

We had killed all but three of the bastard Japs who tried to sneak up on us there on Wilkes Island in the dark. Bob Stevens and I and another guy went down on their flank and fired away at them with our bolt-action Springfield .30-06-caliber rifles. Yes, the ones used in World War I. We captured the last three Japs and took them back up the slope to the three-inch gun we had been using for what little cover it gave us.

The gun had been knocked out in the bombing. There was no ammo, no crew, and no height finder. Just when we got back to the gun, a whole swarm of Japs who came up through the center of the island pinned us down around the gun with deadly machine gun fire.

I don't remember how long I lay there in a small depression trading shots with the Jap MGs. At last I decided to move to my right, away from the others. Corporal Sam W. Raymond was on my left and Gordon L. Marshall was on the other side of the gun. I wanted to get down closer to the Nip MGs, within hand grenade range. Sergeant Joe M. Stowe held down the spot at the back of the three-incher. Sometime after I left the gun, Marshall was killed there.

As I moved toward my new firing position, a Jap rifle round caught me on the side of my head. Hurt like hell. Thought I was a goner. But evidently the round went in and came out quickly. It didn't even knock me out. Actually it straightened me up from my crouched position and I fell forward. I remember I fired the round in my Springfield and moved the bolt to get a new round in the chamber.

But when I tried to lift the weapon, my left arm wouldn't work. Later, the doctors told me that my brain had started to swell and that had led to paralysis on most of my left side. I didn't fire my weapon again. Before it was over that morning, we lost seven men dead. Robert L. Stevens was one of the KIA, and Virgil Martin was another guy near me who bought the farm.

I remember that earlier we had opened new boxes of rifle ammunition for our five-round clips on the Springfield. The boxes were dated with the year of manufacture. Most of them said they had been made in 1918. Even though the rounds were twenty-three years old, I never had any misfire.

When daylight came on that twenty-third of December, I was down on the coral and in the sand and hurting bad. The fighting slacked off when the light improved. We didn't know what had happened. I couldn't move. I knew I was in a bad way.

Staff Sgt. Ralph J. Holewinski, USMC

After that first invasion attempt, the Japs kept bombing us every day
except one. Our two machine guns made a small target from eighteen thousand feet, and they didn't bother trying to hit us. We could-
n't fire back at the bombers, so we sat and watched.

After the second day of bombing, one of the straw bosses from the
civilian workers had been at our gun, and he brought over a bulldozer
and dug us a bomb shelter. He put timbers over the top and piled
dirt and sand on them. Inside, ten of us could lie down. We felt pretty
secure after that during the daily bombings.

The morning of the twenty-third, our machine guns weren't in the
right spot to help prevent the landing, so Lieutenant Hanna was
ordered to take some men and man the three-inch antiaircraft gun
that had been brought onto the beach. We depressed the barrel and
fired it like a rifle, bore-sighting on the enemy. We used it when the
converted Japanese destroyer headed for the beach and rammed into
the coral. We fired at it and set it on fire. I was on the aiming wheels,
turning them one way for up and another for down. Another wheel
moved the muzzle from right to left. We bore-sighted the weapon and
got off thirteen rounds. We hit the second destroyer as it came in
and beached itself near the first one, and Japanese troops poured off
the stern.

When the Jap troops got on shore, they started shooting at our gun
and we couldn't fire anymore. Lieutenant Hanna told us to take cover
under the gun. We had troops fire at us now and then, and when it
got light the action picked up. I had my Springfield rifle and a belt
of fifty rounds of ammo. When it was all over, I was down to my last
three cartridges. One of the civilians with us had a box of grenades,
and he threw them whenever he had a chance. One Jap popped up
out of the brush about thirty feet ahead of us, and I shot him right
in the forehead and he went down. A few minutes later another Jap
lifted up out of the brush and we nailed him, too. The civilian was
throwing grenades, and we took a number of grenades from the Japs.
It wasn't until after the surrender that somebody told me I had been

hit in the back. They said it looked like somebody had scooped a big chunk out of my back.

When it was light the dive-bombers came in and the Jap carrier fighters, and they strafed our gun positions several times. The two civilians beside me were hit. I moved away from them, and on the next pass they were riddled with bullets and both killed. By that time I had been hit in both legs; I could see some bones.

Capt. James J. Davis, USN (Ret.)

We put up with the daily raids from the eleventh through the twenty-second. During that time we built a good wood-lined bunker with bunks in it. I had settled in on the evening of the twenty-second for a nice sleep, but about one o'clock they woke me up and said the Japs were landing on the islands. All that work building the bunker, and then I had only a few hours sleep.

The enemy came at us in force this time. They landed on four places: the South Beach between Kuku and Peacock Points, then to the south closer to Peacock Point. The third group hit the beaches at Camp One. A fourth group landed on Wilkes Island.

The only weapon I had was a .45 pistol I had brought from the ship I came to Wake on. I had it because I would be holding public funds as the paymaster, and regulations required that I be armed. There were Jap troops everywhere but none where we were, near the concrete bunkers behind the taxi strips of the airfield. By daylight on the twenty-third, it was almost over. About nine o'clock the word came down that Commander Cunningham had decided to surrender the island to prevent the deaths of any more marines or of the 1,146 civilians.

I threw my pistol into the ocean, and we waited on the road for the Japs to come get us. The Japanese soldiers took my billfold and my ID, but they let us officers keep our clothes. They marched us up to what was left of Camp Two and put us in the barracks there. We stayed there until we were loaded on board the prison ship, the *Nitta Maru*.

Sgt. Norman Kaz-Fritzshall, USMC

We sat and waited on our machine guns at Toki Point up on Peale, but no Japs landed up there. So we left our guns, took our rifles, and worked down to the bridge and then across it to Wake Island. All the telephone lines were out, so we didn't know how the fight was going. We went looking for Japs. We moved almost all the way to the airport before we found any Japs. We set up a skirmish line.

Then it was all over. We got the word to lay down our arms and wait for the Japs to come get us. They came, and the first thing I knew one of them hit me in the stomach, and another one hit me in the head and knocked me out. When I came to, I had telephone wire wrapped around my wrists and my neck. Then a Jap officer came up to me waving a pistol. He aimed it at me and I thought he was going to shoot me. I wondered if I'd hear the sound of the gun going off before I felt the bullet hit me. Then somebody shouted at him and he put down the pistol.

They marched us down to the airstrip with the other men. I was put on a detail to go collecting all the medical supplies I could find. We took them to the hospital. There a Japanese officer yelled at me and pushed me down to the floor, where there were American magazines reporting that Wake Island had railroad guns—huge ones— to be used for defense. He at last made me understand he wanted to know where the railroad guns were hidden. I tried to explain if a gun that big was fired on Wake, it would sink all three islands.

Sgt. Max J. Dana, USMC

On Wilkes Island, where I was stationed, we heard the roar of engines and a crash against the rocks just before daybreak. Voices were shouting commands in a strange language. We braced ourselves for the landing and received orders to open fire. With just the light from tracer bullets it wasn't very effective, but we slowed them down. However, the Japs made their way inland and found cover. We had a searchlight battery detail, but the light had been knocked out by air raids. As it became lighter, we could see two landing craft beached. We figured at least eighty Japanese to each boat, and we had only sixty fighters on the line to defend the island.

When the firing started, the searchlights from the ships at sea illuminated the sky, which made quite a show. We could see that the island was surrounded. The Japanese boats had searchlights shooting into the sky in all directions. Sixty-three ships and two aircraft carriers, quite a force to take a mere handful of men. Our little machine gun nest was surrounded and took the brunt of the attack. But we got help as soon as other crews heard the gunfire.

Armed with three rifles and a machine gun, we managed to hold our position. When we opened fire with the .50-caliber machine gun, it would mow down brush, rocks, Japanese—anything that got in its way—with a good sweep. It was our only salvation, but it was troublesome. One long burst and it would get hot and seize up. The bolt had to be removed, freed up with oil, and replaced, hopefully in time to ward off another attack. In the meantime, bullets were zinging by our ears and hand grenades were exploding nearby. The two men on rifles kept any diehards with fixed bayonets from jumping into the nest, but one got close enough that when he fell, we could reach out and touch his bayonet. When the captain got wounded and couldn't keep our .50-caliber gun operating, I took over and had my share of fun.

Berdyne Boyd, one of our crew, was hit square in the forehead. The bullet pierced his helmet, hit his skull, and followed around his skull under the skin, leaving through a hole in the skin in back of his head. The bullet had little power left after it went through the steel helmet. He wasn't hurt that bad. We wrapped him up and he kept on fighting.

We had one civilian worker on the island come by our position seeking cover, but he ended up offering to help. I gave him our extra rifle and he did his best. He had to lie along the nest without much cover, and his legs were riddled with gunfire. He still kept on shooting.

I had been given the job of covering the two beached landing craft. A sniper had been left to guard them. He was troublesome. He kept taking potshots at us, and it helped to have someone take a crack at him every time he lifted his head.

I came through the fighting unscathed, but my hands were bloody from frantically clearing the stoppages in the .50-caliber gun. It was around 0900 before the firing slowed down. By 0920 we had the island under control. The entire landing party had been wiped out except for two hog-tied prisoners and another one playing dead.

Gunnery Sgt. Martin A. Gatewood, USMC (Ret.)

On December 21 we had a heavy bomb raid. Platoon Sergeant Johnalson E. "Big" Wright directed the fire of his Battery D ack-ack guns. Big Wright was said to be three hundred pounds, the biggest man in the Marine Corps. Big Wright kept his men at the guns long enough to fire off thirty-one rounds before he yelled for them to take cover. They did, and almost at once the battery was hit with bombs. One of them totally destroyed our directional firing equipment and killed Big Wright. We dug a hole and buried him right there near the guns.

The night of December 23, when the Japanese made their huge landing attempt, no Nips landed on Peale Island. So the major sent trucks and station wagons to haul us three-inch gunners down to the north part of Wake, just below Peale, to set up a defense line. They put us in the brush, facing the beach, but no Japs ever came over that beach.

Cpl. Martin Greska, USMC

When the Nips came in earnest on December 23, it was dark and we didn't have any targets. It looked like the whole Japanese fleet had come in. They landed far south of us, and we didn't fire a single shot during the second invasion. We just sat there in our five-inch gun position until it was all over. We never even loaded a round. We had no targets. We looked out and could see dark shadows of Jap ships but nothing to get a sight on. We saw the two destroyers beach themselves on the coral down by the airfield and knew it was going badly.

Cpl. Carroll Trego, USMC

On the morning of the twenty-third, Major Devereux told me and two other guys to go out to the generator at the west end of the airstrip and blow the charges that had been buried every hundred feet along the runway. The explosives would blow up the strip so the Japs couldn't use it for their planes.

We got to the generator and I started pulling the cord. We needed it running to generate the juice to go along the wires to the charges and set off the electric blasting caps and the dynamite. I almost broke my arm pulling that starter cord. I never did get it started, and that's why the airstrip was never blown up the way we had planned.

Lt. Col. Robert M. Hanna, USMC (Ret.)

I was a second lieutenant back in 1941 and had been in command of the .50-caliber machine guns on the islands. We got in some good shots at the low-flying aircraft the first day, but after that there was nothing we could shoot at until the landing on the twenty-third.

I had been put in command of a three-inch antiaircraft gun we were to use like an artillery piece. I had a mixed crew of marines and civilians. We had to train the civilians what to do, but they served admirably. The morning of the twenty-third we were ready. We lowered the barrel of the usually vertical firing weapon so we could aim it like a rifle, and bore-sighted it at our targets. We had the gun situated between the airstrip runway and the beach on the south side of Wake.

We saw a Japanese patrol boat coming toward shore and our first shot went at it. It was a hit, and we kept firing at it, getting hits on fourteen rounds and leaving the patrol craft a burning hulk in the water. Then we shifted our sights to patrol craft farther up the beach, some of which were now illuminated by the fire on the first patrol boat.

During this time the two converted destroyers had sent nine hundred troops onto the south shore beach, and they began fighting their way inland. We had been taking rifle fire as we worked our three-incher, and sometime during the fight I took a rifle round to my knee. It wasn't bad enough to keep me on the island when the others left on the prison ship. But the wound still gives me trouble some days now, nearly sixty-one years later.

We knew that we were losing the battle, and then we saw Major Devereux come with his sergeant waving the white flag, and it was all over.

SURRENDER

December 23, 1941

Dr. Guy J. Kelnhofer, Jr., USMC
Wesley Chapel, Florida

I was captured on Wake Island after sixteen days of combat. I did not surrender and neither did my fellow marines. We were, like many ex-POWs, surrendered by our commanding officers. We cried and we cursed at that command, because none of us believed that marines surrendered. We obeyed because of our discipline, though we did not expect that the Japanese would spare us. We were stripped and bound and stood facing firing squads armed with machine guns and grenades. At the last moment, an officer appeared and rescinded our execution order. There were times later when some of us wished he had not interfered.

Pfc. Wiley W. Sloman

I don't know how long I had lain there with my head wound when I saw a group of men walking toward us across Wilkes Island. A man in front carried a ragged white flag. As they came closer, we could see that there were some Americans and lots of Japanese in the group. When they came close enough, the Americans shouted that the fighting was over. The island had been surrendered to the Japanese.

We couldn't believe it. We had fought off the Japs to a standstill, and we still had a lot of men and ammunition. Who had called the thing off? Then we saw Major Devereux in the group, and we knew it had to be true. A lot of marines shouted no, and came close to disobeying the orders. But after a few tense moments, we all realized that we had to do what the major ordered, and the marines threw down their weapons.

That wasn't my problem. I was really hurting by that time. The Japanese in the group moved in and rounded up all the marines and lined them up on the sand. Then they tied their hands behind them with wire and put it around their necks too, so if they moved their hands much, the wire pulled hard on their throats.

I watched some of it, then some Japs came and put me on a stretcher and took me away. I didn't know where they were taking me, but discovered they had brought me to a hospital the Japs had set up for their own wounded.

The first day I was there I tried to eat the Japanese food they served me, but I just couldn't swallow it. I'm not sure to this day what it was. Later that first day a Japanese doctor came in and talked in broken English. "You no like our Japanese food?" he asked. I told him I didn't, but what I didn't tell him was that right then I didn't think that I could eat anything.

He left, and five minutes later, much to my surprise, a marine cook came in and asked me what I wanted for breakfast. I couldn't believe he was there. When I got my wits about me, I told the cook I'd like two soft-boiled eggs, toast, and coffee. I wasn't sure if it was a joke or a new kind of torture, but about a half hour later the cook came back with my eggs, toast, coffee, and a bowl of cereal and milk. I was floored. After that, that marine cook came three times a day and brought me food. It was all because the Japanese doctor had showed me a lot of kindness, and I'll never forget it.

Cpl. Jack Skaggs, USMC

From the abortive landing try to the next landing on the twenty-third of December, we had bombings every day but one. We couldn't fire at the planes, so we just had to jump in our shallow holes and hope we didn't get a direct hit. It was a good thing we didn't have to fire. Our battery was down to nothing to shoot but star shells. I don't know about the other five-inch guns.

Another guy and I almost missed the surrender. By 9:30 on the twenty-third, we thought we had mopped up on Wilkes totally. The captain said for everyone to get in a foxhole and wait it out. They were diving and strafing us. We all went to dugouts. The one I went to was made by a civilian. I made friends with him and we went into his cave; it was large. We had no contact with the command post and didn't know what was going on. We were talking about the ships and how maybe we could slip out under cover of night, when all at once we heard Japanese being spoken. We must have missed something.

The other guy looked out and said Japs were out there rounding up prisoners. We sat there trying to figure out what to do. I still had four or five hand grenades inside my shirt and my rifle with a full clip of rounds. Then the other guy looked out the bunker, and he was staring right down the barrel of a Japanese rifle. So he went out. I sat there remembering that they didn't take prisoners. The other guy said, "Jack, come on out, this is a nice Jap." So I surrendered, and they stripped us naked and marched us down to the rest of the prisoners.

Gunnery Sgt. Ed Bogdonovitch, USMC

The first invasion attempt we just sat it out. Nothing we could do. The five-inchers from Battery B near us there on Toki Point got in some rounds that helped drive off the Jap invasion fleet.

When the big invasion came on the twenty-third of December, three other BAR men and I had been positioned near the road on the south shore, just across from the water tower. That was just below Camp One. We had a lot of firepower with our four BARs. Our area held out well and was not overrun. That was because the main landings took place well south of the beach, toward the airstrip. We cut down a number of Japs who tried to come up our way.

Next thing we knew, it was daylight and we saw Major Devereux and his aid carrying a white flag, accompanied by several Japanese army officers. Major Devereux kept hollering something, but we couldn't understand him. When he got closer we figured it out. We had been surrendered. We didn't really believe it. I held onto my BAR as a half-dozen Jap soldiers came up to us. One of them stabbed me in the leg with his bayonet because I still had my BAR. Glad he didn't decide to stick me in the chest. I threw down my weapon, and that was the end of the fighting war for me.

Cpl. Martin Greska, USMC

December 23, before 1000, our lieutenant got word on the telephone to surrender. We spiked our big guns and blew them up, then threw away our rifle firing pins. Before we went to surrender, we all took a swim in the ocean and changed clothes. Then we marched down the island to where we could see the other men who had surrendered.

Sgt. William McFall, USMC

On the last day of the war we couldn't use our antiaircraft guns, so we took our rifles and became infantrymen. We were up north of the airport then, on the lagoon side. We knew things were going badly.

Then somebody came through the brush calling out, "I'm your major, don't shoot." It was Major Devereux and his sergeant with a white flag, telling us to surrender, and it was all over.

Later on I went on the prison ship to Yokohama and then to Shanghai, China, where I spent time at Woosung prison camp. Eventually I was sent to Hokkaido, Japan, and worked in the coal mine. It was the walk-in kind of mine, no elevators or shafts. Those U.S. planes sure looked good when they came over at the end of the war. They dropped a lot of food, including the boxes of Hershey bars. At least I didn't get sick on the candy.

Then it was home, and I took my discharge in February 1946. I'd put in eight years in the Marines, and that was enough.

Sgt. Maj. Robert Winslow, USMC (Ret.)

When the invasion came in the early morning hours of the twenty-third, we couldn't even see it. We were on Peale. They formed the gun crews up on Peale into an infantry defense platoon under Sergeant Ramon Gragg. We were getting ready to join the fighting about nine thirty or so, when here comes Major Devereux in his jeep with the white flag and it was all over. Some of us took our rifles and threw them into the lagoon so the Japs couldn't use them. That was that, the end of the war for us.

At the airport they tied us with our hands in back with telephone wire and made us kneel down in front of a trench, and then set up machine guns behind us. We thought they were going to shoot us and dump us in the trench. About that time a Japanese naval officer in his dress white uniform came and argued with the officer in charge of the guns, and they put the machine guns away.

Gunnery Sgt. Martin A. Gatewood, USMC (Ret.)

After daylight that morning we heard the word that Commander Cunningham had decided to surrender the islands. He told Devereux, who had to tell the troops. Word came down to destroy our

Springfields and throw them into the brush. Then the Japs came and moved us out to the road, where they stripped us and tied our hands behind our backs with commo wire and with a loop around our throats. A short time later, a Japanese officer showed up and the Japs cut us loose, then marched us down the island and behind the airport to the concrete bunkers. We still had no clothes. Later in the day they moved us up to the airstrip, and there we got some clothes. I found a pair of pants and the next day a shirt. That night we almost froze to death sitting on the airstrip. They took us to what was left of Camp Two, and then twelve days later, we were on the *Nitta Maru* and on our way to Yokohama, Japan. After three days there we headed out for China.

Sgt. Fenton R. Quinn, USMC

I remember the big rounds coming in from the ships the early morning of the twenty-third. I was in a dugout, hoping I wouldn't get a direct hit. I was down on Peacock Point most of the time during the fighting. No Japs came ashore down there. They were on the South Beach of Wake, across from the airport. That's where the two destroyers were run aground and the Jap infantrymen stormed ashore.

I wasn't in on any of the actual fighting. I remember hearing that we were not doing well. Then I saw Major Devereux come out of the command post bunker with a man carrying a big white flag. He signaled to us to lay down our arms, the islands had been surrendered to the Japanese. I waved to the men behind me and then took out the bolt on my Springfield and buried it so the Japs couldn't use my rifle.

We held our hands up then, and some Jap soldiers came and herded us up toward the airstrip. Suddenly I realized I still had two hand grenades in my pocket. I took them out and dropped them on the ground and didn't pull the arming pins. One of the Jap soldiers saw me get rid of them, and I thought for sure that he was going to kill me. He just nodded at me and we kept walking. I was relieved.

We came upon one marine who was still fighting. He had a machine gun he had lifted off its tripod and was holding it in his hands and firing it at the dive-bombers. The Jap guards didn't kill him. They just took the MG out of his hands and pushed him into the line of prisoners.

When we got to the airfield, they asked for truck drivers. I figured driving would be better than being tied up. They sent me around picking up marines and bringing them down to the airstrip.

I brought one guy back who was shot up pretty bad. The Japs let me go find something for him to drink. I forget where I got it, but I came back with a big can of tomato juice. The guy really liked that juice. I don't know if he lived or died after that.

Seaman 1st Class Cassius Smith, USN

After we grenaded the landing craft, we went back to the gun, and then later on we watched daylight come. We could hear firing down the beach, around the airport, and above us on Wilkes Island. It was quiet then where we were. But we had no communication, no telephone; we didn't have any radios like they do today. We had no idea how the fighting was going and if we were winning or losing.

Things quieted down, but we stayed there on the beach. Lieutenant Poindexter told us to stay put until we heard something. He had maybe fifty men on guns up and down the beach. Then we heard shouting in the brush behind us. We didn't know who it was. We saw a Jap come out of the brush, but we held our fire. I had at last got hold of a Springfield rifle. A moment later Major Devereux burst out of the brush and yelled at us to surrender. The battle was over, we had lost. A marine came out with a white flag, and then a lot of Japanese followed.

The major told us to throw down our weapons and surrender. I held on to my rifle for some reason, until one of the Japs motioned for me to drop it. Lucky I wasn't shot. Then the major sent me up the beach to tell the next machine gun crew to surrender. I went up there with a Jap who came close behind and pointed his rifle at me all the way. Lieutenant Poindexter told me to take the men up there over to the water tower, where we were stripped. Before we left the water tower I got to put my own clothes back on. I was wearing marine fatigues by then. I also got to keep my shoes. From there they marched us down to the airstrip, where all the prisoners were held."

Maj. Robert O. Arthur, USMC (Ret.)

On December 11 the Japanese tried to invade us, but we fought them off. When they were close to shore, we blasted their ships with our five-inch artillery, then our planes took them on as they steamed away. We sank three or four of them. They came back on the twenty-third with a lot more assets and swarmed all over us.

Our planes were all shot up or shot down by then, and I was an infantryman again. We gathered around a three-inch antiaircraft gun to ward off landing craft. We set one of them on fire and killed all the Japanese around us, then settled in to see how long we could last. I got hit by sniper fire, but I killed the sniper. Major Putnam was hit, Capt. Henry T. Elrod was killed, and gradually they wore us down. At 0830 Commander Cunningham surrendered the island, and at 0930 we were ordered to secure.

We assembled on the airfield. I got to the airstrip alive with most of the VMF-211 personnel who were left. Capt. Frank C. Tharin took charge until Major Putnam could heal. We all closed in as a group and the Japanese let us be.

On the day of our capture, I was left alone on the airstrip with three wounded civilian workers whom I tried to aid so they could join the big group of prisoners of war. The Japs came back and found me there, and forced me to leave the three civilians as they were. Two days later I was on the burial detail, which buried many bodies, including those three men. All three were literally covered with bayonet wounds. I don't know what Japanese officer or noncom was involved in these murders.

Gunnery Sgt. Thomas W. Johnson, USMC

The morning of the big invasion, the twenty-third, we woke up about 0100, only there was nothing we could do. We heard the shelling and

Below: Three of the five marines in this photo taken at Pearl Harbor in September 1941—Lloyd Lane, standing left; Max J. Dana, standing right; and Clifton C. Sanders, seated left—would be shipped to Wake Island by December.
Courtesy of Clifton C. Sanders

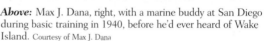

Above: Max J. Dana, right, with a marine buddy at San Diego during basic training in 1940, before he'd ever heard of Wake Island. Courtesy of Max J. Dana

Above: George H. (Bucky) Henshaw, in 1946. In 1941 Henshaw served as communications officer in the effort to set up a base of operations for a PBY squadron on Wake Island. The Japanese attacked before the air base was finished.

Courtesy of George Henshaw

Five marine recruits clowning around during .50 caliber machine gun training at San Diego. Eugene Richter, second from left, and Max J. Dana, far right, would both serve at Wake Island, where, on December 8, 1941, Dana would find himself "in a four-foot deep machine gun nest . . . manning a .50 caliber . . . [with] bombs dropping all around us."
Courtesy of Max J. Dana

Few of the Wake Island fighting marines ever saw this aerial view of the V-shaped atoll from the northeast. T[...] photo, taken on May 25, 1941, shows the lagoon in the center through the clouds. "I used to go swimming ev[...] day in the lagoon and watch the beautiful small fish . . . [never] wondering or questioning why PBYs w[...] wandering around this part of the South Pacific with bombs on their wings and ammo in their guns," rememb[...] Fireman 2nd Class Dare Kibble. National Archives

A view of Wake Island before the war, showing the hotel built by Pan American, center left, and fuel drums in the foreground. Note the heavy vegetation that blanketed the island but grew no taller than ten feet. AP Wide World

The remains of the fuel storage tanks on Wake Island, most of which were hit and destroyed by the Japanese during their first bombing raid on December 8. The fires burned for hours.
National Archives

Floats from ship to shore hold up the pipeline carrying vital gasoline to Wake Island in the last delivery before the attack on December 8. Storage tanks show in the rear, and barely visible on the far right are the tents of the USMC.
AP Wide World

A Marine Corps F4F Wildcat fighter plane and its crew. It took eight men to keep a Wildcat in the air, but the first raid on Wake left marine manpower severely diminished—the Japanese had killed or wounded more than half of the ground crews. USMC

Below: Captain Henry T. Elrod. With all the Wildcats downed, the marines in the VMF-211 fighter squadron, under crack pilot Captain Elrod, joined the infantrymen defending the island against the second Japanese attack of December 23. Elrod was shot and killed at his post. He was posthumously awarded the Congressional Medal of Honor for his actions in defense of Wake Island. National Archives

A wrecked Wildcat. This F4F failed to make it back to the airstrip and came in for a wheels-up landing. National Archives

This wartime painting by
Japanese artist Matsuzaka Yaus
depicts the Japanese conquest of
Wake Island in December 1941.
U.S. Army

Left: "I saw Major Devereux come out of the Command
Post bunker with a man carrying a big white flag. He
signaled to us to lay down our arms, the islands had been
surrendered to the Japanese," recalls Sergeant Fenton R.
Quinn, USMC. In this photo James F. Devereux, now a
USMC lieutenant colonel, steps off a plane at Naval Air
Station, Honolulu, on September 30, 1945, after his
release from a Japanese POW camp. National Archives

Below: This Japanese propaganda photo puts a happy face on the
plight of the servicemen taken prisoner at Wake and in transit to the
Zentsuji prison camp. Commander Winfield Scott Cunningham sits
right center in his dress uniform. The photo originally appeared in the
magazine *Freedom*, published by the Japanese in Shanghai, China.
AP Wide World

Above: Commander
Winfield Scott Cunningham,
USN, the senior officer on
Wake Island in 1941, led the
small naval and marine force
in the sixteen-day battle
against the Japanese. He
escaped three times from
Japanese prison camps,
and three times he was
recaptured.
AP Wide World

Above: Industrial buildings at center and left of this photo identify the Tokyo-area barracks for the Wake Island prisoners with the letters PW painted on the roofs. Housing for the POWs fell far below minimum standards prescribed by the Geneva Convention. AP Wide World

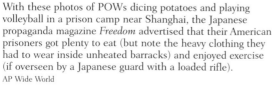

With these photos of POWs dicing potatoes and playing volleyball in a prison camp near Shanghai, the Japanese propaganda magazine *Freedom* advertised that their American prisoners got plenty to eat (but note the heavy clothing they had to wear inside unheated barracks) and enjoyed exercise (if overseen by a Japanese guard with a loaded rifle).
AP Wide World

Battle of Wake Island survivor Michael A. Benedetto is numbered 48 in a photo taken by the Japanese in the POW camp at Osaka, Japan, in 1944.
Courtesy of Michael Benedetto

Left: Yeah! We're going home! American airmen at the Ofuna prison camp near Yokahama, Japan, get the good news that they will be transported back to the United States. Ofuna was reputed to be among the worst camps run by the Japanese.
AP Wide World

Right: At Chitose Air Field in Hokkaido, Japan, U.S. marines await transport after their liberation from the nearby coal mine prison camp. Note the new uniforms, which were dropped to them from B29s when the war was declared over. AP Wide World

Nearly seventy-five ex-POWs crowd the top of the Japanese surrender envoy plane at Nadeat Kisarazu, a Japanese navy airfield twenty-two miles outside Tokyo. AP Wide World

Private Kenneth Eugene Cunningham, USMC, was barely eighteen when he faced the Japanese attacks on Wake Island in December 1941. After the surrender, along with his fellow servicemen and civilians, he endured forty-four months in Japanese slave-labor prison camps. He survived. Hell did eventually stop, and he enjoyed the life he lived to the age of seventy-five. Courtesy of author the gunfire, but our antiaircraft guns were useless. They could be depressed enough to shoot over the rest of Peale Island, the lagoon and Wilkes Island and Wake, but we couldn't see what we would be shooting at. So we were out of action. We left the gun, took our rifles, and set up a skirmish line facing the beach.

The Japs didn't invade Peale Island, so two marines, two civilians with rifles, and I got in a truck and went south, hoping to reinforce somebody down there who needed it. We went across the bridge to Wake, and about halfway down, beyond Camp Two and down near the naval CP. We set up in the brush on the ocean side of the road and waited. There were no landings made on our beach. We had no communications with anybody. That was in the days before radio, and we had no phone lines down there either. We were totally in the dark about what was happening on the other parts of the island.

Later we heard somebody yelling. It was Major Devereux, and at first we thought he said that the Japs were surrendering. We couldn't believe it when he said the island had been surrendered by Commander Cunningham to the Japanese.

We threw down our weapons. We were forced to strip naked there on the road and were tied with wire, hand and foot. About an hour later they cut the wire off our ankles and marched us down to the airport. A lot of men were already there. They set up the machine guns and aimed them at us. A whole lot of us did a whole lot of praying.

We stayed on the airstrip for two days. That first night was the coldest I could remember. I found a bloody bedsheet and wrapped it around me to try to stay warm. We all were still naked. They took us up to Camp Two the third day, and we repaired it as much as we could and stayed in the least bombed of the buildings.

Sgt. LeRoy N. Schneider, USMC

All over the islands I knew men were destroying the big guns. Blankets were stuffed down the five-inchers, and then they were fired, ruining the barrels. Hand grenades were dropped into muzzles. Electric cables were chopped up. At one three-inch battery the height finder and direction systems were riddled with .45 rounds to make them useless.

Major Devereux came with the white flag and a group of Japanese soldiers, and it was all over. We were marched to the airstrip and had to take our clothes off and sit on the coral. It was the beginning of our forty-four months of Japanese captivity.

Fireman 2nd Class Dare Kibble, USN

We didn't know it at the time, 0830, but the island command had already surrendered. The Nips had broken through the line of defense that the marines had established at the east end of the airstrip. That was opposite the end where Moon and I were fighting. The Japs had managed to land a thousand men and had the situation well in hand by the time they worked their way down to our end of the airstrip. They had captured the command post along with Major Devereux, who commanded all the marines.

About this time a couple of sailors from the gun position east of ours came running down the beach and took over our gun. I guess they figured we had deserted our post, or thought they might get credit for stopping the barrage. Moon and I concluded the battle was about over. As far as I could see in any direction, the Japanese navy had enough ships around Wake to enable a person to walk from ship to ship.

You can't conceive the blow to one's psyche that was going through each of us on that morning. About 0930 we heard a voice over in back of the bomb shelter say that we should lay down our arms and surrender. Then the voice identified itself as Major Devereux. I still had two hand grenades on my belt, which I hurriedly buried in the loose coral. Then we crawled out of the dugout, held up our hands, and surrendered to the Nip marines who were with the major.

I am of the opinion I would never again surrender myself in such circumstances. It is so much easier to die than to endure the mental and physical punishment I experienced in the next forty-four months of captivity.

We all had to sit down in rows and take off our clothes, including our shoes. The guards told us that if we stood up, we would be shot. When the sun went down and night descended, it turned cold. Remember, we were naked. The Nips gave us some rolls of roofing paper to cover us. They untied our hands then, and we dug holes in the airstrip. We put down a piece of the paper and lay on it, then pulled another one over us. This was my first night as a prisoner of war of the Japanese empire. They kept lights on us all night long.

As soon as we were captured, the Japanese separated the officers from the enlisted men. They thought the EM were mediocre and without officer's direction couldn't disrupt a camp or plan an escape. In the Nip armed forces, high-ranking officers could kill their subordinate officers and EM without any significant excuse.

The American POW officers were held in high esteem by the Nips. They were not permitted to work. They received all the food their hearts desired. Their food was substantially of better quality. Some of them even received pay from the Japanese. They were allowed to purchase goods from the Japanese commissary. They always had their clothes and uniforms, including good shoes. During our stay in prison I came to intensely dislike the class discrimination between officers and enlisted men.

Gunnery Sgt. Robert F. Haidinger, USMC (Ret.)

On the morning of the twenty-third, our scouting patrol came back with a negative report and we settled in to wait. We heard that Major Devereux had gone up the road with a bunch of Japs and a white flag, but we didn't see him. Then we got on the phone with the other guns and the director position, and the line still worked. They told us the war was over for us. We should destroy our weapons and then come in and surrender.

They said to try to blow up the gun and get rid of any ammo we could in the lagoon. So we pitched all the three-inch rounds we had into the water, then took our Springfield bolts out and threw them in the lagoon. We took the firelocks off the big gun and tossed it in the salt water. Then we tried to blow up the antiaircraft gun. We jammed coral down the muzzle, then stuffed in a blanket and rammed it down, and then fired a round. All it did was spray the blanket shards and the coral out of the muzzle. We didn't have any grenades to drop down the barrel, so we couldn't figure out how to damage the weapon. They didn't teach us in training how to blow up a gun. I didn't see a grenade my whole time on the island.

Then we went down the road to the flagpole, close to where the bunkers were, and we waited there. After a while somebody told us to walk on the road in front of the bunkers, and that's where the Jap soldiers stripped us and tied us up and then tied us together in fifteen-man strings. They took my wristwatch and my rings and a locket that I had around my neck that I was going to give to my mother for Christmas.

We were naked, tied in groups looking at Jap machine guns. If one of us fell, the whole group fell. We tried to hold each other up. I was the only one in my group with shoes; for some reason they let me keep my shoes. We knew we were going to be killed.

It was twelve days that they kept us there on Wake. We were up at Camp Two in a bombed-out barracks with barbed wire around it. Men went out on burial detail and I was on one of them. While we were finding bodies, I came across one of my good friends. Wake was swarming with land crabs. They were always there. They had been feasting on the bodies of the dead marines. After looking at my friend, I didn't go back on any more burial details.

One day the Japs told Mike [Michael N.] Economou and me to teach them how to fire the three-inch guns. We tried hard not to show them very much.

1st Sgt. James O. King, USMC (Ret.)

On December 23 I was on the switchboard. Jimmy Hall was the sergeant in charge. We knew that the Japanese were getting the upper hand, and we heard that they had landed more than a thousand troops. Major Devereux decided to put our men outside in a perimeter guard around the CP in case any Japanese came our way. Several of us went outside and became infantrymen.

After a few minutes I saw a Japanese soldier walking toward us down the road carrying a Japanese flag. I was raised on a farm and did a lot of hunting for food to eat, and I could shoot pretty well. I lifted my Springfield and fired. Three of us shot at about the same time, and the flag carrier sprawled on the ground, dead when he hit. Sergeant Major Laporte came past shortly after and said he had seen the Jap and he had two bullet holes in his head. So I figure that one of us three must have missed. I'm not saying that I shot the guy, but I also can't say I didn't.

A short time later Sgt. Don Malleck came out of the CP carrying a piece of white sheet tied to a stick. Right behind him was Major Devereux. He told us to put down our arms, we were surrendering.

I had heard it from the commander himself, and I still found it hard to believe. Marines never surrender, and the Japanese don't take prisoners. But the major had just told us to surrender. I rammed the muzzle of my Springfield rifle into the dirt and fired a round, ruining the barrel. Then I pulled the bolt out of the weapon and threw it into the brush. I saw Major Devereux and Sergeant Malleck walking out to meet some Japanese.

Moments later Japanese soldiers arrived, stripped us of our clothes, and prodded us with their bayonets up toward the airstrip, where we assembled. They tied our hands behind our backs with some of our own communication wire. That hurt. But some of us held our hands low when they tied us so when they moved on, we could move our hands up and get loose. Several of us were free soon, but we pretended to still be tied.

Pfc. Merle Herron, USMC (deceased)

There was lots of bombing and shelling, and we were just outnumbered, and there was nothing else we could do but raise a white flag. We tore down our rifles and threw the parts into the sand, then disabled our three-inch guns and marched out to the road with arms over our head, as was ordered by our commanding officer. The Jap soldiers made us take off all our clothes and throw them in a pile. They then tied our hands behind our backs with wire. They used our own telephone wire for this, adding insult to injury.

We were lined up five or six deep in front of some machine guns. We had heard that Japs took no prisoners, but it started to rain and the Japs covered the machine guns. Twenty minutes later it stopped raining, and Japs started to uncover the machine guns. But a Jap officer came running down the road yelling something, and the gunners relaxed. They marched us to one of the cement enclosures that had been built by the contract workers.

We were packed in so tight that I couldn't move. Some of the men started to faint and others were vomiting on each other. There was no air, only the odor of stench. Much later we were told we could remove the wires. We did, and that made it easier. Then the Jap guards threw clothes at us. I got a pair of pants. It had a billfold in one of the pockets, with a twenty-dollar bill in it. I kept it, hoping I might use it later, maybe to buy food.

Later we were marched out to the airstrip by soldiers with bayonets, and there we were fed a cup of water that tasted like gasoline and a piece of hard bread. This was our 1941 Christmas dinner. I didn't know that it got so cold at night on Wake Island. I guess if you are wearing only a pair of khaki pants and have no food in your stomach, the cold seems worse.

The afternoon of Christmas Day, we were moved to the bombed-out barracks at Camp Two. There we got more clothing and some food. We also were called out on working parties to bury the dead and to show the Japs how our guns worked. It was an impossible task, because some parts of the guns were gone, and in my case, I didn't know anything about the three-inch antiaircraft guns. They wanted us to fix the weapons. Since none of us spoke Japanese and they didn't know English, it was impossible to understand what they wanted. They started hitting us with rifle butts or poking us with bayonets.

Staff Sergeant John R. Dale, USMC (Ret.)

The third day of the war we dodged bombs. It was the same thing for ten more days until the early morning hours of December 23. We had no targets to shoot at. When the fighting started on Wilkes, we were infantrymen again, taking our Springfields and forming a skirmish line. Our machine guns and riflemen took good care of the two small landing craft filled with Japanese who invaded us. By 9:30 or so we had killed all but two or three prisoners and had firm control of Wilkes Island. Our communications had been cut to the command post, so we didn't know how the fighting was going in the other areas.

We were feeling great and started marching down toward Wake to the channel to see if we could give the others some help. Then, at the channel, we met Major Devereux, who told us to drop our weapons, they had surrendered the island. I couldn't believe it. Marines never surrendered. We also follow orders, so we pulled the bolts out of our rifles and buried them.

After that we went down to the airstrip and faced the machine guns. We were stripped naked and knelt or sat on the hard coral with hundreds of others.

Pharmacist Mate Second Class John I. Unger, USN
Vallejo, California

I was twenty-one years old when I was taken prisoner by the Japanese. I was on Wake as one of seven hospital corpsmen and one U.S. Navy doctor stationed there to take care of the marines.

We beat off one landing attempt by the Japanese, but then on December 23, early in the darkness, they attacked again with far superior forces and effected a landing. Mid-morning of the twenty-third, I walked into the command center just as our commanding officer, Major James P. S. Devereux, received his orders to surrender. He asked one of the marines to carry a white flag and asked me to accompany him. As we were walking toward the Japanese, one of our marines, who had no intentions of giving up, opened fire on the advancing troops, wounding one Japanese. A Japanese soldier, noticing my Red Cross armband, motioned me to attend the wounded Japanese soldier. He was severely wounded, and I simply motioned that I could not do anything for him. I thought my time was up when they stripped my medical pouch away, tore off my clothes, and tied my hands behind me.

Later that day, a Japanese officer inquired of Dr. Kahn, if any medical personnel spoke German. I was pointed out and escorted to the area of the island that was occupied by the Japanese. The Japanese doctor told me that it would be my duty to administer to the wounded Japanese soldiers and to the most seriously wounded Americans, using our medical supplies captured on the island. I was allowed under escort to see Dr. Kahn for consultations and also to bring him some supplies he needed. Luckily, all of my patients survived during my duties there.

Most of the Japanese doctors spoke German, so we could communicate well. We did operations on a regular table. When a patient developed appendicitis, we did the job with whatever instruments we could find. We had little ether and few other drugs.

Once I was beaten severely. One of our Japanese doctors needed some medications, and I knew where the Japanese kept them. The place was closed and the Japanese doctor wasn't there, so I broke in and got the medications. On the way out I was confronted by a Japanese soldier who accused me of stealing. They lined up and took turns beating me. I survived.

When the order came that the prisoners were to be transferred to Japan, I requested that I be allowed to remain on the island, thinking that I would have a better chance of being rescued from there than going to Japan. One of the Japanese doctors granted my request. But just prior to the departure of the ship, the officer in charge of the Japanese ordered that all able-bodied military personnel must leave. Later I learned that the ninety-eight civilian construction workers who did remain were all shot to death. The Japanese officer who ordered their executions was later tried as a war criminal and hung to pay for his crimes.

Cpl. Richard S. Gilbert, USMC

Almost before we knew it, the fighting was over and we had been surrendered by Commander Cunningham. Some say the officers surrendered us so they could save marine lives. Other say that the 1,146 civilians were a factor. The island commander was afraid that the civilians would be slaughtered in the fighting. When the order to surrender came, we worked over our two five-inchers so they would never fire again and then went to the airstrip.

Pfc. Armand E. Benjamin, USMC

Early morning on December 23, we could see the Jap ships hovering in the dark out on the horizon. They moved in closer and started to shell us. Then they landed. By daylight the fighting was still going on. I had been at Major Devereux's command post in what had been an ammo bunker near the short leg of the runway near the hospital. Every time there was a bombing raid the major would go to the doorway of the bunker and stand there watching what was going on. Actually the hospital at that point was in another of the empty ammo bunkers, and Commander Cunningham had his command post in the third one. We had just left the major's bunker and were on the skirmish line along the beach when Commander Cunningham made the decision to surrender. Major Devereux came out of the bunker with Sergeant Malleck, who was carrying a white flag. The major told us to put down our weapons and walk with him out to where a few Japanese met us. They took us to the airstrip, where some other prisoners had been held, and made us take off our clothes and sit down. They tied our hands behind us with some of our commo wire . They made us sit down all together and then set up machine guns all around, pointing at us with rounds charged into the chambers ready to fire. We stayed that way for a long time, and then an officer came and talked with the other officer in charge and the machine guns were taken away.

We sat there for two days without any food or water. Then on Christmas Day they gave us a small piece of bread and some water from a barrel. The water was strongly tainted with gasoline. But we drank it and it tasted good after two days in the hot sun.

Cpl. Carroll Trego, USMC

On the morning of the twenty-third, our side was not doing all that well. Commander Cunningham decided it was time to stop killing Americans and surrender. I was walking along a road up near Wilkes Island when a pickup truck came along with Devereux in the back. His aide held a large white flag on a pole. They were headed up to Wilkes Island across the ferry to tell them to surrender. I watched them go and knew it had to be all over. I walked on down toward the airport, where I knew other prisoners had been gathered.

Down there a Japanese soldier spoke to me in English. We started talking. He had been an exchange student in Berkeley before the war. It was weird talking to a Jap whose English was as good as mine. Years later I was talking with some friends in Berkeley who said they remembered a Japanese exchange student. We figured it might have been the same one.

Sgt. Max J. Dana, USMC

There on Wilkes Island we had no idea what was happening on the main island. We had lost our communications with the command post before dawn. About ten o'clock Major Devereux came riding up in a pickup with a large white flag and told us the island had been surrendered to the Japanese. He told us to destroy our big guns to prevent any use by the Japanese. Our war was over. The Japanese had won. We joined another group and headed for the channel.

With all the forces and firepower and fighter planes buzzing around strafing and dropping bombs, we knew we were doomed and would never see the sunset. You couldn't help but wonder just how you would get it—bomb, bullet, or bayonet—as we slogged along, dog-tired, toward the channel. We also knew marines never surrendered.

Well, we were wrong on both counts. Just past the channel on the Wake side we met more marines, who said we had to surrender. It was hard for us to believe, and we were suspicious that it was some sort of trick. Finally convinced it was not, we threw down our arms and moved forward. We found out later the officers had surrendered the main island hours before. Cut off from all communications with Captain Platt, the major and his staff had mistakenly assumed that Wilkes had fallen. We soon met a squad of Japanese soldiers.

They just weren't friendly and immediately made us strip to the waist and get on our knees, then they bound our hands behind us with wire. Any unusual movement was rewarded with a rifle butt or a saber to the side of the head. They marched us to the airport, which seemed to be their headquarters, their bayonets and swords waving over our heads. The march was a gruesome sight. We passed by where most of the fighting had taken place. Bodies were strewn about, and one of our gun emplacements had dead Americans sprawled over the gun. We saw they had been brutally bayoneted.

In the distance I saw the water tower, where I had stood many watches in the main camp. It now had a huge Japanese flag hanging from the top, waving in the breeze. It was hard to believe what was happening. All in all, this was our first taste of being prisoners of war, and we began to have hope that we might see the sunset after-all. It was quickly dismissed when we arrived at what was left of the airport. We were lined up against a bank, with bulldozers running above us and fully manned machine guns in front of us. One guard with a smirk on his face said, "You have one hour to live," but at the last minute a high-ranking Japanese navy officer appeared and saved us. They had decided to use us for propaganda purposes in the homeland. All huddled together, we did not know what to expect next.

We were kept at the airport for two days and nights without shirts. The days were hot and the nights were cold. It was particularly hard on me because of my fair skin; it sunburns easily. We had no food and little water for those two days. Later we were fed potatoes boiled in ocean water and a little peanut butter with plum jam.

Gunnery Sgt. Artie Stocks, USMC (Ret.)

Before daylight on December 23, we lost our communications again with the command post. We were on Kuku Point on Wilkes Island on a machine gun. About 0900 the marines defending Wake Island could no longer hold out. The commanders must have figured they could save a lot of American lives by surrendering. The odds were overwhelming.

On Wilkes we had no idea the Americans had been overrun, so we kept on fighting. Then, later that morning, Major Devereux came up to us with a big white flag and a bunch of Japanese. We were all pretty well dispirited when we saw them coming. We were out of ammunition and supplies, and since there were about twenty Japanese marines surrounding us, there wasn't anything we could do but surrender.

They stripped us and marched us to the airfield. There a Japanese officer told us that they were waiting word from their high command to see if they could take prisoners. If Tokyo said take no prisoners, we all would be killed. We marines hastily formulated a plan to rush the guards and try to get their rifles away from them if Tokyo said no prisoners. We figured that if we were going to die, we might as well take as many Japs as we could with us.

Then the word came through—they would take prisoners. The guards removed the wire that had tied our hands behind our backs. From that moment on we were POWs.

Maj. Robert M. Brown, USMC (Ret.)

The amphibious landing by the Japanese on Wake's three atolls on that December 23 morning lasted about six hours. We then received orders to surrender, primarily because of the presence of the 1,146 contractor's civilians. We had never heard of marines surrendering before, but an order is an order. So we threw our rifle bolts far into the brush and waited.

With my hands in the air and my heart in my feet, I was sure that my final hour had arrived, and I expected a bayonet thrust to end it all. Instead, we were marched to the airfield and ordered to strip naked. We were then trussed in a hog-tie, with our hands behind our backs and tied at the wrists. Then the telephone wire went around our necks. We could choke ourselves with the slightest movement of our arms. We were herded into a group and made to kneel on the coral next to the aircraft revetment. On top of the revetment a dozen Japanese troops set up machine guns. It was obvious what their purpose was. About the time they were ready, one of those sudden tropical squalls so common in the Pacific descended with torrential rain. The Japanese troops covered their machine guns and hunkered down. We continued to kneel on the coral with immense discomfort.

The squall lasted fifteen minutes and the blue sky returned. The troops uncovered their machine guns and were working with ammunition boxes when one of our marine trucks drove up and a Japanese officer in a dress-white naval uniform got out. He got into a screaming match with the officer in charge of the machine gun party. Finally the navy officer won, and the troop commander angrily shouted orders and the Japanese machine gunners secured their guns and left the revetment.

If it had not been for that rain squall, the naval officer would have been too late. Apparently he was relaying a message from Tokyo that they would take prisoners.

The next two days we spent sitting on the airfield with no food and little water. The third day I was lucky. I was chosen to be a member of a burial team. We used a truck and went from place to place looking for American bodies. The Japanese had already removed their dead and burned them in pyres on the beach. When we finally convinced our guards that we needed water, they detoured to a large barrel of good water and let us drink our fill. It was warm but still tasted like nectar.

At Camp Two, where the contractor's men stayed, it was worse than around the airfield. We found the remains of forty men, both military and civilian, who had been killed during the early bombing and strafing attacks. They had been stored in a large walk-in freezer that had been used for holding fresh meat. Our job was to empty it and bury the remains, which were in rubber body bags. The problem was that later bombings had destroyed the generator, which cooled the reefer, and it had been sitting in the tropical sun for two weeks with no cooling. When we opened it, the stench was indescribable. We hesitated, but the guards fixed their bayonets, so we had no choice. By this time the remains in the body bags had liquefied, so loading them on the truck was not a pleasant task.

On the morning of December 26, we were moved from the airfield to what was left of the living quarters in Camp Two. The next seventeen days were relatively uneventful. We had plenty of water and were able to gorge on canned food from the contractor's stock of tuna, corned beef, and vegetables.

I interviewed more than seventy survivors of Wake Island's sixteen-day battle, but I couldn't find any of them who remembered my brother Kenneth. Some said they had a vague idea who he was, but they didn't know what his duty station was during the fighting. While I didn't learn what I had hoped to, I could fall back on the manuscript that he wrote shortly after he returned to Oregon in 1945, to learn about the rest of his experiences. He began with the surrender.

Private Kenneth E. Cunningham, USMC (deceased)
Forest Grove, Oregon.

On Christmas Day of 1941 we stood in the boiling hot sun on a white coral strip two thousand miles from nowhere in the middle of the Pacific Ocean. We were fifteen hundred hungry, naked, tired men who, after battling overwhelming air, sea, and land forces, had surrendered to the Imperial Japanese Navy of DiNippon.

We were told we were prisoners of His Majesty, the Emperor Hirohito, and as we had surrendered while fighting, we had no right to live, so we should ask for no mercy. We had been stripped of all our clothing, tied together with telephone line wire, and left to stand in the blistering tropical sun.

Many of the men were so weak from lack of water and food that they could not stand. They were beaten with rifle butts or bayonets until they either stood or passed out. Some hours later, we were marched, as we were, to the airport, where we lined up so close together there was only room to sit down. We were badly in need of food, but, worse than that, we needed water. After having been burned, blistered, and beaten, our mouths and throats were parched. Men asked for water and were laughed at or beaten until they were unable to talk or see.

The first night it was chilly, and the chill was welcomed until it started to rain. We had scooped out shallow holes in the coral, where we lay four or five deep with no covering to keep off the pelting rain and the driving wind. Our sick, wounded, and half-starving men were the worst off of all. They had no covering or any medical attention of any kind.

The next day came hot and clear with a surprise and a lot more misery. We were lined up and separated, the civilians on one side and the military men on the other. We were then told that permission for us to live had been granted from the admiral of the Japanese fleet, Togo. As long as we would do as we were told, and cooperated with them, we would be very well treated and would learn to love their country and their people. I guess they thought we would, because they set five heavy machine guns up out in front of us, loaded them, manned them, and got all prepared to hold a grand Roman holiday. About that time we began to whisper among ourselves, wondering just how long we had to live. God must have been watching over us that day, for we all had prayers in our hearts and they never fired those guns.

That night came cold, with more rain, and we were herded into part of an old hangar where there was hardly enough room for half of us. We were piled in on top of each other and the stench was horrible. The air was heavy, and the men screamed all night from the pain and agony caused from their wounds and sunburn. Knowing that we were no better than slaves, we prayed for a speedy rescue.

How that night ever ended, I do not think I will ever know. Somehow the light of morning came and we were once again taken back out on the hot, white coral, where for the first time in nearly seventy-two hours we were given the food and water we had longed for, begged for, but never got. It was a small piece of bread and some water, which had been stored in gasoline barrels and was so foul that we could hardly drink it. Despite all of this we were glad to get it, and it sure tasted good. Many times after that, we would wish we had some of that same kind of bread, for it would have tasted just like cake.

The next morning at 0430 we were herded onto the bomb-damaged road and pushed along two miles to the former camp of the civilians, who were there as navy contract workers. Upon our arrival we were divided into five groups and put three hundred men to a bombed-out barracks, which had been built to house one hundred. We were then told again it was a special privilege to be kept alive after being taken by the Japanese navy. They tried to convince us we could never hope to get home, for the great Nippon air force was bombing New York, San Francisco, Washington, and Chicago. They told us we would be their prisoners all the rest of our lives, for the Japanese would soon have all of America and her people for their slaves.

We were kept on the island until the twelfth day of January. During this time we were worked from ten to fourteen hours a day. We were ordered to build up the island defenses, which were to fight our own forces, the men who were to someday come and rescue us. We had to install gun positions, put up barbed wire, and repair all the damaged buildings. Some men repaired the runway so the Japanese could land their planes. They brought in supplies by ship and began to prepare to make a move on toward Midway.

There were tons and tons of good American food in cases and tins hidden in the scrub brush and in shallow holes all over the island. The Nips destroyed about 90 percent of it and loaded the rest on their ships, presumably to take to Japan. The rest of our time there they gorged themselves until the day we were taken away; eight of ten Nippon soldiers had dysentery and fever so badly that they were completely indisposed. But the ones who were well did all they could to make our life as miserable as possible.

We couldn't speak their language, and if we were unable to understand them, we were beaten and tortured until we were unable to do any work at all. This made them all the worse, and they would deprive us of two or three meals when this happened. They were like children who were mentally unbalanced and loved to torture the things in their power.

On the eleventh day of January 1942, we were each questioned on our ability to do technical work. Three hundred and fifty men were separated in this manner from the rest. These were the men who were going to stay on Wake and finish the work of fortifying the island. I wasn't one of them. We did not know where the rest of us were going to go, but we thought anyplace would be better than Wake Island. If we had only known it, we were only beginning to have a tough time. The worst was yet to come.

Douglas D. Gardner, USMC (deceased)
Helendale, California
(*from Katherine Gardner*)

My husband, Doug, didn't talk a lot about the fighting on Wake Island during World War II or his time spent as a prisoner of war, but he did have one story he liked to tell. It was near the end of the fighting on December 23, when he knew that they would have to all die or surrender. Then he heard about the surrender order from Commander Cunningham. He had a hoard of several bottles of whiskey that he was determined the Japs wouldn't capture. He dug a hole in the sand and the coral and buried them. Only after that did he surrender. He didn't tell me if anyone else was in on the project. He always laughed when he told the story and enjoyed the idea that he had pulled a fast one on the Japanese.

These accounts by individual sailors and marines of the American surrender of Wake Island on December 23 compose a vivid, personal, and intense
chronicle but from a restricted viewpoint. The servicemen knew what was
happening near them and to them, but they could not see or evaluate the
larger picture. That was up to Commander Cunningham, the ranking military man on the atoll, and Major Devereux. Their writings reveal that the
events that day went something like this:

Devereux reported to Commander Cunningham about 0700 that the situation was critical. Positions with which he still had contact were in danger
of being overrun. Wilkes Island, Devereux thought, had fallen, since all communications with them were out. Because he had had no contact with Lt.
Arthur Poindexter on the western end of Wake, Devereux also assumed that
group had been overrun. He ticked off the other units and areas he knew
were in trouble. The enemy was advancing on Maj. George Potter's last formal line of defense on Wake. Japanese navy planes were bombing and strafing what units were left functioning.

Devereux reported everything to Commander Cunningham, and they
talked about the chances of surrendering. Cunningham told him that the
relief force had turned back to Hawaii, so there would be no last-minute reinforcements. Devereux told Cunningham that all they could do in that case
was spend more lives with no hope of winning. Cunningham was the ranking military officer on the atoll, so it was his decision. He decided they had
to surrender, and Devereux said he'd pass the word.

Commander Cunningham went outside his headquarters and dropped his
.45 automatic in a latrine. He then drove to his cottage, where he shaved,
washed up, and put on a clean uniform before driving south to surrender.

Devereux had the job of notifying the various units that their war was
over. The phone rang. It was Lt. Clarence Barninger from his battery at Peacock Point. Devereux told him to cease fire and destroy the big guns. He then
called all the units he could still reach and told them the same thing. After
that, he had Sergeant Malleck make a white flag on a broomstick, and they
walked out to surrender.

A short way from the command post, Devereux and his aide met a single Japanese soldier. He advanced on them, then motioned with his bayo-

net. Devereux took off his helmet and pistol belt and dropped them; he emptied his pockets. The three men walked on to the hospital, which had already surrendered.

Soon thereafter, Devereux and his entourage of Japanese proceeded to each unit and gave the surrender order.

PRISONERS OF WAR

The brutal treatment of the marines and sailors during those first terrifying hours of surrender set the horrendous pattern of behavior that they would experience with the Japanese guards over the next forty-four months of captivity.

Here is a directive posted in the *Nitta Maru* prison ship that applied to all the captives on the ship. It was written in English, and some of the sentence construction would be funny if the message were not so terrible.

COMMANDER OF THE PRISONER ESCORT

Navy of the Great Japanese Empire
REGULATIONS FOR PRISONERS

1. The prisoner disobeying the following orders will be punished with immediate death.
   a. Those disobeying orders and instructions.
   b. Those showing a motion of antagonism and raising a sign of opposition.

c. disobeying the regulations by individualism, egoism, thinking only about yourself, rushing for your own goods.

d. Those talking without permission and raising loud voices.

e. Those walking and moving without order.

f. Those carrying unnecessary baggage in embarking.

g. Those resisting mutually.

h. Those touching the boat's materials, wires, electric lights, tools, switches, etc.

i. Those climbing ladder without order.

j. Those showing action of running away from the room or boat.

k. Those trying to take more meal than given to them.

l. Those using more than two blankets.

2. Since the boat is not well equipped and inside being narrow, food being scarce and poor, you'll feel uncomfortable during the short time on the boat. Those losing patience and disobeying the regulations will be heavily punished for the reason of not being able to escort.

3. Be sure to finish your "Nature's call," evacuate the bowels and urine before embarking.

4. Meals will be given twice a day. One plate only to one prisoner. The prisoners called by the guard will give out the meal quick as possible and honestly. The remaining prisoners will stay in their places quietly and wait for your plate without order will be heavily punished. Same orders will be applied in handling plates after meal.

5. Toilet will be fixed at the four corners of the room. The bucket and cans will be placed. When filled up a guard will appoint a prisoner. The prisoner called will take the buckets to the center of the room. The buckets will be pulled up by the derrick and be thrown away. Toilet papers will be given. Everyone must cooperate to make the room sanitary. Those being careless will be punished.

6. Navy of the Great Japanese Empire will not try to punish you all with death. Those obeying all rules and regulations, and believing the action and purpose of the Japanese Navy, cooperating with Japan in constructing the "New order of the Great Asia" which leads to the world's peace, will be well treated.

The End.

Lt. Cmdr. Glenn E. Tripp, USN (Ret.)

As I boarded the *Nitta Maru* on January 12, 1942, I came over the side up a Jacob's ladder. At the top of the ladder Captain [Toshio]Saito and several of his crew stood searching and inspecting the prisoners as we came on board. I was searched by the guards, and one of them stuck his hand in the breast pocket of the coveralls I was wearing at the time. When he pulled his hand out of my pocket, it tore and a class ring fell out and hit the deck. Captain Saito grunted, then said something in Japanese and bent over and picked up my ring and placed it in his pocket. Years later I received the ring from the War Crimes Branch in Tokyo. The ring had been found in Captain Saito's house in Tokyo.

After being searched, I was given a strong shove by one of the guards standing in the group about Captain Saito. This shove started me down a passageway leading across the ship. This passageway was about twenty feet long and then led forward another twenty feet. Along these two passageways members of the crew of the ship stood about three feet apart. They were placed alternately on sides of the passageway, and each of them was armed with a ball bat or club. The first man in the passageway was four feet from Captain Saito. As I reached this man, he gave me a blow with the club and told me to move and clubbed and shoved me to the next guard in line. Each man in turn clubbed and beat me about the head, shoulders, and arms as I went along the line. There were thirty guards in the two lines. I started running after the first few blows, so I can't identify any of the guards in the passageway. At the end of the gauntlet we were directed down a ladder leading into the hold. As we entered the hold, many of us nursed cuts and bruises suffered in the passageways.

During my stay on board the ship, while en route from Wake Island to Yokohama, Japan, I received two beatings. A Japanese guard, a member of the merchant marine crew of the ship known to me only as "Square Jaw," administered these beatings. He was about five feet eight and weighed about 140 pounds. He was a petty officer third class. The first beating occurred on or about the sixteenth day of January. From his station at the hatch cover "Square Jaw" observed me whispering and obtained a relief guard. He came down into the hold and told me to stand at attention. Then he struck me several times in the face and head with his fist. Some days later he caught me whispering to another prisoner and came down into the hold. He called me to the center of the hold, directed me to stand at attention, and struck me several times about the head and face, again with his fist. I was bruised and sore from the effect of these wounds.

On January 20 we were inspected and searched while in the hold. This search was conducted by four of the guards, members of the merchant marine crew of the ship. One of the guards was known as the "Captain's Orderly." He was about five feet nine and weighed about 145 pounds. This man was always at Captain Saito's side when the captain inspected the prisoners.

On January 21, three of our men—Wilford J. Lindsay, USMC, Phillip Buford, USMC, and Richard L. Hotchkiss, USN—failed to stand at attention while the inspection was being made. A Japanese guard, one of the ship's crew, grabbed these men one at a time and, using a judo hold, threw the men over his shoulder, each of them crashing to the deck. They did not get up immediately after this treatment; they remained on the deck, unable to move. They were battered and had bruises visible upon their bodies. "Judo" was about five feet eight and weighed 175 pounds. He was husky and strong and swaggered about, showing off his strength. Another guard there at the same time was known as "Sword Happy." He was the ship's leading petty officer and always carried a sword. He was in charge of the inspection details when Captain Saito was not present. He would always draw the sword, brandish it, slash it through the air, and act as if he would cut some prisoner. No one provoked this guard.

Commander Winfield Scott Cunningham, USN (deceased)

by Gregory Cunningham, his grandson, from his pamphlet, "The Life of Winfield Scott Cunningham"

The grueling years of imprisonment were about to begin. On January 12, 1942, it was announced that the prisoners would be leaving on the ocean liner *Nitta Maru* to begin confinement in prisoner of war camps. Three hundred civilians were kept on the island as a labor force, in clear violation of international agreements. Two hundred of these civilians were later transported to imprisonment, but ninety-eight were found murdered on the island after the war. The ninety-eight civilians had been lined up and shot in 1943 when the Japanese feared an American invasion was imminent.

The captives on the *Nitta Maru* were ordered to pass through two lines of the ship's crewmen. Commander Cunningham said, "I had barely picked up one of my bundles when a Jap struck at my hands and tore it from them. It was like a signal. The double line erupted in hate, and as we ran the gauntlet we were dealt kicks, blows, and slaps by men who had no part in our capture."

Cunningham and twenty-nine other officers were herded into the ship's mailroom. They were lucky. The enlisted men and civilians were confined in the cold cargo spaces in the hold. In the months ahead, it became apparent that for the Japanese keeping prisoners half-starved was a studied policy. Cunningham said, "In all our long record of semi-starvation as prisoners of war, the thirteen days we spent in the voyage from Wake were, at least in my estimation, the worst. If the prisoners did not follow directions fast enough, a resounding slap on the face would follow. Since none of us knew any Japanese, we had difficulty understanding what was expected of us. There was a great deal of slapping."

The guard commander, Toshio Saito, was especially cruel. He relieved Commander Cunningham of his Naval Academy ring, "in the name of the emperor." The emperor never received the ring. After the war it was found in the residence of the former commander of the guard. They were looking for Saito to try him for war crimes.

On board the ship in Yokohama, Saito gathered 150 spectators and brought out five military prisoners, who were bound and blindfolded. Saito said the men had killed many Japanese soldiers in battle. "For what you have done, you are now going to be killed for revenge," Saito said. "You are here as representatives of your American soldiers and will be killed. You can pray to be happy in the next world." Each serviceman was then beheaded, bayoneted, and mutilated before he was thrown overboard. After the war Saito was never found to stand trial.

On January 24, 1942, Commander Cunningham arrived at his destination, his first prisoner of war camp. It was located outside Woosung, China, and a few miles downriver from Shanghai. They were marched three miles from the ship to the camp in freezing cold. The enlisted men and civilians were packed thirty-six to a barracks, and the two or three officers were put in the smaller rooms. All the area was unheated and extremely uncomfortable. Colonel Yuse commanded the prisoners' new home.

Commander Cunningham said, "I thought of the brave men who had died under my command on Wake Island, and the others who were now mistreated prisoners because I had made the decision to surrender. Over and over I reviewed that decision and others I had made, and I wondered whether different ones might have saved us." His thoughts turned to escaping. He believed it was every prisoner's duty to try to escape. He had an extra reason to get away. He wanted to get back to the war and fight again and avenge the humiliation of Wake Island's defeat.

Lt. Cmdr. Glenn E. Tripp, USN (Ret.)

Each night we were on the *Nitta Maru* a Japanese petty officer would come about 6:00 P.M. and tell us there would be an inspection. He would tell us how to sit and in what formation we should place ourselves. This would be different each night, and each night the instructions would be to sit in a posture that would become uncomfortable after a few minutes. We would be compelled to sit in that exact position until Captain Saito came. The captain usually didn't come until two or three hours later. If any man, due to weariness or any other reason, slipped or fell out of the position while the captain was present, he would point at the man and a guard would beat the offending POW.

While we were stationed at Wake Island, I had known John William Lambert, seaman first class, and Roy H. Gonzales, seaman second class. Lambert ate at the same table at mess that I did, and Gonzales was at the next table. We were on friendly terms, and when the three of us were put in the same hold, we kept together and slept side by side. We were all asked to fill out questionnaires during the voyage, and on two occasions the questions covered practically the same information. Two of the forms asked for information as to former occupation and specialties, both in naval and in civilian life. Lambert and Gonzales had attended aviation machinist mate school before going to Wake Island and were aviation mate strikers.

We docked in Yokohama on January 19, 1942. All aviation and radiomen were told to leave the ship. The next day I saw Lambert and Gonzales leave the hold under guard. They were gone about two hours, and when they came back they appeared excited and frightened. When we could talk, they told me that they had been called topside and accused of lying about their experience and had been told that they would be punished for not telling the truth about being aviation men. A short time after this talk, both men were ordered by a guard to go topside and were told to bring their blanket and shoes. They both left with the guard, and I never saw them again.

We were soon heading for China. At Shanghai we were counted out by holds. The count in our hold was 277. It had been 279 when we'd reached Yokohama. The guards who made the count were not concerned about the two missing men and made no search for them.

I watched the prisoners disembark near Shanghai, looking for Lambert and Gonzales, but I never saw them. I was curious as to where they were. I watched for them again on our three-mile hike to the prison camp. I asked men in the other holds, but no one had seen them since they had gone topside in Yokohama on January 19. I continued to search for them in Woosung prison camp, but I never found anyone who had seen them after they left the hold in Yokohama on January 19, 1942.

Fireman 2nd Class Dare Kibble, USN

On the *Nitta Maru*, we were ordered into the hold of the Japanese ship. A ship is made so the hold goes from the weather deck down to the hull. Actually, the hull is covered with what is termed a double bottom to give the ship a flat deck at the very bottom instead of a vee. The hull really looks like a vee if you see it in cross section from the bow or the stern. The hold is divided into a number of decks or floors. It has a hatch port or door on the side, by which persons can enter the hold and climb down a ladder to the next hold or floor. The top of the hold is usually covered after the cargo is loaded and battened down or secured.

In the hold of the *Nitta Maru* we spent the next seven days on the high seas, with the top hatches battened down, so there was no way out for us if the ship sank. This actually was the case with a number of Nip prisoner of war ships; while transporting POWs from the Philippines and Asia proper, several of these ships sank with no POW survivors.

Around the time of an enemy submarine alert on the *Nitta Maru*, a Japanese officer came into our hold with an interpreter. They wanted to know if there were any U.S. Navy men who had been trained in the Navy Air Arm of our armed forces. Well, after volunteering for Wake Island, you couldn't get me to volunteer for a free night in paradise with the best babe Hollywood had to offer. Anyway, three men I knew around the island stood up. I'll call them Chunky, Max, and Hotdog.

I remember Chunky was a nice, young, fat and happy Mormon boy from Ogden, Utah. I liked him very much. He was one of the three Naval Air type sailors who were lying right next to me during the voyage. I also knew Max fairly well. He was braver than almost any man I had ever met. He was always charging around on Wake with a different gun. Where he managed to acquire them, I don't know. Every time I saw him, he would be looking to see if the Nips had arrived. He was only about five feet tall, but, boy, what guts. Hotdog was a sailor I had seen around the island but didn't know too well.

All three of them were lying close to me when they volunteered to go topside with the Nip interpreter. This was the last moment in life I was to see these men. We didn't know it then, but the Nips took the three of them up to the weather deck, made them kneel down, and tied their hands behind them. Then the Nips had a big crowd of Japanese gather around to exalt the superiority of the Nip navy as evidenced by the conquering of Wake Island. We heard there were two marines also in the group. One of the officers then took his samurai sword and hacked the heads off all five of the men. Except the heads of the men didn't come loose from their necks on the first whack, and the Nip had to hack and hack until they were finally beheaded. The Nips then took the bodies and heads and dumped them overboard.

In the postwar crime trials, some of the Nips at the beheading ceremony said even the witnesses were sick at their stomachs from viewing the gruesome atrocity. All five of these men should have been awarded the Navy Cross. [The five men beheaded were Seaman First Class John W. Lambert, Seaman Second Class Theodore D. Franklin, Seaman Second Class Roy H. Gonzales, and two marines, Master Sergeant Earl Raymond Hannum and Technical Sergeant William Bailey.]

In 1945, after I'd returned home, I was at my folks' house when we heard a knock at the door one afternoon and an older couple, about forty-five or fifty years, was there and wished to talk to me. They introduced themselves as the father and mother of the beheaded sailor Chunky. They had ridden the train all the way from Ogden to Idaho just to talk to me. I don't know why, but the U.S. government didn't have information diddley-squat about prisoners lost or missing in the Orient. These people had not heard a word about their boy even in November 1945. I told them what I could about their son and what I had heard about the executions. I felt so sorry for them. I still have a tremendous hatred for causes, that initiate such sadness and pain.

The world called them prisoner of war camps, but they were not. They were slave labor camps where thousands of Allied prisoners were forced to work ten to fourteen hours a day; where men were fed as little as possible, from 800 to 1,000 calories a day, so they could continue working; where Japanese Army guards treated the prisoners like cattle, with little in the way of clothing; where there usually was no heat in the winter months, and blankets were made of sticks and leaves. Slave labor it was for as long as the war lasted, as the men of Wake Island worked in mines, foundries, steel mills, on the railroad, on docks, and on the building of a mountain firing range. No attempt was made by the Japanese to adhere to the Geneva Convention regarding prisoners of war. The POWs were slaves and were treated like slaves.

Pfc. Merle Herron, USMC (deceased)

(written January 1988)

Today, January 12, 1942, the Japs told us to get ready to board ship. We could only take one extra pair of clothes and two blankets. We marched down to the dock. There was a small boat, which we were loaded onto. There was a large ship, the *Nitta Maru*, about five miles out. The sea was very rough. It took four or five tries before we could tie up to the big ship. Then a rope ladder was tossed down and we were ordered to climb up the ladder. If you ever have tried to climb a rope ladder with something in one hand, it is not easy. When I got to the top of ladder, there was a line marked on the deck, and on each side of the line were ten or twelve Japs with rifles or boards. Yes, they used them across our backs or wherever they could hit us. The line led to a hole in the deck of the ship where they loaded on supplies. We were forced into the hold. The thirteen days on the ship were dark, cold—a starvation ride. We could tell that we were running into colder weather and in what direction by feeling the sides of the ship. The food was two bowls of gruel rice or rye a day; it was lowered down in a bucket.

On the thirteenth day, we docked and started to unload. Some of the older marines said we were at Woosung, China, close to Shanghai. The weather was rainy and cold. The wind went through the summer clothes that I was wearing. We marched on a muddy road for three miles. When we got to the rundown camp, it was getting dark. Later we learned that it was the barracks the Japs last used back in 1937. There were seven wooden barracks, and a barbed wire fence surrounded the buildings. The first meal was a small bowl of curry waterlike soup. It really burned going down. For the night, we slept on the floor wherever we found a place to lie down. The next day we received mattress covers that we filled with strawlike hay. Some of the stems were the size of pencils. We also received four thin, used cotton blankets. The food rations consisted of tea, a cup of unpolished rice with a few small pieces of fish, and cabbage or whatever vegetables were on hand. Sometimes we ate a lot of fish. I worked around the compound to help improve the living quarters, but about a month later, I started to work on the road to the camp. I was filling in potholes with a pick and shovel. A month or two later we stared digging a canal. It was for transferring supplies by smaller boats through the canal to bring in freight to the warehouses.

We could only work on the project when the tide was out, because the water was too deep to dig. For tools, we used a shovel and bucket. I was wet most of the time, and if it rained, we still worked a ten- to twelve-hour day. The completion of the canal required about a year.

The marines from Wake Island and a few army and navy enlisted men had only the summer clothes that we'd brought along from Wake. The back-breaking work and near-starvation diet started to take a toll on my body. I lost weight; my rib cage was protruding. We all looked alike, for we had no way of shaving or getting haircuts. We found out it was better to stay dirty than try to wash up, at least in cold weather. There was no heat in the barracks. Sometimes I would walk in the hallway to try to keep warm, if I had the strength to walk.

A Jap guard got shot during the night while he was on guard duty. That same day we were told to pack up again, we were moving. We marched to a camp called Kiangwan, which is about four miles out of Shanghai. It was December 5, 1942. This place didn't look much better—same old barracks—and we had a brick wall with an electric fence around the camp. I kept the three thin cotton blankets and straw mattress. I was given a pair of pants, shirt, socks, a thin cotton jacket, and a pair of shoes, in two different sizes, of course—all had been used. The clothes we had were worn out. The food wasn't any better, and living quarters were crowded, with no heat, and our friends, the rats, were there. Ishihara, the head interpreter in our section, carried a sword around and was a wild, vicious fanatic. We all hated him. He thought nothing of hitting us with the sword or his riding crop, whichever he was carrying.

Yes, I was hit more than once by him and other Jap guards. We started work on a project we called Mount Fuji. This was a rifle range. Its size, as I can best remember it, was six hundred yards long and forty-five yards wide, and it tapered to a height of forty yards. There was an area ten yards across called the butts. There were six ramps that started at the height of the butts and rose to ten feet high after they ran out three hundred yards. We used carts that ran on narrow-gauge rails. They were like the old handcars that were used on railroads. We used shovels to load them up with dirt. There were three to four men to a cart. After the cart was filled, we pushed it to the spot where the dirt was needed and dumped it. No, we didn't set our own speed. We had so many loads to do in a day during our twelve- to sixteen-hour shift. The work didn't get any easier, and the men started to get weaker.

All the men got dysentery or diarrhea. Some got TB, and some couldn't take the strain and broke up mentally. What happened to them, we never found out. They were taken from the camp. One of the times when I had diarrhea, they were working me harder than ever and I was pushing up a cart full of dirt, when I slipped and fell, hitting a track with my right knee. The skin was broken, and it looked like the kneecap had been pushed out of place. I didn't see any doctor, there weren't any around. The best I could do was push the kneecap back into place and keep working. The working was easier than the beating I would get for not working. Yes, I kept at it and walked the three miles to work and back every day. After a month the swelling went down, but my knee is still weak and aches to this day.

We didn't work on the Fuji project every day, because sometimes it rained so hard that the dirt would be too wet to move. But we did not get out of working those days. They marched us in rain and mud to a building that had no walls. The cold air blew through, and we stood there and polished empty shell casings. We had so many to do

a day. If we tried to make it easier for ourselves, the Japs increased
the number of shells we had to do in a day. I had learned by then to
handle the hunger pains by drinking more water and by wearing
something tight around my waist. I slept on my stomach, which
helped relieve the hunger pains at night. That also kept rats from running across my face.

After two and a half years at Kiangwan, the word came. Get
packed up, we're leaving. It was May 14, 1945. The Japs didn't tell
us any reason, but we could see the B-29s and fighter planes flying
over the Shanghai area. Those of us who could walk to the train were
loaded into boxcars like cattle. The best thing about leaving was that
the greatly hated interpreter didn't come along. We spent five days
packed into boxcars. The food was not any better, but at least we did-
n't have to work twelve to sixteen hours a day. We ended up at a place
they called Tengtai Camp, near Peking, China. The housing was an
old warehouse building. We were on the end of a shovel once more,
digging foundations for a building. The food here was no better, and
there wasn't enough to go around. About then my mind started to
block out a lot of things I didn't want to remember. One thing I
couldn't ignore was always being hungry and weak. Why I wanted
to keep going, I never could find a reason. It must have been to show
the Japs that we were "True Americans." They said we didn't act like
prisoners.

On June 25, 1945, we had to get ready to move again. We were
loaded in the same-sized boxcars like cattle for a six-day trip. We
ended up in Pusan, Korea. There we filled salt barges. Living conditions got worse. We had to brush flies away to eat the garbage they
fed us. Then less than a week later, we were marched to the dock
and put on a ferry steamer. It wasn't very big and we had standing
room only. The temperature was hot, and a half deck below us were
Koreans packed in like we were. The odor that came from them was
unbearable. That was one of the worst trips I have ever taken in my
life. I was thankful that it took only twelve hours to get to Honshu,
Japan. There we unloaded. The Japs let us wade in the ocean. That
was the first bath we'd had since leaving Shanghai. We were then run

through a delousing tank. Next, they gave us different clothes. It all was used and some of it fit, but most was too big or too small. After that, we boarded railroad day coaches. We were jammed into cars built to hold 88, but they loaded 170 to a car. We had no idea where we were going, only north. The change in food was somewhat too different. Instead of raw fish with rice, we were served fried grasshoppers. We had a five-day train ride and then went on a ferry and at last landed at Tashimsi, Japan. We were on the northernmost Japanese Island of Hokkaido, in Hokkaido Branch Camp #3. The first night there we found out we had friends: fleas and bedbugs. They began crawling on us and biting. Sometimes I had to get up and take off my clothes and shake off the fleas and bedbugs. The Japs found jobs for us in a cold, damp coal mine that hadn't been worked for years. Our transportation was the same, we walked. The food was no better. Sometimes we received a little more meat and stew, but that came from old horses that were overworked and underfed. The working hours were just as long, twelve hours or more a day. If it had been wintertime, most of us would not have seen another spring.

Thank God that President Harry Truman ordered the atom bomb to be dropped. Food and treatment got much better. Then, on August 15, 1945, the U.S. First Cavalry Division liberated the camp. Forty-four months of brutal prison camp living were over.

Looking back after forty-two years, I often wonder how a human body and mind could withstand such a beating, lack of food, and terrible living conditions. It is my belief that the body gradually breaks down from lack of food, cold, and overwork; but if you can keep your sense of humor by thinking and talking about better things to come, you will overcome many things that can destroy you.

I didn't escape completely the bad effects of such treatment. I have trouble with my stomach, and arthritis has been gradually settling in my back, knees, and hands. But I have learned how to live with it.

★ ★ ★

Gene A. Fleener, USMC

I joined the marines right out of high school by adding six months to my age. After basic in San Diego I went to Pearl Harbor in Honolulu, then to Midway Island, back to Pearl, and then to Wake Island in October of 1941, just two months before the Japanese attack.

I was on a five-inch gun during the fight and came out without getting wounded. The surrender came on December 23, and two days later it was Christmas. It wasn't an Iowa Christmas. We were stretched out on the Wake airport, some just wearing shirts and no shorts. I had shorts and no shirt.

Our Christmas feed was a piece of bread the size of your fist with a thin spread of jam on it. The water they gave us came from a gasoline drum and tasted mostly of gasoline.

The Japs put us on board a ship on January 12 and took us to Yokohama. We were there for three days while some officers and enlisted men were taken on deck and questioned.

We got to Shanghai on January 24, 1942, and were taken to a prison camp about three miles north of the city. For a year we did nothing but work in a garden. Then our old Japanese colonel died and we were moved to Kiangwan, a camp four miles the other side of Shanghai.

There we had a mountain-moving project. We moved dirt in great heaps. It turned out that we were building a one-hundred-target rifle range. The Japanese officer over us was a former teacher in Hawaii, and he knew the ways of our men even better than he knew our language. He set us a certain quota of loads of dirt to move each day, and then kept increasing the quota day by day until it was almost unbearable.

If we did anything wrong, we had to stand at rigid attention for anywhere from five to twenty-four hours. I did only one twenty-four-hour stand. It's rugged. Every time the Allies won a battle or victory of some kind we paid for it. They gave us front duty, which we could expect once a week. This was an extra load of work.

★ ★ ★

I weighed 155 pounds when I went into the marines, and was worked and underfed down to 115 pounds by the Japs by the time we were released.

In May of 1945 we started our long trip, mostly by train in crowded boxcars and overloaded coaches. We were taken to Peking, China, for a week and then traveled by train again through Manchuria to Korea. Finally they put us on Hokkaido Island, where we remained until liberation.

B-29 bombers dropped food to us in August and kept us well supplied. Then, later on, torpedo planes began bringing in supplies. They'd cut a torpedo in half and stuff it with food and things and then drop it. One of them fell right on a little shack where we got our lamps. There were eleven Japs inside and the "food bomb" killed nine of them.

I made a big mistake by grabbing a carton of twenty-four chocolate candy bars from one of the deliveries. I ate them all. Boy, were they good. And boy, was I sick.

My trip home was from one hospital to another from Tokyo to Guam, then Honolulu, then Oakland, and on to Chicago. I spent from three to eleven days in exams and checkups at the hospitals. Then home.

Senior Master Sgt. Ernest Rogers, U.S. Army (Ret.)

Once we had surrendered the island, we were ordered to go outside and sit on the road until the Japanese came for us. We did. First thing the Japs did was rob us of our rings and watches; they also went through our wallets. Then they stripped us down to our underwear and shoes and marched us up to the airstrip, where there were a lot of other men.

I went with the rest on the prison ship to Yokohama. There I was taken off along with the navy radiomen. I wasn't questioned and was never asked to work the Japanese radios. Instead, I was sent to a prison down on the southern island of Shikoku. For a while we cleared trees and brush from mountain areas to make the land ready for planting crops. Then we worked on the railroad. I was there until the end of the war.

We learned the war was over on August 16, but it was almost a month before U.S. military personnel came to lead us down to a port and eventually to a hospital ship. Then we went to Okinawa and then home to San Francisco. I was at Letterman Army Hospital in San Francisco for a week, then a hospital in Stanton, Virginia.

I stayed in the army. Spent thirty years in the communications department that progressed from Morse code and telephones to computers. I retired as a senior master sergeant in 1969.

Pvt. Kenneth E. Cunningham, USMC (deceased)

The log of the *Nitta Maru* recorded a trip of thirteen days from Wake Island to Shanghai, China. She was a converted first-class luxury liner of the Japanese steamship lines, but we were not riding first class. We were jammed into a stinking, rotten little hold. There were four decks with about three hundred men to a deck.

We left the island in our own motor launches and were taken to this big liner. It looked good from the outside, but it was the biggest floating hellhole that was ever made by man. We were pushed and thrown down ladders and hatches until we ended up in the hold "where we belonged."

They gave us two blankets each and said we were to lie down and if we moved or talked, we would be shot on the spot. There was no room for all of us to lie on the deck, so we had to pile up on each other. In some places we were three and four deep.

The Japanese sailors seemed to enjoy torturing us. One of their tricks was to make us stand on our knees for hours at a time while they walked between the rows and beat with a heavy club anyone who so much as batted an eye. We had been degraded to an existence lower than that of an animal.

The place was sickening, and for the first three days, while we were still in the tropics, it was so hot that we nearly died. We were dressed in little clothing, and then, after the fourth day, it began to get cold. This floating prison was going north, where it was winter. The steel decks of that ship were cold and brittle, and we began to freeze. We could not move, so we just lay there and froze our fingers, and toes, then our feet and our hands and ears.

On January 19 we tied up at Yokohama docks in Japan, where we stayed for three freezing days. During this period we were asked more questions, and a few men were taken off. The morning of January 22, 1942, the ship moved out of the harbor for three more days of rough weather at sea between Yokohama and Shanghai, China. On the afternoon of January 24, we saw daylight for the first time in thirteen long, miserable, cold days. We were told we were to be turned over to the army and we were to work in central China to help build Nippon's Greater East Asia Co-Prosperity Sphere.

After standing in the rain for two hours, we started on a three-mile march to the camp where I was to stay for the next year and a half. It was cold and rainy, but the walk got our blood starting to circulate. Although it was a painful process, the feeling finally came back to our fingers, toes, and ears. Some of us got the first smoke we had had for nineteen long days. We were quick to notice the soldiers were inclined to be better to us than the navy men had been. After standing in mud and mire nearly knee-deep for two hours, we were told to go into a pigpen of a barracks. It was then that we were given blankets, dishes, and the first food we had to eat for what seemed like a long, long time. The food consisted of rice and a very poor soup with so much curry in it that it was nearly impossible to eat. But it was hot and we had gone without food for so long that it tasted mighty good.

This place was called the Woosung prison camp. This was where we were to try to make our homes for the next eighteen months. It was about five miles from Woosung Forts, which are on the Wang Poo River, and three miles from Shanghai. It was on low ground with rice fields all around it. There were no windows in the buildings and there were cracks between every board. The floors were broken in and there were no lights.

Not getting the food we needed to keep us warm, we were always cold, so we were in our beds as much as possible. You could not call them beds. They were only long board platforms about six feet wide where everyone slept together. I had four thin blankets that I rolled up in, and we all rolled close together. We did not know what it was to be warm, and sometimes we wondered if we would ever see the next summer.

From the day the war started, December 8, 1941, until sometime in March of 1943, there were a good many of us who did not have our hair or whiskers cut. We had it done only when we were made to shave our faces and our heads. From that day on we were never allowed to let our hair grow.

Early in the spring of 1942 we were put to work in a huge garden that was to be for our benefit. That's what they told us then. There were twenty-five acres and we had to turn it over with picks and shovels. The tools were so crude and so clumsy that it was impossible to do much with them. The ground was filled with graves and the ruins of old Chinese homes. The graves, and the incessant driving of the Nips who forced us to work ten hours a day, made the whole project quite a task. We worked at that until the next fall, when we were put to work building an earthen monument that the Japs called little Mount Fujiyama. We really went to work then. We used picks and shovels and big bamboo baskets in which we carried the dirt to the outlined area, and began to build.

To make things real pleasant, we also had an interpreter who was crazier than the rest of the Nips. His name was Ishihara, and he had a special mania for beating Americans. At one time he had been a taxi driver in Honolulu and had been deported for that very thing; he had a pet hate for all Americans. He beat many men badly. Some were injured for life, and some even died from the aftereffects of the beatings. He used to tell us how much he hated us and often said he would kill any of us if he could find a good excuse.

He was in charge of the job we were doing and drove us like slaves, making four men do the work of ten. If the men were not doing the work well enough or fast enough to suit him, they received miserable beatings. Then they were locked in solitary and made to go without food for a few meals. Food being short, we needed every meal we could get to keep us alive. If you did not work, you got just half the amount the rest of the men received.

The barracks were surrounded by a high-voltage electric wire fence. We had three men accidentally fall into or touch this fence, and they were killed at once. One night a prisoner was shot by one of the sentries for no reason at all. The next day the Nips took pictures of a hole they made us dig under the fence so it would look as though the dead man had been trying to make his escape. They even printed this picture in one of their propaganda magazines that came out of Shanghai. The sentry was never relieved, and he made signs like it was very funny and he would like to do it again if he thought he dared.

In November 1942 an International Red Cross representative got into our camp. He'd been trying for eight months. He started to make arrangements for our Christmas. The twenty-fifth of December 1942 is a day that will stay in my memory for a good many years to come. There was food and clothing sent out to us from civilians of Shanghai who were not yet interned. To save face and to try to put up a front, the Nips gave us two days off. We were sure happy to get the rest, and we had the best food that I had to eat over the whole forty-four months of my internment. The International Red Cross was responsible for the whole of it, and the Nips gave us absolutely nothing. For two days, though, we could forget what we were going through.

At that time, the American officers were still fairly decent to us enlisted men. They always seemed to have plenty of smokes and a little better chow than we did. They did not have to work. On Christmas Day they gave some of the men a few cigarettes, but on the whole they turned out to be a no-good bunch. Everyone lost all respect for those American officers and hated to see them around in the same camp. They seemed to think they were so much better than we were that they did not even have to speak to us when we asked them a question. Of the sixty-five officers in that camp with us, there were only half a dozen that I would even call men fit to be officers.

Cpl. Jack Skaggs, USMC

I was on the *Nitta Maru* and the thirteen days of hell there. Then we got to Shanghai and into the old barracks at Woosung. I was on a detail to go and get blankets. When I got back, the men had been served our first good meal since our capture. The food was all gone by then, so I didn't get any.

One day I heard we were going to have soup. All the good things went to the bottom. The guy next to me said to stir it up and get some of the good stuff off the bottom. The server did, and when the ladle came up and was emptied in the guy's bowl, it held a good-sized rat. He ate it and was as healthy as the rest of us.

At Woosung we had a garden. We grew vegetables in the summer, and that helped to feed us a little better. We had our own prisoner cooks, but they could cook only what was given to them by the Japanese. The cooks had a good deal and they kept the jobs as long as they could. Naturally they ate better than the rest of us did. By the time we were freed, some of the cooks were looking a little fat.

One of our staples was cracked wheat with worms. The cooks told us we were getting a little protein with our wheat. It came from being swept up out of freight cars after the sacks of grain were unloaded. The wheat also had a lot of dirt and small rocks in it.

The officers had their own mess. Their food was brought to their rooms. They ate better than we did.

The International Red Cross in Shanghai brought us packages now and then, and that helped us along. We had sports, softball especially. Often the prisoners played the officers. We had some guys who were really good. I forget where we played. I remember one man got killed when he reached under the electrified fence to retrieve a softball. He touched the fence and was electrocuted on the spot.

For Christmas in Shanghai, a civilian American who hadn't been interned yet, Jimmy Jones, convinced the Japs we should have a good Christmas dinner. They kept suggesting things to the prison officials until we had a feast of roast turkey and all the trimmings. It was the best meal we ever had as prisoners. Thanks to the civilians in Shanghai.

Sgt. Maj. Robert Winslow (Ret.)

At the Woosung prison camp near Shanghai, we stood in the rain while the camp commander talked to us for at least an hour through an interpreter. He listed all of the things we couldn't do and said if we did any of them, "You will be shoot." He said it several times that way.

One of the guards, Ishihara, the "Beast of the East," yelled at us one day because we had blankets around our shoulders when we were exercising. His favorite name for us was "you individualists." He kept yelling that at us: "What are you doing, you stupid individualists?" One of the men said that we were wearing the blankets because it was cold. He said: "It's wintertime, you're supposed to be cold."

At Woosung it wasn't as bad as it was later. Woosung was a model camp, because the International Red Cross came and inspected it. They would pretty up the camp before the Red Cross people came. But we did have contact with them, and we were in touch with people in the international settlement there in Shanghai. That was before they locked up all the Americans and other foreigners who lived in Shanghai. They were responsible for getting us a big turkey dinner for Thanksgiving the first year we were there.

In 1943 I left with a detail that went to Osaka. The reason I was along was because I had listed my job on Wake as "truck driver." There weren't many trucks in Japan then and most of the people couldn't drive, so they needed me to drive a truck.

Staff Sgt. Earl Barnes, USMC

They moved us from the airstrip to the civilian barracks there on Wake. On January 12, 1942, they took us on board the *Nitta Maru*, a luxury tour ship, for the trip to Japan. When we boarded the ship, we were herded down a hatchway into the hold, where we had barely enough room to sit. We couldn't stretch our legs at all. Conditions during the voyage to Japan were brutal, diarrhea and seasickness were common, and the stench was awful. We were not allowed to get out of the hold during the entire voyage. I later found out that there were 1,235 prisoners on board the ship.

After seven days at sea, the ship arrived in Yokohama. We stayed there three days, then we were taken on a three-day voyage to Shanghai, China. They took us across the river to the Woosung prison camp, an old Japanese army cavalry barracks.

Conditions at Woosung were very bad. We were put to work carrying soil in baskets at a construction site. I was there until November of 1942, when I was one of a group of seventy moved to Japan on a small cargo ship. Our destination was Moji, on the island of Kyushu, where we went to work in a steel mill carrying iron ore to load on railroad cars. We were kept in barracks and worked from dawn to dark seven days a week. Later the Japanese put twelve of us in an auto repair shop working on marine and auto engines. There we got better treatment, along with rice, thin stew, and hot tea. I was working in the steel mill repair shop when Hirohito made his surrender speech to the Japanese people. Soon after, we were visited by a navy officer and an International Red Cross official, who asked us to remain there until transportation could be arranged.

I weighed 180 pounds when captured, and when released I was down to 120. They beat us with bamboo canes, rifle butts, and steel rods, anything they could lay their hands on, and the threat of bayonets was always there. The old Japanese guards who had fought in the war against China were the worst.

Fireman 2nd Class Dare Kibble, USN

In Woosung prison near Shanghai the buildings we lived in had six sections. In each section there were four built-up wooden platforms. Eight men slept on each of the four platforms. There was a hallway, which ran down the full length of the building. Half of the section bay was on each side of the hallway. Sixteen men were in each half of the bay.

In our section I was quartered with our section leader, whom I called Brownnose, along with Louie, Red, Jackie, Dutch, Oldman, and Hardway. I was to sleep, eat, work, fight, freeze, and pray with these guys twenty-four hours a day for two years, until I left China for Japan in 1943. In those days I would get so sick and tired of their faces and problems, I thought I would go insane. Louie was the only one I could really talk to.

In POW life, in almost every case, when the men were assigned to groups or sections, they would pair off, always seeking someone to cleave to, as if some supernatural force demanded that each individual recognize he was not sufficient unto himself. In our quarter bay the pairs were Brownnose-Oldman, Hardway-Dutch, Jackie-Red and Louie-Kibble. The men didn't always break down into pairs. I've seen them break off into threesomes, often leaving a single somewhere. The groups of three never lasted long, and I never saw any group with four.

By the winter of 1942, after ten months as prisoners, we were a miserable gang. For the months of January through April, it was cold and, at times, snowy. The Nips allowed us to stay in the barracks for those first few winter months. We stayed in bed to keep warm. Have you ever tried to remain in bed twenty-four hours a day? We had two blankets each. If you lost a blanket, you would be shot immediately, without a trial. The blankets were made of coarse wood fiber, and when you tried to fold them down around you, they would stick straight out like a starched apron.

To correct this quirk in the blanket industry's quality control, all eight of us would sleep huddled together. In this way we had sixteen blankets, and the sheer weight of the wood tended to curl the edges of the blankets. We took turns seeing who had to sleep on both outsides. We learned the best way to sleep on the hard boards was on our sides. After so long on one side, someone would say "shift," and we all would turn over to the other side. You either cooperated or got some fists in the ribs. It didn't take long to get everyone's cooperation. If you lie on your side for three or four months on a wooden bed, you get vicious infected sores on your hips and legs. Also your skin begins to resemble fish scales. Remember, we did not wash, change or remove clothes, bathe, brush teeth, comb hair, or shave in those four winter months. We relegated our activity to three areas: eating, sleeping, and pissing.

Anonymous (an unidentified Wake Island marine)

Our food at Woosung was almost the same every day. Three times a day we received a small teacup of boiled barley. Sometimes we got daikon soup. A daikon is similar to a large white radish. The soup was one daikon, a dash of soy sauce, and gallons of water. We got a small teacup of the sorry, thin soup. We figured we were taking in from eight hundred to one thousand calories per man per day.

For proper distribution of food and to make certain no one received more than his portion, a practical system was strictly enforced. A wooden bucket with a food ration for sixteen men was distributed twice a day. Each bay contained sixteen men, and we would elect by voice vote the man who would serve the food for a couple of weeks. The duty rotated through the group. The server set up our sixteen metal bowls and dispersed the gummy barley. Each man had his own bowl. Some were clean and some grimy. The *toban*, or server, dispensed the barley. If there was any complaint, a person could speak up and any unequal distribution would be fixed so no one thought he was given less food than another. Each man at any time, could elect to trade his portion with any other person's ration with no questions asked. There were some problems at first, but we soon settled down. With thirty eyes watching the *toban*, he quickly became expert at the food distribution.

You heard about food parcels being sent to prisoners by parents and the Red Cross? Sent but almost never delivered. I received three food parcels from the International Red Cross during my forty-four months in prison. The IRC sent enough packages so each prisoner in Japanese captivity would have one food parcel a week. The Japanese prison officials received them and kept them in warehouses, and sold much of the goods on the black market or ate them themselves. Hundreds of tons of such parcels were found in Japanese warehouses by U.S. troops after the war.

The IRC parcels were a superb model of planning ingenuity. Each item fit its own little space in the box. Some of the items were two packs of Chesterfield or Camel cigarettes, a can of powdered milk, several Hershey bars, cheese, cookies or hardtack, several types of C rations, a can of corn willy or fish.

You may wonder how long a food parcel would last. Normally, when supplementing the barley ration, an IRC parcel was meant to last a week. However, some prisoners would take all the items out of the parcel box at mealtime and fondle them, never eating a bit of the parcel food, only the barley ration. Some kept the IRC food for years. After a shipment of packages, we often had prisoner guards in the sleeping quarters during the day when the rest of us worked; so if you wanted to save your food, you had to take it with you to work.

The International Red Cross did another good thing for us. In 1942 they shipped into Woosung prison a number of milk goats. Their milk was reserved for the sick and dying prisoners. It helped many of them. But the goats needed a reserve supply of hay for the winter months. Thus I was blessed with the best job of any I enjoyed in my forty-four months of captivity. I was assigned to the hay detail. Actually, when I think back over those years and the tasks on which I labored, I usually was assigned to a job because it appeared to the men in charge that it would be a shit detail. Even so, this job materialized into the best I'd ever had. I loved the hay detail. There were only five men on it, one honcho and four coolies. I was a coolie. We were on the "honor system," and we could go anywhere within sight of the prison without a guard and work at our own pace.

We had scythes, a barrel-shaped wooden box, and plenty of straw rope. We had a two-wheel cart, called a *yucca*, to haul the tied bales of straw into the camp. The sequence of production was to cut the grass, stuff it in the box, trample it with our feet, and then tie it into a bale. It was wonderful to be out in the fields with no guard around.

We could scour the land for wild onions, volunteer crops of peanuts, rice, and daikons. Also we could wade for crawdads in the drain ditches. Of course, all the time that we were exploring for food, we had to keep cutting hay. But we were able to stay out in the field all day by hauling all of the bales in at the close of the work day. This enabled us to take a little nap in the sunshine at noon, after we had eaten a small amount of barley saved from breakfast. I was on the hay detail until late in the fall of 1942. Those days were great after the horror of the winter hibernation and the fearful beatings in the barracks. I don't do too well mentally unless I can fight back.

Gunnery Sgt. John S. Johnson, USMC (Ret.)

I had been writing notes of what happened since the start of the war. When we went on board the prison ship, luckily I put the notes in the sole of my shoe, so I didn't lose them. In China I met some Englishmen who hadn't been interned yet, and one of them supplied me with some paper. After the war, when I was briefed by the U.S. military in Yokohama, they took some of my notes for evidence. I'd kept a record of some of the men killed in prison camp. One marine, who was an old hand from earlier China service, was ordered to cut the grass under the fence. He had a scythe and was doing it when the Japs turned on the electrical current on the fence. He didn't know the juice was on and he touched a wire with the scythe; it electrocuted the man in an instant.

Gunnery Sgt. Robert F. Haidinger, USMC (Ret.)

I went with all the rest of the troops on the *Nitta Maru* to Shanghai and then on to Woosung Fort Prison Camp. When we arrived we marched to the fort. It seemed like fifty miles, but they tell me it was only about three miles. The Japanese had Chinese on both sides of the road to watch us go past. Somebody said they were showing these Chinese that the great Japanese army had humiliated and whipped these white men into submission and they put us on exhibition to prove it.

One of my work details at Woosung was on road repair. Mostly we filled in potholes. We overdid it and made good-sized humps out of each hole. When the trucks went over them, they bounced all over the place. The guards never caught on. We worked the road from Woosung up to North Station in Shanghai. Later we were moved to Kiangwan, on the other side of Shanghai, to a different camp, and there we built Mount Fuji. They said it was going to be a rifle range, and I did my share of hauling dirt in those carts.

Later on I was one of five hundred prisoners who was sent to Osaka. That was about August of 1943, as I remember. We wound up in Kawasaki Camp and worked in a steel mill there, the NKK mill. (The American planes flattened Kawasaki and the steel mill with bombs and firebombs in April of 1945.) Then they sent us to Niigata on the Sea of Japan side of northern Honshu, the largest Japanese island. It was a port city, and we worked as stevedores, unloading ships at the docks and putting the goods on trains. This included unloading coal as well.

At Niigata we had an interpreter who was handsome enough to be a movie star. He was an Australian who'd been captured in Hong Kong. He could speak Japanese better than the Japs could. Somebody said he had gone to a Japanese university. They wouldn't let him out of camp; they were afraid that he would vanish and blend into the community. He listened to the Japanese radio at night and then told us what the news was the next day. He told the fire watch in each barracks what was going on, and they told the rest of us. When he told us about the nuclear bomb explosion, we didn't believe him. We didn't think that any one bomb could cause that much destruction. When the second bomb was dropped, we knew about it the same day that it happened.

The Imperial rescript came out on August 15. We were chopping wood in a lot to take back to the barracks to cook with and to use in our stoves, when the Jap guards told us to march back to camp about one o'clock in the afternoon. They ordered us to stay in the barracks. The next day our camp's highest-ranking man, a U.S. Army major captured in the Philippines, told us that the war was over and we were to stay put and not to harm the guards.

The next morning we woke up and all of the Jap guards were gone except one Jap sergeant major who gave his short sword to the major to show that he was surrendering.

A few days later we were bombed by B-29s with barrels of supplies. They welded two fifty-five-gallon drums together and put them on a pallet board and dropped them. But they were so heavy they ripped right through the parachutes and came down like huge bombs. We gorged on the food, put on new uniforms and even high-top shoes. What a treat.

Later we went by train to Tokyo, then into hospitals and then to ships that took us to Oakland. I took a discharge in 1946; then a buddy and I learned that if we went back in within three months of our discharge, we could keep our rank. So I went back in and stayed for twenty-nine years total, retiring as a gunnery sergeant in 1968.

Pvt. Kenneth E. Cunningham, USMC (deceased)

In the Kiangwan prison camps we soon fell into a rut, but somehow we kept plodding along, getting some news and a lot of rumors. Most of us always believed that sometime in the dim, dark future we would see the end of it and would get back to the place that was our home and to our families and our friends we had left so long ago.

Everyone stayed in this rut, for there was no getting out of it. You had to ride along and keep your head and keep up your spirits. A good many of the boys got to the place where they thought they would never get out of that place, so they gave up hope and didn't care what happened to them. The biggest share of those men started downhill physically and never stopped. They got sick and would not fight. They died and were unceremoniously hauled out of camp and cremated. All we ever saw was a little white box that the Nips said held the men's ashes. Most of us kept up our hopes and spirits, and somehow we knew that someday we would get out of there and back home.

Slowly, surely, the cold started to become less and less bitter. It began to warm up and our working days started to get longer. The warm weather made us feel better, and our hopes rose as to our chances of getting the war over in twelve to sixteen months. That was the summer of 1943. We were still working like slaves and not getting nearly enough to eat, but the warm weather put a little heat into us and gave us a little more energy, so it made things easier all the way around.

Thanks to the International Red Cross, that summer some of us got a letter or two that had been written a year to eighteen months before. But they were from home, and that was what we wanted, this news from home. A lot of the boys stopped and thought about it and they quit feeling sorry for themselves. They got along pretty well for a while.

On August 15, 1943, five hundred of us were picked out at random and given instructions to get ready to leave on August 20. No one seemed to be sure where we were going, but we were fairly certain it would be to Japan. Our luggage, such as it was, had been gone through half a dozen times, and we were finally ready to leave.

The morning of August 20 we were piled into trucks and taken through the dirty, crowded streets of Shanghai to the docks on the Wang Poo River. We were herded into a big warehouse and quietly relieved of half of our luggage, which we never saw again. Then we were packed onto an old Japanese freighter like a bunch of sardines. We were ordered not to talk, smoke, or move around until we were under way and out to sea. The ship untied and left the river at 9:00 P.M., and we were told that any act that looked like violence would be punished by death.

We put in four hard days with little food between there and Osaka, Japan. We arrived in Japan at 8:00 P.M. and were put in large motor launches, which took us ashore. On shore, there was a big commotion with Japs running around and shouting and running us from one group to another. Finally there were 124 men were singled out one by one and put in a separate group. I was one of them.

We were given a small box of rice and started down the road at a fast walk. They said we were going to a train station. We walked about five miles through the streets of the city, where we were booed and screamed at by the Japanese civilians. Some even threw rocks at us as they cried out their curses. Having learned the language pretty well by then, we could understand what they were saying. Upon reaching the station, we were dry and thirsty and asked for water. It was refused. We were shoved into small boxcars, where most of us had to stand or sit on someone else who was already sitting on luggage.

We rode in this manner for twelve hours, with plenty of starting and stopping and switching to bounce us around. Finally we reached Shinagawa station. At that time it was the biggest railroad station in Tokyo and about the size of a small city station in the United States. There we were unloaded and shifted to an electric tram.

Almost 60 percent of the trains in Japan then were electric, and all ran on the same main power unit—a fact that made transportation an easy mark to destroy when the time came. On the tram we were taken fifteen miles to a small manufacturing district of Tokyo called Kawasaki. We arrived there on the afternoon of August 25, 1943. This turned out to be a lot worse hole than the one we had just come from. We all knew we were sunk, but we little suspected the hell there was in store for us for almost two years to come.

It was called Kawasaki Camp D-5. It was set right in the middle of a huge steel mill known as NKK, or Nippon Kawasaki Kokan. The NKK was one of the largest steel plants in Japan. The part of the plant we were in was nine miles long. Here they smelted metal, made various steel products, and manufactured coke and coke gas. The plant was run by the lowest class of people in Japan. They knew no morals or what it was to be clean. These were the people we worked for.

The civilians in charge of us used to preach to us how clean and honest the Japanese were, yet we got only one small bar of soap once every four months—if we were lucky. About a third of the time we couldn't get water to wash with. We wore the same clothes, the only ones we had, for months at a time because there was no way we could wash them. After six months we got used to the filth—and to the lice, fleas, and bed bugs. We would come in at night dead-tired from work, and lie down on straw mats that were alive with the vermin. We were lucky to get two or three hours of good sleep a night.

A word about the honest people we worked for. We POWs used to steal cigarettes and food for our own use, but the Japs would steal anything they could get if they wanted it, or thought they could sell it on the black market. The one that was in charge of our food sold on the black market half of what we were supposed to be getting. They allotted us just enough to keep us alive in the first place, and when this was cut in half we had trouble working ten hours a day on it. After the bombing started, I saw a good example of Japanese honesty. We had occasion to see miles of burned-out residential areas, and nearly every house had a small blackened safe sitting in the ashes. They trusted each other like wolves in a pack.

In camp life we were awakened every morning at 4:30 by a ringing bell. A sentry marched up and down the barracks ringing the bell and shouting at the top of his voice for us to get up. We had only ten minutes to get up, get dressed, fold our blankets, and be ready to stand for inspection and roll call. This lasted about ten minutes and left us just twenty minutes to eat our meager breakfast and get ready to go to work at 5:10 A.M. Then we fell in according to work details and marched away in their military-style goose step. My work was about four miles away.

We had to be on the job by 6:00 A.M. sharp. If we were over five minutes late, we were usually made to go without our lunch. We got forty-five minutes off for lunch, and sometimes an hour. Then it was back to more work until 6:30 or 7:00 P.M.

At work there was no loafing around. There was a Jap or two standing over you with a club ready all the time. We figured out that it took five Japs to keep three of us POWs working. But we were doing all of the jobs that the Japs didn't want or couldn't stand to do.

After work we were marched back to camp and given our supper. As soon as we entered the gate of the camps, we were searched for stolen goods or weapons. If anyone was caught with anything he should not have, he was in for some rough times in the next few days.

We were given thirty minutes to eat our supper and prepare for another inspection and roll call. At this ceremony we had to stand at rigid attention, Japanese style, and count off in Japanese. If the Jap taking roll didn't like it, we had to repeat it two or three dozen times. Then maybe he would slug a few of the men he didn't like. After this proceeding was over, it was nearly 8:30, and that's when the lights went out. Everyone had to be in bed at that time and keep his mouth shut. A Jap sentry patrolled through the building all night long; they wanted everything quiet and no one out of bed.

It was the same routine day after dreary day without any change. You just automatically fell into the monotonous pattern and stayed there. You did what you were told and got to take things as a matter of course. You automatically kept out of trouble, for there was plenty of it to get into if you wanted to.

This dull, dreary grind went on for a year and a half with no change. Men got sick, and because of no medical aid, they died. Nearly everyone had malnutrition, beriberi, and pellagra. There was also a lot of flu and pneumonia. After that kind of life for three years, it was still hard to see your buddies lie down by your side and die. At the same time, it was not something we could see or believe, but it is very plain now in 1961. The men who kept up a little hope and always figured they would get home are the ones who did make it home. The men who did not care or doubted they could make it are the ones who just gave up, are the ones who are over there in those small ash-filled boxes, the ones who never did come home.

Seaman 1st Class Cassius Smith, USN

Two days after our capture, the Japs marched us up to the bombed-out buildings at Camp Two. We stayed there for almost two weeks. We raided the canned goods the civilian cooks had in the storeroom. I remember the last thing I ate on Wake was a gallon can of pickled beets. Yes, I still like them.

We were loaded on the *Nitta Maru* prison ship on January 12 and sailed for Japan. At a stay in Yokohama some of us were taken on deck, where Japanese journalists talked to some of the men through interpreters. They didn't talk to me. At least I got out of the hold after a week down there. The fresh air and sunshine were a welcome change.

Then it was on to Shanghai, China, and Woosung prison camp. We had various work projects while there. One of mine was to go to the Kiangwan racetrack. Out there in center of the track they had us bury sixty-five-gallon drums of alcohol. We dug a hole, put in the barrel, then laid split bamboo over the top and put sod back on the bamboo. It was camouflage so American pilots and cameras wouldn't see them. They used the alcohol for fuel for their cars and trucks. Yes, I drank some of it, even though it was 180 proof.

The alcohol got me in trouble. The corpsmen in the camp asked me to bring back some of the alcohol so they could use it in the clinic. Some guys got tire inner tubes and melted the ends together and made water bottles out of them. I filled some of them and carried them back to the medics. One day I got caught. The camp guards inspected every prisoner when he came to camp. They found the alcohol. They stripped me naked, beat me up, and threw me in solitary confinement for three weeks. I had half rations of a cup of rice and a cup of water a day. They also beat me up every day.

In May of 1945 I went with the bulk of the prisoners into North China, then down to Pusan, Korea, and by boat to Japan and then on up to Hokkaido Island. There I worked in the coal mine. I was there when the war ended. We waited for somebody to come rescue us. Nobody came for several days. Cecil Doke, a couple of marines, and I decided to rescue ourselves. We took off and wound up at an airport where there were U.S. military. They asked us who we were and where we were from, then began treating us like kings. We had medical attention and lots of food, then began our trip home.

When I was weighed for the first time in forty-four months at the hospital, I checked in at 98 pounds. Usually I weighed about 160 pounds. I'm seventy-seven years old now. I was just seventeen when

I enlisted and had only been in the navy for five months when I was sent to Wake. I got one rank promotion and was discharged in July of 1946 and went back to my family in the San Francisco area.

Gunnery Sgt. Martin A. Gatewood, USMC (Ret.)

At Woosung Camp near Shanghai, China, the Japs questioned us. They wanted to know how many marines were on Wake and what we knew about the other U.S. islands. During the summer of 1942 we worked in a vegetable garden and raised a lot of food supposed to be for ourselves. It wasn't. While we were there I had a bad attack of appendicitis, and a navy doctor, using his bag of instruments, gave me a spinal and then cut out my appendix. I didn't feel a thing.

On November 3, 1942, I went from there on a ship to Yawata, Japan, on Kyushu Island. There we worked at a steel mill. At first I unloaded iron ore for use in the mill. Later I went into the automotive shop, where I worked repairing cars and motorcycles. I stayed at that job until the end of the war.

When the war was over, a lot of the guys just took off and headed for U.S. troops wherever they could find them. The marines took over management of the camp when we got word to stay put until the army or navy could come and get us. We were there two or three weeks before some military came and took us on a train to Kobe, where we boarded a ship that took us to Okinawa.

At Okinawa my hernia kicked up, and they put me in the hospital for a week. The rest of the guys went by another ship to Guam. They flew me to Guam, and I almost beat the rest of the POW's there. At Guam we got some back pay, and I stuffed it into my pocket and kept away from the dozens of big-pot poker games.

I went to Oakland to the hospital for a day, then flew to the naval hospital at Norman, Oklahoma. After an overnight there I was given a ninety-day leave. When I got back, they operated on my hernia. After that, they sent me to a casual company, where I reenlisted. I stayed in for twenty years, retiring from the Marine Corps in 1960 as a gunnery sergeant."

1st Sgt. James O. King, USMC (Ret.)

I went through the usual hell on the prison ship to Japan. While we stopped at Yokohama, I was selected to go on deck and talk to about twenty Japanese reporters. We talked through interpreters. I don't know why they picked me, and I don't remember what I said, but after seven days of being jailed in that stinking hold, it was great to be on deck and to see the blue sky and the sunshine. The good time lasted only about a half hour, then I was back in the hellish hold again.

Then on to Woosung prison camp near Shanghai. One thing we did there was to clear out a swamp. We turned part of it into a recreation area and part of it into a garden. I don't remember seeing anything from the garden that we ate. Neither did I play any sports on the field. But I understand that's where the softball games were held.

On November 3, 1944, they picked seventy of us and shipped us to the southern Japanese island of Kyushu, to a little town called Yawata (now named "Kita Kyushu"). There they had us doing menial work. First, we were loading large rocks, twenty to thirty pounds each, on a flatbed train in freezing sleet and rainy weather. The next day we offloaded the same rocks. This went on for several days and they finally took a few of us in communications inside, and we sat around a charcoal stove, splicing wire all day. Included with me was Sgt. Randolph M. June, our senior NCO in charge of communications on Wake Island; his second in command, Sgt. Edward B. Rook; and Armand E. Benjamin, Dennis C. Connor, and Thomas J. Andrews Jr. However, that lasted only a few days for Andrews and me, who were put to work repairing high-tension cable wire in place on poles; with no protective gloves, we were working high up between poles. Thankfully we finished this job. We were then placed in a "blacksmith" shop, swinging an eight-pound sledgehammer all day every day and were there until the second A-bomb was dropped on Hiroshima, which saved all POWs' lives as well as perhaps millions of Allied forces and Japanese lives, had an invasion taken place. The Japanese POW camp commanders had written orders to the effect, "Kill all prisoners of war, and leave not a trace!" The civilians, woman, men, and even able children would have fought until the death with sticks, knives, and other weapons.

We were in the factory working when all the POWs were "escorted" back to the train to return to camp. But the train was stopped for a broadcast by Emperor Hirohito. The Japanese had never even heard his voice before that day, when he announced that the war was over and that Japan was surrendering to the USA. Of course we did not understand the speech, although we had figured out what had happened.

There were four cities; now they are all together and named Kita Kyushu. But then one of the four had a "red light" area, and Sergeant June figured that this would be an area where trouble might break out. So he appointed us communicators "military police" to patrol that area. Sergeant Rook and I obtained a Jeep from the U.S. Navy to use, and we used the local police department offices as our joint headquarters. We never had any problems in that area.

After a couple of weeks we decided that all was secure, since the vast majority of POWs had evacuated the area. I caught a ride on a train that went near Nagasaki, and I saw firsthand the destruction. It was unbelievable! A few poles were still standing and intact, and the rest was rubble as far as I could see.

I boarded an English ship for Okinawa, disembarked, had lunch at a marine mess hall, and caught another ship to Guam, where they paid all of us a five-hundred-dollar advance. I also found a fifty-dollar bill. There were some marine planes heading to the States via Hickam Field, but the navy spokesman refused to let marines travel with the planes, since they had a ship going to Oakland, California, and we were scheduled to travel via ship. There were wild poker games on board, but I steered clear.

Upon arrival in the bay, it was already getting dark and we were kept on board until morning. I heard that a marine or two went overboard and did swim the short distance to shore and managed to "disappear." We were taken to the U.S. naval hospital, Oak Knoll, where we were issued some new khakis, paid another five hundred dollars, and given liberty overnight. I decided to visit a great-uncle I had never met; he lived in Vallejo. I finally went back to Oak Knoll on the fourth day. Nothing was said or done about my absence.

Cpl. Jack D. Hearn, USMC

I went with the rest of the group on the "cruise ship" *Nitta Maru*. We stopped for three days at Yokohama, then on to Shanghai and Woosung prison. Nothing too terrible or memorable happened to me there. I was one of the seventy prisoners taken to Osaka, Japan, then to Hokkaido and the coal mine. I worked deep underground with a pick and shovel.

Then the war was over and I was on my way home. I drew only ninety dollars of my pay and figured I'd spend the rest of it after I hit the States. I went to several military hospitals and was discharged in February 1946. I had spent over five and a half years in the marines.

Master Sgt. Walter T. Kennedy, USMC (Ret.)

After the surrender, I didn't go with the rest of the guys on the luxury liner *Nitta Maru*. They kept about twenty of us seriously wounded in the hospital, because there were no medical facilities on the ship. We stayed on Wake until April 1942. Then they took us on the *Samurai Maru*. We slept around the indoor swimming pool. The ship was really a tour luxury liner. My arm and leg were pretty well healed up by then. We had about four hundred civilian construction workers on board with us. They were the lucky ones who weren't left on Wake. Ninety-eight men who were left on the island were massacred when the Japs thought an invasion of Wake by U. S. forces was imminent. The Jap general there was later hanged. We had good food on board the ship, but that wouldn't last when we hit prison camp.

I wound up in Hokkaido at the coal mine prison camp. One day I was put on a detail to load up a dump truck with coal. The guard told us to stay busy but not to work too hard. He said if we got it full quickly, he'd have to take it back and dump it and then we'd have to do it again. He got us working, then curled up under a tree and went to sleep. We worked slow, at last got it full, and he took us back to camp. His superiors never found out about it.

Staff Sgt. Ralph J. Holewinski, USMC

In the battle on the twenty-third I had been hit in both legs; I could see some bones. And shortly after that, I saw Major Devereux and the man with the white flag. The island had been surrendered.

A couple of marines carried me over to the airfield. We were there for most of two days. The second day, somebody found a cot for me to lie on. I was hurting. We didn't have any morphine or sulfa. The Japanese doctors did wrap up my legs and stopped the bleeding. The third day, they took me to the Japanese hospital at the old Camp Two. Both of my legs were bandaged from ankle to knee, and my back had a big bandage on it, too. Every day an American doctor came and changed my bandages. There were several Americans in the hospital. I think we had better food than the other prisoners had.

On the tenth day I was transferred to the American hospital. I was outside on a stretcher when the other POWs were put on the *Nitta Maru*. The doctors asked the captain of the ship if he could take me, but he said they had no place for me.

I stayed on Wake until May. I started to walk a week before they shipped us out on the *Asuma Maru*. It was a cruise ship that had been in Los Angeles harbor on December 5, 1941, and had been ordered to leave before it could unload its cargo of pure silk. It had sailed down the coast of South America before it had been ordered back to Japan. It stopped at Wake to pick up twenty of us prisoners from the hospital.

They had no cabins for us on the *Asuma Maru,* so we were quartered on the swimming pool deck. Some of the guys even swam. At least we weren't in the hold and had fresh air and sunshine. I went to sick bay, and the ship's doctor dressed the wound on my back, which hadn't healed yet. There were Japanese women and children on board, and they were curious to see these Americans. We ate pretty well during the trip. We stopped at Yokohama, where six of us were taken off the ship and moved to an interrogation camp about fifty miles away. I had been on Palmyra, and the Japs wanted to know about the defenses and the strength of the military stationed there. I stayed there for a month. The other prisoners were from many different countries.

We were sent to Cenzsurie on the southern Japanese island of Shikoku. My back still hadn't healed; the doctor said that I couldn't work. We stayed there for eight months, and the conditions were the best there of any prison camp I was in. Many times we got a small loaf of bread with our soup.

In January we went to a camp near Osaka, where a lot of Bataan and Corregidor prisoners had been sent. They were physically in bad shape, and one or two of them died every day. I still couldn't work, my back wound was still draining. The work parties put their time in on miniature submarines in a shipyard about two miles from our camp.

Later we went to another camp near Osaka. The prisoners at this camp broke up larger pieces of coal into small ones so the trucks could burn them. There were a lot of coal-burning trucks at that time in Japan; the fire produced the steam that ran the small engines on the trucks. When I felt better, they put me on a cook detail that went to the place our men were working, and we cooked their noon meal. We stole what we could to cook and get more food for our men to eat.

In May of 1945 we moved again, this time to Osaka Two, the prisoner headquarters camp. After two weeks we were bombed out of Osaka and they sent us to Hokkaido, the northernmost island. There we worked on the docks unloading boats and barges until the war ended.

Then the army rescued me and sent me home. I got a promotion and was discharged on March 21, 1946 as a staff sergeant.

Pfc. Armand E. Benjamin, USMC

We were taken on board a ship, the *Nitta Maru,* on January 12. We climbed up the cargo net to get on the ship, then went down ladders into the hold. I was in the bottom of the four holds that our men used. It was hot at first, but got cold as we went farther north toward Japan. We stopped for three days in Yokohama. It was while we were there that three sailors and two marines were beheaded on the ship's deck, though we didn't find out about it until after the war was over. We never saw daylight until we landed in China.

My first prison camp was at Woosung, near Shanghai. While there I worked mostly on the roads. But in November of 1942 I was sent to another camp, this one on the southern Japanese island of Kyushu. It was called Yawata. There were seven of us in the crew, and we were all linemen. They picked us out for this special job. We were working on telephone cables, getting them ready for a new telephone exchange that was being built but wasn't done yet. We didn't work too hard or too fast sometimes. A civilian was our immediate boss. One day he told me he was cold and ordered me to build a fire for him. "If you're cold, build your own fire," I told him. He picked up a two-by-four and came at me. I got to him before he got to me and beat him up. He told the army guard, who came and slapped me a couple of times. After that we had no trouble.

Some of the men with me on Kyushu were E. E. [Eschol] Davis, POW #449, James A. Fitzpatrick, #451, "Rocky" [Robert L.] Deeds, James O. King, #448, a man named Adams from the North China marines and Chick, a Korean. Another guy with us was John R. Himelrick, #450. He died while we were in prison camp. I stayed at that same camp for the rest of the war.

On August 15, 1945, the Japanese guards all vanished, and eventually American officers took over the camp. Most of the POWs waited for the army or navy to come find them, but three of the men left the next day and took a train north toward Tokyo. Three of us left camp the day after that; we boarded a train that was going south. We'd found out that the Fifth Air Corps was at a Japanese airfield down near Kagashima, and just walked on the train, not bothering with tickets. When we came to a large town, the Japanese police chief came to us and asked where we were going. We told him the air base at Kagashima. He gave us a place to stay for the night and put us on the train the next morning.

At the airbase the MPs asked us for our serial numbers. We said, "What serial number?" They said then, 'Where are your dog tags?' We said, "What are dog tags?" We didn't have either one when we entered the service. They must have had our numbers at Washington, but we didn't know what they were back in 1941.

We stayed with the Fifth Air Corps overnight, and the next day they flew us to Okinawa, then on to the Philippines. There we were checked over at a hospital and sent to an army recreation camp for ten days. We even got a one-night liberty in Manila. They gave us some of our pay in Philippine victory money. Back in 1941 I was making fifty-one dollars a month—thirty-six regular pay and fifteen dollars a month specialists' pay. But when the war broke out, they cut out all specialists' extra pay.

I decided to leave the Corps and was discharged in 1946. The army and navy and air corps all gave their POWs automatic promotions when their time in rank was up. The marines didn't do that. I started the war as a PFC, and after five years I was still a PFC. Congress is trying to do something about compensation for those pay grades we missed.

In 1950 I was called back into the service and took a tour in Korea and then later in Vietnam. I retired in 1969 after twenty-eight years as a master gunnery sergeant. I get to the reunions of the Wake Island Defenders every year. This year I went to two of them.

Sgt. Max J. Dana, USMC

When they loaded us on board the hell ship *Nitta Maru,* we had no idea where we were heading, although there were rumors that we might be taken to a distant port and exchanged for oil. We all had hopes of repatriation or release. Also that the war would end in less than a year with an Allied victory. Little did we know what had to be accomplished before this could become a reality. Better that we didn't. We soon figured we were going north, as the nights kept getting cooler and cooler. The one blanket per man wasn't near enough to keep us warm, so we started doubling up. They held us in Yokohama for three days.

While we were there, my bunk partner and blanket sharer, John W. Lambert from Utah, was pulled out and taken up on deck. We didn't know why. He never came back. It was a long time before we knew that he and four other GIs were executed that day.

We left Yokohama and sailed to Shanghai. At our new home in Woosung prison, a Japanese interpreter met us with a short welcoming speech. He said, "If you try to escape, we will shoot you." Later a camp commander told us prisoners, "From now on you have no property, you gave up everything when you surrendered. You do not even own the air that is in your bodies. From now on, you will work for the building of a Greater Asia. You are the slaves of the Japanese."

Our toilets at this camp were slit trenches that you straddled. They were in separate cubicles. Underneath each cubicle was a large bowl. Local Chinese emptied the bowls by what we called the honey bucket brigade. They would dip the crap out of the bowl and put it in buckets attached to *yeh-ho* shoulder poles. Then they'd haul the buckets to a boat we called a "shit barge" on a nearby channel. This fertilizer would later be used to nourish their crops. Nothing was wasted in China.

They finally decided that we needed some more clothing. They gave us worn-out Japanese uniforms and shoes. The pants I got came just below my knees, and the shoes were terrible.

To pass the time we did various things. One was playing cards. I learned to play bridge. We gambled, playing blackjack or poker and using cigarettes and bread for chips. At one time they issued us a loaf of bread a day in place of a bowl of rice. The loaf was actually a big biscuit about the size of a grapefruit that we cut into quarters. It was in reality about two bites and worth ten cigarettes. We were issued three cigarettes a day, so the gambling was for high stakes.

Some of us also studied Spanish. We were fortunate to have a Peruvian merchant marine in our camp who had been a professor. Three officers and myself were the whole class. We learned vocabulary and how to conjugate verbs. It let me know how little I had paid attention to grammar in school, so I had to learn English grammar before I could learn Spanish. I lucked out, as I had a friend who was a whiz at it and gave me a crash course.

Punishment, such as solitary confinement and standing at attention in front of the guardhouse overnight or longer until you were ready to drop, was handed out quite frequently for the slightest infraction. If they wanted information or to get you to squeal on someone, they would resort to torture such as twisting thumbs or the water cure. The most common form of punishment was beating.

While on a working party outside the compound, I strayed just a little out of the prescribed boundary in search of some small buds that grew on weeds and were edible. We had two guards, and they immediately marched me back. One held a bayonet on me while I had to stand at attention and the other guard used me as a punching bag. When his knuckles got numb, he let the other guard have his turn. He used his rifle butt against my head, so it didn't take long to drop me. Failure to bow to an official, which was the same as a salute to them, was another reason for punishment. If you looked a guard in the eye, it was considered contempt. Then you would have to stand at attention and get beaten.

Maj. Robert M. Brown, USMC (Ret.)

On board the *Nitta Maru* our water allowance was a half a ladle per man twice a day. Food was a small bowl of barley gruel and a small piece of pickled bamboo shoot twice a day. The first six days on board were hot and stifling, but as the course went northward it became extremely cold lying on the steel deck. We were so scantily clad that the cold was brutal. I had only a short-sleeve khaki shirt and khaki trousers. We attempted a blanket pooling system, but everyone was so cold we had no body heat to share. Since my only footwear was a pair of shower clogs, my feet stayed like ice.

Next stop was Woosung prison, near Shanghai, China. It was cold and we were issued two blankets made of wood fiber. After two weeks we were issued Japanese army uniforms and shoes. They were really too small for us, but they did give us some relief from the cold.

Our biggest problem there was boredom. In mid-summer the International Red Cross in Shanghai was able to get some clothing and toilet supplies into the camp. This enabled us to shed our Japanese uniforms and get into real clothes and shoes. We also cut our beards and, for the first time since the war started, brushed our teeth and took our first showers. We rigged the shower from a pipe on the edge of the roof. We never knew how bad we smelled, because we all smelled the same. After this late June cleanup, we felt like new men.

In December 1942 they moved us to a different camp, Kiangwan, about three miles the other side of Shanghai. This was a marked improvement over the Woosung buildings. They even had stoves for the winter months.

It was in Kiangwan Camp that I encountered Mr. Ishihara, the camp's chief interpreter. He had lived in Honolulu before the war, so his English was perfect, but he hated Americans and his actions were those of a maniac. He always carried a large riding crop, which he used to slash prisoners whether there was any reason for it or not. He was in charge of the Mount Fuji project and seemed to take delight in increasing our quota of dirt to be moved before we could return to camp. This led to eleven-hour days, plus an hour's march each way. He originally earned the title of "One-Man Reign of Terror" and then various other names, but the one that stuck was "The Beast of the East."

By the spring of 1944 small amounts of mail were getting through to us via the International Red Cross. I had never received any. One happy day I was told that my name was on the list of mail received. Instead of a letter, I got a message to report to Mr. Ishihara's office that afternoon. Five of us showed up at the appointed time.

The "Beast" lined us up, then leaned back in his chair. He had several letters in his hand. He stared at us for a while before he erupted. "You are the cause of an insult to the Japanese empire," he screamed. "You leave your cheap, common women at home and they dare to write you here. Your whores dare to speak of love. This is not a time for love, this is a time for war. Maybe you marines think first of love and then of fighting. Maybe that's why you now live in this camp." He went on and on. When he subsided, he smiled at us. One by one he tore the letters into tiny pieces and threw them in our direction. "Here," he said. "Take them and be ashamed."

I doubt that I will ever recover from the hatred I felt and feel still for Mr. Ishihara. It doesn't help to know that he died a very painful death from cancer while in prison. He still lives on in my nightmares.

Both 1943 and 1944 were a combination of work and illness for me. The work was pick-and-shovel duty, mainly on the infamous Mount Fuji project. Also we repaired roads and dug a tank trap near an airfield. I was hospitalized for malaria two or three times, and was in the hospital again for what they called infectious hepatitis. I had considerable trouble with my legs and feet, and for an extensive period I was excused from work due to the painful swelling of my lower legs and ankles. Our navy POW doctor diagnosed it as beriberi.

Soon we were moved again, this time mostly by train and boat to Japan, and then all the way to the northernmost province of Hokkaido. We were in Hakodate Camp #3 on the southwestern part of the island.

Our work assignment was in a nearby coal mine, access to which was by a sloping ramp about six hundred yards long. At the base of it we had to wade through ice-cold, chest-high water. Then we worked ten hours in wet clothes. We were "muckers," using jack-hammers and then removing the loose coal from the tunnel facing. The mine was said to be forty-two years old and in terrible condition. Many of the support timbers were rotten and broken, and cave-ins on a small scale occurred constantly. We were lucky we didn't get caught in a major cave-in. The food there was the worst we had had so far. We had one small teacup of dirty rice three times a day, with seaweed so slimy it was almost inedible, and for the evening meal a tasteless broth with a cellulose reed called *fuki*.

It was the camp steward, a civilian named Kikuchi, who made life miserable. He was so bad that he made Ishihara look tame. He was in charge of the galley and any work details inside the camp. He was loud, arrogant, sadistic, and always hostile. He beat buddies of mine unmercifully. Our prisoner cooks knew that he daily carried out of camp a portion of the rice intended for the prisoners.

My personal experience with Kikuchi was on a day when I was taken off the mine detail for "camp work." That meant carving an air-raid shelter out of the side of a hill just outside the compound. Kikuchi personally supervised the project. To this day I do not know what I did or failed to do to upset him. He came at me with a long-handled shovel, and as I turned away, he hit me on my right upper back and shoulder with a blow that knocked me off my feet. I was just lucky he didn't hit my head, or I might not be here today.

I was happy to be one of several dozen who had the opportunity to detail Kikuchi's actions to the U.S. intelligence officers on our way home. I understand he received twenty years at hard labor at the Tokyo War Crimes Trial. I still dream of this man from time to time.

Pvt. William B. Buckie, USMC

You've heard it before, the prison ship from Wake to Japan and China was a hellhole. We were packed in like sardines in too small a can. We were elbow to elbow. Almost no food, and no sanitary facilities other than the overflowing slop buckets that were supposed to be emptied regularly but weren't. Then it got cold, when we moved north toward Japan. The whole trip was threatening, physically degrading, dangerous, and scary. Hey, I was only twenty-one. But I hadn't seen anything yet.

Woosung prison, just outside of Shanghai, China, was our first prison camp. We worked every day, polishing shell casings, repairing the roads, even working in our garden. Later we were transferred to Kiangwan Camp, also near Shanghai. Conditions there were primitive, the guards were brutal and sadistic, and the work was unending as we struggled ten to twelve hours a day on building a huge rifle range that we called Mount Fuji. I was in the second shipment of prisoners to go from Shanghai to Osaka, Japan. In Osaka we worked in the shipyard. Mainly our job was to unload steel from the barges that brought it alongside. We took it off the barges and spread it out in the yard so the shipbuilders would have it when they needed it. The work was hard and long.

As in every camp, the prisoners tended to pair off with a good buddy for self-protection and companionship. I had several good friends in Shanghai: Willy Williams from Louisiana, John P. Moore, and John F. Blandy. His uncle was Admiral [W. H. P.] Blandy, who worked on the nuclear testing after the war. I heard that John Blandy stayed in the Corps for thirty years before he retired. In Osaka "Jake" Jacob R. Sanders was my buddy. He was from Texas, but he moved to Seattle after he got out of the service. He died a couple of years ago.

After the Army Air Corps bombed the steel mill in Osaka into rubble and we couldn't work there, we were shipped out to Niigata up on Honshu Island. We had especially brutal guards there. One guy was particularly hard on the Australians. After the war was over, I heard that the Aussies killed that brutal guard. Not sure if that was true or not, but that was the story going around.

We knew the war must be over when we didn't have to go to work one glorious day and the whole guard force was changed. The brutal ones were gone, and kinder and more polite ones came in. We really knew the war was over when the American planes came over and dropped food, clothes, and all sorts of things we hadn't seen in years, like toothpaste and soap. Then we broke down the fences and wandered about a little, but we stayed in that camp for about two weeks. By then we had all the food we could eat, new clothes, and even shoes. We shaved and showered and looked more like marines.

Then an officer came and led us down to the railroad station, where he put us on a train, and eventually we got to Tokyo. There the medics took over and examined us. I had bad cases of beriberi and pellagra at the time and felt terrible. On the ship out of Tokyo I went into the hospital. We were at Guam for a couple of days, but I stayed on the ship. I felt a lot better when we hit Pearl Harbor. From there it was another ship to Oakland. What a great feeling when we sailed into port and saw the good old U.S.A.

I was in the Oakland navy hospital for a week, then took a train to the Great Lakes Naval Training Center. There I got a ninety-day leave. Back at the base they wanted us to sign a paper saying that we were physically well and healthy. A bunch of us refused to sign the paper or take the discharge. They at last gave us honorable discharges that were marked "Under Protest." Those two words meant that the Veterans Administration would take care of my many physical problems after I left the service. They did.

At home I went into the family business, graphic arts, and spent the rest of my working days there.

Capt. James J. Davis, USN (Ret.)

On board the ship they put us in the parcel post mail room. It was not in the hold. There were about twenty officers in the area. We had it easier than the enlisted men in the holds.

In Yokohama they took off all the radio communications men and anyone who had served on Midway, Johnson, or Palmyra Islands. They wanted any information about defenses on those points that the men might have. I don't know what happened to those men taken off at Yokohama.

Then we went on to Shanghai and the infamous Woosung prison camp. The officers in camp were given the job of making a garden. We did pretty well. Some kinds of vegetables we grew produced well, and we had more than we could eat. Later we went with the rest of the camp to Kiangwan, on the other side of Shanghai. After that stretch we went by train up into north China and down to Pusan, Korea, then to Honshu Island, and by another train all the way to the top of Honshu and by boat over to Hokkaido. Up there we were at an old coal mine. The officers worked above ground, stockpiling gravel and timbers to be used for braces in the mine. There was usually six feet of snow in the area during the winter, so they had to have the braces ready.

We had arranged with our guards that we got fifteen minutes of rest each day—seven in the morning and eight in the afternoon. We would sit down to rest and nobody checked the time. We never went back to work until the guards told us to. Often we had a half hour of rest.

The night of August 15, 1945, it was my turn as camp rotating adjutant. One guard came and told me there would be no work in the mines the next day. I asked why and he said, "No more work, ever." Then he turned and ran away. The guards we had then were the lowest class of reserves that Japan had. They had called up everyone.

The next day a Japanese officer told us that the war was over, that we had won, and he asked us what he could do for us. What a switch in attitude. He brought us some beer and saki and better food, and we all promptly got diarrhea from eating too much. Then the planes came dropping supplies and food. I took sick with an attack of malaria on the train down to the seacoast town. There we were back in the command of U.S. troops. I spent some time in the hospital and eventually was flown back home. I stayed in the Navy, received promotions, and retired in August 1, 1966, with the rank of captain.

Radioman Chief Petty Officer Marvin Balhorn, USN (Ret.)

After we made the long, cold trip to Yokohama on the *Nitta Maru,* the eight navy radiomen were all taken off the ship. They didn't do any questioning of us. Our officer was not with us; we never knew where he went. They took us to a big radio station between Tokyo and Yokohama. There they brought in the typewriters we had used on Wake and told us to start taking down the U.S. military radio transmissions. They were all in five-letter code. We took them down on the typewriters, but often we would change some of the letters. The Japs were trying to break the U.S. encrypting code. As far as we know, they never did.

We had our own little prison camp, for the eight of us. Sometimes we got plenty of food, sometimes not much at all. I understand our situation was much, much better than that for most of the Japanese prisoners. We just sat there taking down the codes on the military radio messages for the whole course of the war.

In June of 1945, after a large firebombing of Tokyo, one of the guards came in screaming mad. His wife and two daughters were in Tokyo and he didn't know if they had survived the bombing. He took his hatred out on me, pounding me with his fists and breaking out many of my teeth. Blood was flying all over. There wasn't any medical or dental help for me.

On August 15, when the war ended, we were told to stay where we were. When the marines landed in Yokohama some of them came and got us and took us to an airport, where we were given new uniforms and food and flown to Okinawa. From there they flew us to the Philippines, and then we island-hopped our way across the Pacific to Pearl Harbor. The next step put us in an air station below San Francisco, and shortly thereafter to a naval hospital near Chicago. The medics said they would fix my teeth, but not quite yet.

First I had a leave. I arrived home in September of 1945 to a big homecoming. My parents came to Cedar Rapids to get me and I went home to Garrison, Iowa. I stayed in the navy for twenty years and made Radioman Chief Petty Officer.

Anthony Lepore, USMC (deceased)
Crestview, Illinois

I lived a nightmare in the Japanese POW prisons. It's hard for me to believe what happened; how can I expect anyone else to believe it? I enlisted in the marines in August 1941, before the war started. I was assigned to an antiaircraft battery that hauled supplies to other units. I was later reassigned to a fighter unit on Wake Island, where I was taken prisoner along with the rest of the servicemen on December 23.

I have learned to talk about my experiences because of help of a psychologist and social worker at the Veterans Administration. I have turned to them for over forty-six years. The painful memories are the hard part. But even now there are some experiences that I will not discuss.

I remember waking up many mornings to find drool on the straw mats we had to sleep on. We had dreamed about bakeries. Part of that was because our rations consisted of six ounces of rice.

I had a shrapnel wound on Wake and the Japs didn't do anything about it. A doctor who was also a prisoner dug it out and removed the poison. Of course we had no anesthesia, so it was painful.

Torture by the Japanese guards was common in all of the four POW prisons I was in during my forty-four months as a prisoner. One of my legs is a half-inch shorter than the other as the result of a rifle beating that affected my spine. The Jap guards constantly sought ways to maintain power over us, mentally and physically.

They called us barbarians. They told us it was America's fault the war was on, and that the Japanese were winning.

My prison camp years were hard on my family. I was listed as missing in action for three years. My father repeatedly refused to accept my life insurance benefits. He had hope that I had made it. And he was right. A letter told my parents that I was a POW in China or Japan. Another year later my older sister fainted when she heard my voice on the telephone. I told her I was free and coming home.

Yes, I partied when I got home. It took a while. Usually I weighed 175 pounds. When I came home I was in a 96-pound body. My neighbors and family greeted me with tears and food. That's when I realized that I had to learn how to eat again. Also I had to adjust to functioning in this new, to me, American society in 1945.

Like when I started dating. The girl who I would marry scolded me one night. "You don't talk, you don't do anything," she told me. She was right. My mind was wandering. I wasn't the same person I had been when I left town.

In my later years I have learned to appreciate life more. I have a hard time throwing away any food. I make it a point to help a person who is needy. Also I have not and never will buy a Japanese-made car. By now I'm a grandparent, and I've learned to talk about some of the wartime experiences with the grandchildren. I tell them a little bit, but not too much.

Brutality by the Japanese camp guards was the norm. They delighted in punishing the "western white men" who had no honor, because they had allowed themselves to be captured. The water cure, bamboo slivers driven under fingernails, a half-hour beating for stealing an apple, guards taking turns drubbing the prisoners with clubs and fists, hard slaps to the face for minor infractions—the pattern soon emerged, and just the threat of cruel corporal punishment kept the POWs walking the line and doing exactly what their Japanese guards told them to do. There would come a day of reckoning, but it was many months away.

Private First Class Leonard G. Mettscher, USMC (deceased)
Wright City, Missouri

We disembarked from the *Nitta Maru* at Shanghai, China, and marched three miles to Woosung prison. My clothing at that time consisted of a pair of khaki shorts and one shoe. We were assigned to the working parties and repaired roads and drainage ditches. During that winter I contracted malaria and severe dysentery. My bowel movements were as frequent as twenty-five times a day, and that made me very weak. It got so bad that I was passing lots of blood. My only medication at that time was ground-up charcoal, which didn't help. My weight loss that winter was 60 pounds, down from my usual weight of 180 pounds.

During April of that next year, due to exposure from working on the roads and in the ditches without any proper clothing, I contracted pneumonia and was so weak that the Japs let me off work and I stayed in the barracks. They called it the hospital barracks, but all it was was a place to lie down. You had to be too weak and sick to walk to be allowed in there.

In the early part of 1943 we were transferred to Kiangwan prison, also near Shanghai. There we worked building a combination shrine and rifle range. The work was extremely hard, pushing loads of dirt up an incline in terribly harsh weather for twelve hours a day, with one day off work a week. The food was terribly inadequate—a cup of rice in the morning, a bowl at noon, and a cup of rice at night. Sometimes some bread and slimy soup made from boiled okra was served. During that time I also contracted hookworms. I had round-worms so bad that I even spit them up.

In 1944 I was nearly beaten to death. I was in charge of a horse that was used for hauling away debris. The guard made me overload the cart. I protested, but to no avail. The horse stumbled and fell, hitting his head against a post. The fall paralyzed the animal. Later it died. They blamed me and gave me the water cure. They put a tube into my throat with a funnel attached and poured liquids down it. You could either swallow it or drown. When my stomach became dis-tended after much liquid, they beat me with a rubber hose until I was unconscious.

In May of 1945 we were transferred to another camp, this one close to Peking, China. The food there consisted entirely of steamed bread. They had no oven, so they put it in a pot and steamed it, and it made everybody sick. In a camp of twelve hundred men, nobody could get up because of the terrible stomach cramps. We stayed there about a month and then left for Pusan, Korea. They didn't have any barracks. The only protection from the weather was poles with rice mats across the top to keep the rain out. Rice mats were laid in the mud for our beds.

When we left there we went by ship to Japan, then by train and a ferry up to Hokkaido. We went to a little town up in the mountains called Utashinai, where we worked in a coal mine twelve hours a day. Our only food was a bowl of rice three times a day. We worked there until the end of the war, when we were released. By the time I got to Guam I weighed only 87 pounds, down from my normal weight of 180.

Some of the diseases I suffered in addition to the mental and phys-ical torture were amoebic dysentery, hookworms, roundworms, pink worms, pellagra, beriberi, pneumonia, and malaria.

Later in my life I suffered from a serious heart condition and a stroke with paralysis. I have blocked this all out from my mind for many years. There is no way to describe what forty-four months of living under such conditions is like, and how it has affected me and the other men all the rest of our lives.

Sgt. Norman Kaz-Fritzshall, USMC

I was on the prison ship with the others. One Japanese guard was inspecting lots of prisoners. When he came to me, he nodded and made me take off my shoes. I have small feet and so did he, so he got himself a new pair of shoes.

When we at last got to Shanghai, China, and stepped off the ship into the cold fresh air, it was wonderful. The cold got to us at once. All I had was a shirt and khaki pants. By then my socks were worn out, since I didn't have any shoes. We had to stand in the rain that first day we got to camp at Woosung prison to hear a talk by the commanding colonel. We couldn't understand what he said, and my feet were turning blue from the cold.

One day in camp some Japanese guards grabbed me and tied me down to a big shutter on the floor and jabbed bamboo slivers under my fingernails. They watched me suffer and roared with laughter. After a while they untied me and threw me outside. In the process they had pulled my shoulder out of the socket. It took two days before the other men helped me get it back in place. That shoulder still hurts today.

I hit all of the prison camps the other men did on our route up through China and down to Pusan, Korea, then by boat to Japan and in railroad cars up to northern Honshu. I wound up in Hokkaido and the infamous coal mine.

I was too sick to work for quite a while. I had malaria, beriberi, and dysentery and was so sick I couldn't walk. When the American planes came over dropping food after August 15, I was too sick to go out and get any of it. I remember that one of the torpedoes they dropped filled with food, hit close to the men, skidded and spun around, and killed three of the POWs.

The military rescue units came and took us down to Sapporo, and from there we went by boat to Tokyo and then on home. I spent nine months in the Great Lakes Naval Hospital. At last I got my sergeant stripes and a regular discharge.

Cpl. Richard S. Gilbert, USMC

I remember one man who was beaten on the prison ship as we went to Japan. I don't know what he did. He had a big gash on his back, and they pounded on the gash, punched him, and beat him with a club until he couldn't walk. He wound up paralyzed from the waist down. I don't know what happened to that guy.

My biggest problem was one day in prison camp a guard kicked me in the stomach. Later a knot developed there, and then it grew larger. We had no medical people in camp to look at it. It's still there but is a lot larger now, like a big orange. Just won't go away. Doctors say if it doesn't hurt, leave it alone.

The Japanese? I don't like them. I won't buy a Jap-built car. I try not to buy anything made in Japan, which is getting harder all the time.

My one gripe? The marines didn't give us time-in-rank promotions the way the army did their men. That costs us quite a bit of extra pay, especially if they make it in 2002 dollars. Also we never got paid for the work we did in Japanese factories and firms. The companies told the government they were paying us, but they never did. There are some class action lawsuits about that now.

No, I didn't stay in for twenty. I enlisted in April of 1941 and was discharged in April of 1946.

Maj. Robert O. Arthur, USMC (Ret.)

On January 12 we left Wake Island on board the luxury liner *Nitta Maru*. We were crammed into four holds, and conditions were sub-human. We arrived in Yokohama on January 19, and I celebrated my twenty-third birthday. I wore a tropical hat, a bathrobe, and shorts.

What a sight. Someone took a picture of me in the get-up as I was thanking the Japanese people for the parade and helping me to celebrate my birthday. I'm sure they thought I was crazy.

The officers and pilots were taken off the boat there, and we were quartered in a Standard Oil Company executive house while the Tokyo CIA questioned us at length. They were particularly interested in Midway Island. It wasn't hard to figure out where they wanted to go next.

After that we were split up. Some were sent to Shanghai and the rest of us to Zentsuji, a German POW camp, where we were questioned again. This camp was ideal compared to what we had later. They served us decent food, and the buildings had heat enough to keep us warm. The Japs just hadn't decided yet how to treat us. I have no complaints about our treatment there. Later that would change.

On March 11, 1942, Commander Cunningham and three others escaped from Woosung prison, near Shanghai. At once the Japanese insisted that we all sign a paper saying we wouldn't try to escape or we would be killed. The Wake Island personnel refused to sign, even though we knew we would not be held to this. So we were labeled "dangerous prisoners" and shipped to a prison camp at Kawasaki, a town between Tokyo and Yokohama. This camp was to be my home for almost four years. We were quartered in a flophouse with bedbugs and lice, eight men to a room with one small window for air. It turned out that after ten to twelve hours of work on the railroad, we were so tired we just didn't care.

On September 1, 1942, we were transferred to Kawasaki Camp #1. We were greeted by Lieutenant Takiuchi, or "Bamboo," as we called him. We were there only five minutes when this Japanese officer called out a squad of soldiers with fixed bayonets. He told us that if we didn't sign the non-escape pledge, he would kill us. This Lieutenant Takiuchi was quick-tempered. We didn't sign and he didn't have us killed. Later I saw him beat a young Scotsman for a half hour. Finally in despair for not knocking him down, the Jap used his fingernails on the boy's eyes. This attack took place at the Kawasaki railway. The young Scot was being punished because he had stolen some saki and was drunk.

I had my turn at being beaten for half an hour in October 1943 at the Kawasaki railroad yards. I had stolen an apple and I and another man were caught. He was Mechanic First Class Tattrie, a navy man. A civilian guard called "Tin Ear" and Mr. Takasara, or "The Pig," did the job on us. "The Pig" beat us with a stick and his fists until he was tired, then "Tin Ear" took his turn, and then they alternated. At least they didn't break any of our bones.

One of the civilian guards, Mr. Tagiuchi, or "The Gook," was head of all prisoners of war who worked on the railway. He was the biggest racketeer in Japan. We stole things for him, then he'd slap us for stealing, take it, and bury it somewhere. In one instance he made everyone on one platform go without food and slapped them all with his stick because something was missing out of a food crate. He beat a merchant marine for an hour because he stole some sugar. Any time there was cruelty to the prisoners working on the railroad, Tagiuchi was responsible for it. This Japanese lieutenant was directly responsible for misdirecting and stealing International Red Cross goods. He allowed all Japanese in camp to steal the U.S. woolen shirts and blankets that had been intended for the prisoners.

Despite our harsh treatment, many of us were allowed considerable freedom of movement in our capacity as laborers. Because of this, we were able to commit acts of sabotage and destruction that served to produce a strong sense of accomplishment and a high level of morale. In the Kawasaki marshaling yards we soon worked out an elaborate system of thievery and sabotage, in which many of the Japanese guards and workers enthusiastically helped.

There were 350 of us prisoners, and we worked fourteen to sixteen hours a day loading and unloading all kinds of freight. We stole anything we could get our hands on. What we couldn't use we traded or used for bribes. The prison camp commandant was one of our best customers. He lived in high style on the champagne and fancy foods we supplied, and in return he looked the other way when we helped ourselves.

In over three years at the Kawasaki yards hardly a freight car went through without being raided or its cargo sabotaged in some way. The sugar and acid we stole were used to "service" any number of vehicles and equipment. The sugar we poured into the gas tanks and the acid was poured into thousands of vehicle tires and tubes.

I know it sounds amazing, but they never caught any of us at it, and I don't think they ever tumbled to who was doing all the damage.

Heavy equipment was worked in the yards by Japanese civilians. One of the crane operators was devoted to rice wine, and that made him a bit unsure on the job. We would get him drunk on stolen saki, and in three years he wrecked more stuff than he moved. In his drunken state he'd take signals from us. If he was hoisting a tank high over some important lathes or factory equipment and we gave him a sudden halt sign, he'd stop the rig. The wood-lifting beam often snapped from the terrific strain. Then one heavy piece of equipment would fall on another expensive and heavy piece of equipment. Just getting the mess cleaned up shut down operations for hours.

Things began to get a little difficult about two months before the war ended. I could speak Japanese pretty well by then, and I had been labeled a troublemaker because I was propagandizing the Japanese workers to take it easy on the job. I told them that as long as the bombs were going to destroy all the food and stores anyway, they might as well steal all they could while they could get it. There wasn't any use working when the war was almost over. A lot of them believed all this, and whenever I talked to them like that, the work would stop all around me.

It's funny, there we were doing everything we could for over three years to sabotage their war effort in the rail yards, and then, with the war nearly over, they come down on me and a couple of others for talking too much. Another man and I were sent by special guard to work in an open-pit iron mine near Mount Fuji. We were rescued at the end of the war from that mine in the mountains near Tokyo. Fortunately the atom bombs were not laid in our area. We watched as the big bombers burned Tokyo and Yokohama to the ground.

We went from the mine to Yokohama, where we were back in American military hands. We were deloused, issued new clothes, and debriefed. I took a ship to Guam for shots, medical exams, and rehabilitation. I was still six-foot-two, but I barely weighed a hundred pounds. We found we couldn't get a steak down or anything greasy. We tried but spent a lot of time running to the bathroom or throwing up.

When we got back to San Francisco, we went to the Oak Knoll Naval Hospital. In 1946 I was transferred to the Marine Corps Recruit Depot in San Diego and then to Marine Corps Air Station in El Toro, California. I stayed in the Corps. Kept flying, checked out in all the planes that the marines flew. I went back to Japan twice on normal tours with different squadrons, usually R4Qs, and retired as a major in 1968 with thirty years in the Corps.

Many of the officers in the slave labor camps believed strongly that every prisoner had the duty to attempt escape. A few tried. Most were caught. Some tried again and again. The longer the men were interred in the slave camps, the greater grew either their inertia (and they did nothing) or their urge to get out, to be free. Toward the end of the war, the attempts to escape increased steadily. Five officers got away by slipping off a train in China, contacting local Chinese forces , and successfully escaping the Japanese. Others shared the experience of Commander Cunningham, who got free two times, was captured twice, and was courtmartialed three times. For almost all of the servicemen in the camps, the only escape would come with the end of the war.

Cmdr. Winfield Scott Cunningham, USN (Ret.)

By Gregory Cunningham from his pamphlet, "The Life of Winfield Scott Cunningham"

Commander Cunningham's roommate at Woosung was Lieutenant Commander C. D. Smith of the Naval Reserve. He had been called to active duty a few weeks before Pearl Harbor to take over all the U.S. Navy interests in Shanghai when Rear Admiral William Glassford sailed for the Philippines. Smith commanded the gunboat USS *Wake,* which was in Shanghai harbor waiting to be blown up if the Japanese attacked. Commander Smith hatched a plan to escape and Cunningham jumped at the chance. Commander John Wooley of the British Royal Reserve; Dan Teters, head of the Wake Island contractors; and a Chinese boy named Loo, who was from that area of China and was a ship boy on the *Wake,* rounded out the plotters.

On the night of March 11, 1942, they made good their escape plan. They avoided the guards and carefully dug under the electrified fence. They reached the banks of the Yangtze, and Smith convinced everyone to move downstream in search of a sampan and they would ride the tide to Pootung and the friendly Chunking Chinese forces.

Cunningham said, "Strangely enough, we paid no attention to Loo. Convinced that Smith knew what he was doing, we ignored the advice of a man native to the area and took the word of the Occidental who said he knew better." After hours of searching for a sampan without luck, they decided to contact a local Chinese farmer for help. The local man betrayed them to the Chinese government troops. Soon they were surrounded by the Japanese troops and all hope was lost.

They were taken to the city jail in Woosung and interrogated by the feared Kempeitai, who were the Japanese army elite. Surprisingly, no brutalities occurred. Commander Cunningham said, "Our interrogators actually seemed to be in good spirits about something." They learned later the reason the Japanese were so happy. It was the simple fact that the Kempeitai looked with disdain on other army elements, represented in this case by the miserable Colonel Yuse. Commander Cunningham said, "The fact that we had escaped from him and then were recaptured by the Kempeitai filled them with such glee that they were almost grateful to us for the chance to humiliate him."

They rubbed it in Colonel Yuse's nose one more time when they were brought back to camp and showed him how easy it was to escape. Then Commander Cunningham and the other escapees were taken to Shanghai on March 14, to be confined to the infamous Bridge House, headquarters of the Kempeitai and the scene of its most terrible torture sessions. There they awaited trial.

Each man was placed in different cells that already contained about twenty prisoners. They were required to keep seated at all times except for a few exercise periods when they walked Indian-file around the cell. No talking was permitted. Commander Cunningham said, "It was hard to keep still, for the cells were full of lice and the odor of filth and decay were always present. Plumbing facilities consisted of a wooden bucket in the corner of the cell. Most prisoners were Nationalist Chinese soldiers and they were receiving exceedingly brutal treatment. The Chinese were given no baths, no medical treatment for injuries or disease, and were constantly beaten. On two occasions during the first ten days I was there, I woke up to find one of the Chinese prisoners dead."

On April 14, 1942, after a month at Bridge House, Cunningham and the other men were sent to Kiangwan Military Prison, near Shanghai. There they faced a Japanese army court-martial. They were now considered part of the Japanese army, since they were now captives of the army. The trial lasted several hours. They were not given a public defender. The court officers were trying to find the ringleader. The accused said they were all the ringleaders with the exception of Loo. The court said they would all be punished as if they were the ringleaders. They had to wait seven weeks in solitary confinement before sentencing. Cunningham said, "A single day of solitary confinement can be torture in a cell that had a small window that was too high to look out of. Seven weeks can feel like a lifetime."

They went before another court to hear their sentences. Winfield, Wooley, and Smith all received a ten years' imprisonment. Teters got two and Loo, one. Commander Cunningham was relieved. He said, "It didn't sound good, but it was better than being shot. We almost beamed at the senior officer." A week later the five were moved to Shanghai Municipal Gaol to serve their sentences. Now they were not prisoners of war, but common criminals serving out their time.

Prison conditions were generally better than they had experienced up to that point. For the first time since their capture they were allowed to write home once a month. They were not allowed to receive packages from home or the Red Cross, but they did receive short letters from their families.

By February 1944, Commander Cunningham's physical condition had deteriorated badly. Escape plans were put on hold. No one had ever escaped from this jail. Cunningham was determined to be the first. But that had to wait. His weight dropped from 185 before Wake Island to 129 pounds. He went to a hospital for three weeks and his diarrhea stopped. A new rule let prisoners buy food through the Swiss Consul. Gradually his weight came back to 160 by summer.

On October 6, 1944, the commander made a second attempt to escape. Eight men with Cunningham split into two groups and tried to make it to friendly Nationalist Chinese in the countryside. The other group made it to freedom, but Cunningham's team was captured. He wondered if his second escape try would lead to a death penalty for him. He was sent back to Kiangwan prison under the eye of the Kempeitai. It meant eleven weeks of cold solitary confinement, hunger, and sickness. The commander said, "The only thing that gave me cheer during the frightful winter of 1944–45 were the bombings near the prison. Eight days after I arrived at the prison, the bombs started falling. Some were close enough to shake the building."

Six weeks later, on December 11, Cunningham went before a general court-martial for a third trial. It was over quickly. He had no lawyer and was sentenced to life in prison. He was sent to Nanking Military Prison. "I was relieved that it wasn't death. This was the third time I faced hard-looking Japanese army officers. I am prepared to claim the honor among United States Navy officers of having been court-martialed the most times by the Japanese."

Fireman 2nd Class Dare Kibble, USN

In the spring of 1943 the Nips gave the military prisoners aptitude exams. I was not quite sure what the purpose of the exam was.

Maybe all those flunking would be executed. Or maybe all those passing would be shot. However it worked, in August of 1943 I was listed among one hundred prisoners to go to an undisclosed destination. That brought my spirits crashing into a bottomless pit. The only thing I had to take with me was my rice bowl and my cup in my little cloth bag.

I never did understand why, but for the next week, during our travels, the Nips seemed almost human. The day we left camp, some trucks pulled up to the main gate and we were told to load up. We had always walked everywhere we ventured in the past. Riding was a luxury unheard of in the life of the POWs. The truck took us down to the docks near Shanghai and stopped beside a small intercoastal ship, which, I believe, was called the *Murote*. It was about two thousand tons.

We were told to get aboard, and the guards took us down into the hold. But the hatch was not battened down, nor were we given any instructions about our movements in the hold, only that we could not go on deck without permission. Now you could have knocked us over with a feather. At first we were certain the war was over, and then the outreach conclusions began to fill our thoughts. Maybe this was a new method of eliminating the POWs and we would soon be killed and thrown overboard, as had happened to many Japanese-held prisoners.

The ship got under way the same evening. The meal was out of this world. It was a stew of sorts, with nice white rice and a reasonable ration. It had to be the same food the crew was eating. We wondered if this was to be our last meal. We were uneasy when we lay down in the hold to sleep that night. However, God's day broke over the sea as usual, and we had rice for breakfast. I neglected to say earlier, but I was the only one from my section in Kiangwan prison who was on board the ship. I was never to see my friend Louic again.

As the day progressed, to our great astonishment, we were allowed to go up on the weather deck in the beautiful ocean-going sunshine and walk around. If you have never been to sea and bathed in the luxury of the sun in the salt air, you have missed one of God's most beautifully created moments. Instead of reveling in the moment, we were all so suspicious we didn't fully appreciate the opportunity of the freedom and the extravagance being offered at the time, albeit unknowingly, by the ship's captain.

Also, instead of buckets in the hold to be used for toilets, we were allowed to go to the *benjo* in the ship's heads. The johns were built on platforms out over the side of the ship. The total supporting structure was made of wood and held to the side of the ship by hemp lines. When you were in the structure, you used a slot in the floor to straddle and the excrement dropped into the ocean. If battle stations were sounded, a crewmember cut the lines and the john and anyone in it fell into the ocean. I remember each time I stepped into one of the little houses, I said a prayer asking the Supreme Being to command any U.S. submarine skipper to postpone any torpedo shot for at least twenty minutes.

Gunnery Sgt. Edward M. Bogdonovitch, USMC

I was the only one of the four of us Brown automatic rifle men to get hurt when we surrendered on Wake on December 23. The bayonet jab into my leg wasn't too bad. I used some sulfa on it and kept walking. We were near Camp One, and the Japs marched us over to the medical facility and held us there for a time. The corpsmen put some more sulfa on my leg, but it was never bandaged. Later they marched us to the airfield, where they stripped us and made us sit on the ground.

It was seventeen days later, as I remember, that they loaded us on the *Nitta Maru*, a Japanese cruise ship serving double duty. We didn't have the first class cabins; we went into the second and third holds, where we were jammed and crammed in like ten pounds of potatoes in a five-pound sack. I kept packing my hurt leg with sulfa, and the miracle drug healed it up for me with no infection.

We took the usual cruise, with a one-day stop in Yokohama, then on to Shanghai, China. Woosung was our prison camp. They were tough on us. One of our jobs was to level an old Chinese cemetery where the bodies were buried on top of the ground in humps. We leveled it and then planted vegetables. I remember we harvested sweet potatoes and green beans. They added to our meager diet of rice gruel. We also went on details to repair roads.

I was in the move to Kiangwan, where we worked on building what we called Mount Fuji, a large rifle range for the Nip marksmen. A bulldozer could have done the job quickly, but the Japs didn't have any, not around there at least. We worked ten to twelve hours a day and barely had enough food to stay alive.

We were there for a year and a half, then they transferred 150 of us to Osaka. We worked in a shipyard there. My job for a while was as a drill press operator. That didn't last long; then I had to push loaded carts with parts and supplies up to the point on the ship where they were needed.

In January of 1945 the American bombers came. First the navy and marine aircraft from the carriers, then later the B-29s. They burned the shipyard to a cinder and leveled it. Our barracks area caught on fire, too, and the guards told us we had to put out the fire or they would shoot every one of us. We put out the flames.

With no work for us there, the Nips moved us to a small town on the China Sea side of the Japanese island of Honshu. It was January of 1945. I worked at the foundry in the steel mill there. It was good to stay warm inside, but outside there was lots and lots of snow. We shared our camp there with a group of Australians. We also shared it with millions of fleas, bedbugs, and other crawly creatures. We ate what they gave us, we existed, we worked, and then on August 15, 1945, the guards told us we would have a vacation day.

At once the mean, vicious guards took off. We tried to find them, but couldn't. New guards came who were much softer, kinder, and far less strict. We knew something was up. They told us the war was over and we would soon be going home. In a few days the planes arrived. The B-29s dropped fifty-five-gallon barrels filled with food and clothing and all sorts of things we hadn't seen for years. One of my good buddies at the camp rushed out to get one of the barrels, and it tipped and rolled on him, crushing him to death. What a waste, after all the years of torture, to get killed by a friendly barrel.

Then we took a train to Tokyo, stopped at a hospital ship, then took a boat to Guam and on to Pearl Harbor. At last we arrived at San Francisco. I stayed at the Oak Knoll hospital in Oakland for two or three weeks. Then they flew us to Great Lakes Naval Hospital. After a stay there, I took a thirty-day leave and had a promotion of one rank. My discharge came through on February 11, 1946.

Sgt. Fenton R. Quinn, USMC

On the prison ship I hurried through the gauntlet of club-swinging Japanese and into the hold. We touched at Yokohama and then sailed on to Shanghai and Woosung prison camp. I never played softball in camp, but I did play poker. I bought a deck of cards from one of the Chinese prisoners. We used food and cigarettes for markers. The Japs issued us three cigarettes a day. Some of the guys who had never smoked before started. I was a pretty good poker player, so I ate a little better for a while.

After a year and a half I was sent to Japan with about seventy other guys. We landed in Osaka and worked in a shipyard. A couple of the guards at the fire station took a liking to me, and I spent a lot of my working days with them. We'd sit around and smoke the cigarette butts I found on the way to work, and eat soup. It was real easy duty there for a while. I never did find out why they liked me. We finally got bombed out of the shipyard. The navy and marine fighter-bombers came over and caused all sorts of damage. They bombed our barracks there in Osaka too, but they didn't know we were inside. Several POWs were killed and a lot injured. We knew that if the air-craft carrier planes were coming over, the rest of the U.S. forces must be closer to Japan itself than we realized. We had been at Osaka for about a year and a half.

They shipped us to a little town on the west side of Honshu on the China Sea called Neuetsu. There we worked in a steel mill. They put us to work making sixteen hundred-pound ingots of carbon, which were used as fuel to fire the huge furnaces in the steel mill. One night while at the mill, two of us sneaked out and broke into a storeroom and stole a bunch of apples. We got them back into camp and cooked up some applesauce. It was good. We hadn't tasted applesauce for three years. We also stole salt. It came in big cubes. We melted it down and then boiled the water off and dried it out and had salt. Salt was one thing that the Japs never gave to us, and we craved it.

After August 15, and the end of the war, the guards were much nicer to us. They were still there. One night a buddy and I sneaked out of camp and went into the little town. We found a woman outside her house and talked with her. She knew a little English and we had learned enough Japanese, so we had a good talk. She invited us into her house. The B-29s had been dropping food, more than we could ever eat, so we had brought along food to give away.

It was about a month after the surrender before we saw any American officers. One finally came in by train and up to our camp. He got us on a train down to Sapporo and they flew us into Tokyo. Then we went to Guam. The first morning we were there, they started serving breakfast about six o'clock, and by ten they had to stop. Our guys had been eating, then getting back in the chow line and eating again. The regular troops there hadn't had their breakfast yet.

My stomach was ready for it. One day back in Japan, when the B-29s dropped their barrels, I found in one a carton of twenty-four Hershey bars. I ate all twenty-four. That chocolate on my shrunken stomach and touchy digestive system didn't work. They went right through me; I was sick for two days.

In Guam they gave us three hundred dollars in back pay. There were some poker games, and before we left Guam I had over two thousand dollars in my pockets.

After that we went to Honolulu and then Oakland and Chicago, where I put in some time in various hospitals. I was discharged in March of 1946 after almost six years in the Marine Corps.

★   ★   ★

Gunnery Sgt. Artie Stocks, USMC (Ret.)

The prison ship dropped us off at Shanghai, where I spent the next three years at two POW camps. We did a lot of work building roads. Then one day they put us on trains and headed us north toward Bejing, then down the peninsula to Pusan, Korea. It was winter and we rode in boxcars with the doors removed. The openings were strung with barbed wire. The guards stood on platforms outside the wire. I don't believe that I have ever been so cold in my whole life. In Pusan we loaded salt onto ships headed for Japan. We had bags strapped to us that were loaded with salt. We had to walk a plank over a cargo hold and dump the salt into the hold. If a prisoner was caught eating any of the salt or if he fell into the hold, he was beaten or killed.

After several weeks of loading salt, about two hundred of us were ferried over to Japan. There we were put on a train and headed north. We came to a spot where the tracks had been bombed out. We were taken off the train and walked about a mile to get on another train. A sea of civilian women, children, and old men lined the path the entire way. The Japanese guards left us to the mercy of the civilians. They hit us with clubs every step of the way. I lost several friends at that time. We tried to help those who were knocked down, but we had to keep moving.

We wound up on Hokkaido, the northernmost Japanese island, working in a coal mine. The mine was cold and damp and the tunnels so low we had to constantly bend over to work. Then one day the war was over.

We were just left on our own, and it took the Americans a while to locate our camp. When the navy finally found us they dropped torpedoes full of food. A group of American doctors came and put us on a diet of rice and canned hash so we could get used to regular food again. They gave us all the rice we wanted, with a teaspoon full of hash mixed in. Each day the doctors increased our amount of hash. In thirty days we could begin eating other kinds of food.

We were soon flown to Tokyo and got new uniforms. An officer asked us to count off one day, and we did it in Japanese out of habit. We had almost forgotten how to count in English.

I left the Corps in February of 1946 and went back to the family farm in Bridgeland, Utah. In 1950 when the Korean War started, I reenlisted in the Marine Corps. The reason I went back in was to get even with the Koreans who had treated me so badly. But I soon realized these weren't the same ones.

Later I had a tour of duty in Vietnam and served a total of twenty-six years in the marines. I have no animosity toward the Japanese people. Those were times when the whole world was in turmoil, and soldiers did what they had to do. I felt it was my duty to serve this country to the best of my ability, and I believe that I did.

Gunnery Sgt. Thomas W. Johnson, USMC

On January 12 they put us on the *Nitta Maru*, a luxury liner converted into a prison ship. We were in the three holds, without any facilities, and crowded in like cattle.

From there we hit Yokohama, then Shanghai, and I stayed in the usual prisons and took my share of punishment. Early in 1945 they sent us by rail, boat, and ferry to Hokkaido Island, the northernmost of the Japanese group. There we worked in an abandoned coal mine. My job was driving a rig that pulled the loaded coal cars out of the mine. One day an electrical cable broke and dropped on my head. It jolted me off my truck and paralyzed me. The men carried me back to camp to the "Dead House," where men who were sick or injured went. The name implied that most of the men who went in never came out of it alive. I did. We had medics from the China marines and a navy doctor from Wake, Dr. Gustav M. Kahn, who helped me. They had no medicines or equipment. Mostly they talked to me and massaged my body. I got better; the paralysis went away.

We welcomed the navy and marine fighters and dive-bombers who came over the camp after August 15. We were liberated on September 16 and headed home.

We were treated like kings all the way home across the Pacific. It seemed every time we turned around they sprayed disinfectant on us and gave us new uniforms.

I stayed in the marines until September of 1948, when I received a medical discharge with the rank of gunnery sergeant.

1st Sgt. Franklin D. Gross, USMC (Ret.)

At Yokohama some POWs were taken off the *Nitta Maru* for questioning, and we went on to Shanghai, China. We marched to the old Chinese fort of Woosung, our first POW camp. There we worked on the roads and in the spring planted a garden in a plot of ground they gave us.

Next we went to Kiangwan, on the other side of Shanghai, where we worked at building Mount Fuji, a giant rifle range. While there I had an attack of appendicitis. We had a couple of doctors in the camp; the younger one wanted to operate, but the navy commander medic said no, they didn't have the right instruments and no anesthesia. They put cold packs on my abdomen, and eventually the swelling went down and the pain stopped. The appendix hadn't ruptured, which was a great thing.

In August of 1943 I went to Japan with 520 other marines and some civilians. We landed near Osaka and worked in the shipyards there. We had eight riveting crews who worked beside the Japanese putting the ships together. We built mostly coastal freighters two hundred to three hundred feet long. I think most of them were sunk as soon as they splashed into the ocean. We worked on ten ships in the twenty months I was there—until the first of May in 1945, when fifteen of us who said we had been carpenters in civilian life were selected to go to a new camp. We picked up fifteen more carpenters and went by train for several hours up into the mountains to a place called Rokukroshi. We were to work on quarters for an officers' POW camp. Most of it was built by the time we got there, so all we had to do was pick up and clean up. It was the best three months of duty I had while a prisoner. I stayed there until the end of the war.

We stayed in camp after the war was over. On September 9 two nurses and twelve army men came to rescue us. They took us by train down to Yokohama. That started a long series of hospital stays and island hopping by plane, until I landed in Oak Knoll hospital in Oakland. Later they flew me to the Norman, Oklahoma, navy hospital, where I got my ninety-day leave. After that I reenlisted and stayed in for twenty years, retiring in 1958.

Pharmacist Mate 2nd Class John I. Unger, USN

I went on board the *Nitta Maru* with the rest of the men and remember the horrible conditions and the beatings that were endured during the thirteen days we spent on the ship. This was the ship where five Americans were selected, taken to the deck, and beheaded. Later I learned that the *Nitta Maru* was torpedoed and sunk by our submarine the USS *Sailfish*.

I worked in the prison camps as a corpsman the entire period of our captivity and remember the suffering and deaths of those in the camps. I was never hospitalized during our prison time, but worked many long hours. Toward the end I was losing my strength and had trouble breathing after exertion. At last I felt I couldn't take all the death I saw and asked to be relieved of my medical duties and put back with the other prisoners. Major Devereux talked me out of it.

During the imprisonment, my stomach shrank in size due to the small portions of food we had. If a cat or a dog wandered into camp, it was promptly killed and cooked by the inmates. I stayed away from that food. I probably avoided getting malaria because I could get quinine pills and took them quite often.

On the day of our liberation, we marched to the nearest airport, with our fighter planes overhead to insure our safety. On the flight to Tokyo I developed a severe stomachache, hard breathing, and nausea. I had an acute attack of appendicitis and had an ambulance waiting for me at the airport. I was taken to a field hospital and operated on by an American doctor. What timing. If it had happened a few days earlier, I might not have survived.

I didn't go home with the others from my camp. I was on a hospital ship, but I never forgot one thing . . . I was going HOME! We were going home because we were rescued by the atomic bomb. Thank you, President Harry S. Truman.

Staff Sgt. John Doyle, USMC (Ret.)

Twelve days after our surrender we were on the former luxury liner
Nitta Maru, but we didn't get the luxury cabins. In Woosung prison
in Shanghai, China, we did a lot of work projects. One was to level
an area near the prison where the POWs could play soccer and softball. I got in a few soccer games.

I went to a series of camps and prisons. Once, in China on a train
we heard that we would go near the Great Wall of China and that
friendly Chinese forces were only fifteen miles away. Four of us
planned an escape, but before we could do it, it began to rain hard
and ended our chances.

I'm glad about two things that happened when I was in China.
One, I got to see the Great Wall, and two, I saw some of the great
camel caravans.

A bunch of us wound up in Hokkaido, the northernmost Japanese island, where we were coal miners deep underground. Then the
war was over and B-29s dropped barrels of food and clothes. We
went down to Sapporo and were flown to Tokyo. There I was lucky
and got to fly home to Oakland via several mid-Pacific islands. I
wound up at the navy hospital at Norman, Oklahoma, and was discharged on February 26, 1946, as a staff sergeant.

Brig. Gen. Bryghte Godbold, USMC (Ret.)
Dallas, Texas

In the prison camp at Woosung, near Shanghai, China, our recreation situation was really quite good. There was a large contingent
of American and British nationals in Shanghai who had not yet been
arrested and imprisoned in the years of 1942–43. They knew of our
plight and provided us with a great deal of recreation equipment,
including that for softball, football, basketball, and volleyball.

I became the recreation officer for the camp, and set up games
and soon had leagues going for both softball and volleyball. There
were a lot of pickup football games going on. We played our games

on Sundays and sometimes on Saturday afternoons if the workers were given that time off.

We had a lot of lively games. The Japanese guards and camp officers loved baseball, so they took to softball quickly. Most of the Japanese came out to watch and cheer on the teams and even made bets when the men played softball. It was a good outlet for the men, and I'd estimate that about 30 percent of the prisoners in camp took part in the athletic events. These games went on in the spring, summer, and fall.

As long as we were in Woosung we had all of the athletic equipment we could use. We had a group of men come from a captured merchant ship. One of the men was one of the premier softball pitchers in the world. He and others helped us organize the league and we had top-notch softball.

Another benefit we received from the American-British community in Shanghai was the library that they provided. They brought us over two thousand books in English that the men could check out and read. The librarian at camp was the same man who had run the library for the civilians on Wake Island, so he knew his business. He told me that he figured that 75 percent of the men in camp used the library at one time or another.

The civilians from Shanghai also brought us playing cards, chess, and checker games, and we set up tournaments. There were several bridge tournaments going on most of the time. We had an ex-professor among us, and soon we had organized classes to learn Spanish.

As time moved along, and with the near-starvation diet the men were on, we had to cut back on the athletic events, because the men were just not physically able to perform. This hurt morale and made a difference in how well the men could work. When we moved to Kiangwan, we kept up the athletic activities, but they declined as the health and stamina of our men went down.

In all of the camps there was always talk and plans for escaping in the officer quarters. The senior American officer in the camp, Colonel [William W.] Ashurst, discouraged us. He told us if we tried to escape and made it, the Chinese would kill us for our shoes alone. We didn't believe him. He told us that even if two or three men escaped and made it, the retribution on those prisoners still in camp would be extreme. He figured the war wouldn't last long and we'd all be sent home.

When we were in Kiangwan, we heard rumors that we were to be moved to Japan. That was early in 1945. By then we had been reading newspapers that were brought in and getting news reports on a clandestine radio, and we knew that there were Chinese "bandits" who were working the area near the railroad to the north. The radio we got the news on was in my room in the barracks, but I didn't operate it. The best information we had was that when we moved, we would be taken by train into northern China. This would take us directly past the area where the Chinese Communists were still fighting the Japanese. This was a stretch about a hundred miles long, and if we wanted to escape, this would be the area, since we could move north or west and contact the Communists.

One day we heard from the guards that we would be moved and it would be north by rail, exactly as we had hoped. They would move us to Peking, then down the peninsula to Pusan, Korea, and then by boat to Japan. If escape was possible, it had to be on the train during that one-hundred-mile stretch somewhere between Nanking and Peking.

To get ready for the move, they brought in railroad boxcars and had us work on them, putting up barbed wire over windows and down the center, and making them escape-proof. They also let us put straw on the floor to make sitting and lying down easier. I managed to get on the work team for those cars. The officers discovered that one car had some loose bars on one window. They worked at loosening them even more so that they would be easy to remove when the time came. The room with this window could be curtained off by a blanket to give the men privacy when using a toilet bucket. The lieutenants would ride in this particular car, but captains and higher ranks would be in another car. The colonel wasn't about to let any higher-ranking officers try to escape.

We got on the train and all was ready. When we hit that favorable stretch of tracks, five officers used the toilet and then dropped off the train, one at a time, out the unbarred window. All five of them made it and they were not caught. Within twenty-four hours they were in the hands of the Chinese "bandit" Communists and on their way back to the U.S. The escape was discovered, but there was little the Japanese could do about it. Later the Japanese claimed that they had caught all five of the officers and they were being punished. We didn't believe that either.

Cpl. Carroll Trego, USMC

On the prison ship going from Wake to Yokohama we were packed into the holds of the big ship. There were about three hundred of us to each of four holds. We were so jammed in that we couldn't sit down. Everyone had to stand up.

My first job in Woosung prison camp, outside of Shanghai, China, was polishing shell casings. I managed to get a gouge in each of the rims of the shells I worked. I hoped that would make it misfire. Others must have done the same thing, because they didn't keep us at that work very long. I did a lot of road repair around Shanghai, mostly with a pick, a shovel, and a bucket.

They moved the whole camp out of the falling-down Woosung Camp in December of 1942. The old Chinese cavalry base was coming apart. Bad even by Japanese standards. They moved us about twenty miles to the other side of Shanghai, to the Kiangwan camp. It was in much better shape.

In camp most of us didn't like Major Devereux. As an officer he didn't have to work twelve to fourteen hours a day the way the rest of us did. Then, when we came back after a long day, he wanted us to salute the officers in camp. Most of us didn't. I bet I got fifty citations and marks in his little book for not saluting.

In the prison camp the food was almost always the same. We had thirty-five pounds of meat for three thousand five hundred men. We got that only once in a while. American cooks made our food, but what we ate depended on what supplies they got. We had rice every day, and usually a thin soup. And yes, to this day I still love to eat rice.

For a particularly bad infraction of some rule, the Japs used what they called the Japanese "teapot treatment." I had it several times. I was laid on a board with my feet above my head, then they filled a three-gallon teapot and pushed the spout into my mouth and held my nose closed with their hand. The idea was to bloat the prisoner with more than he could hold, then jump up and down on his stomach. Many men took a great deal of water and then vomited, which ended the torture. I learned that the secret was to push your tongue into the spout to stop the water, then hold your breath as long as possible. This cut down on the amount of water you had to drink. At least nobody tried to jump on my stomach afterwards.

Early in my enlistment I applied for flight school, so I could go to Pensacola and be a Marine Corps aviator. When I was in Hawaii, word at long last came though channels that I had been accepted for flight training and I was to report to Pensacola for the starting class in February 1942. In February of 1942 I was rather tied up and couldn't make it. The Japanese wouldn't let me out of prison camp to go. Too bad. John Glenn and I would have been in the same class.

In 1945 I tried to escape. It was when they were taking a lot of people from our camp at Shanghai to Peking. The Japanese controlled the two large towns, but they owned only a narrow corridor, about ten miles wide, along the railroad tracks between the two towns. We figured that if we could get off the prison train. we'd have only a short way to go before we found friendly Chinese people who would hide us.

The train cars we were in were set up especially for prisoners. On each side there were platforms and no seats. Down through the middle was a corridor where the guards walked. This hallway was partitioned off with wire. Two windows on each side of the cars were covered with heavy wire and fastened securely. Outside the windows was a long wire with tin cans tied to it. If someone tried to get out the window, he would jiggle the wire and set off the tin can alarm.

As soon as we got on the train, I tried to talk somebody else into escaping with me. No takers. At last I decided to do it myself. I got the wire off one window, and when the guard wasn't in our car, I started to crawl out through the window. I was half in and half out when the tin can alarm went off. Five officers had escaped before I made my try. A moment later our guard had his rifle pointed right at my heart. I said, "Okay, Okay," and crawled back inside.

We were only in Peking from May 11 to June 19, 1945. While there I was hauled out of the barracks and told I was going to be court-martialed. Why?

It takes some explaining. Back in 1944 my work for the Japanese masters was managing a battery shop. I had ninety Japanese workers under me. The owners thought I should have some status, so they put some epaulets on my shoulders and told me now I was a sergeant in the Japanese army and I had status. The workers would be more respectful of me. As soon as we left that camp, they jerked the epaulets off and I was just a lowly POW again.

When I tried to escape, my records showed that I had been this phony Japanese sergeant, so I was part of their army and I was charged with being AWOL for my escape attempt. I had a full colonel for my defense council. The prosecutor was also a full colonel. There were two generals on the court-martial board. The trial took three days. I didn't understand a word of what was said. I didn't get to testify. They convicted me. My sentence was to suffer ten days with no food or water in a jail of my own making.

The guard towers at our prison were four feet off the ground. I built a box four feet square and four feet high under the tower and crawled in. I stayed there for ten days and nights. I had no food and no water. It was July and hot in China. I played mind games to pass the time. I memorized new multiplication tables. I tried everything. The last two or three days I was probably only semiconscious from lack of water. When they pulled me out after the tenth day, I came alive and stood straight and tall. "I'll show these bastards how tough I am," I said. Then I promptly fell over in a dead faint.

The U.S. air raids, which leveled whole factory complexes and forced Japan to move the prisoners, did much more than burn down and blow apart many of Japan's vital industries. They also fired the imagination of the POWs and raised their hopes that the war was nearing its end. The ghostly specter of Tokyo after the bombing raids, with miles and miles of burned-out paper and wood houses and businesses, buoyed the spirits of the Wake Island vets. They had battled deprevation, disease, and depression, but now they had a faint glimpse into the end of the tunnel. Their spirits surged with the news that the U.S. had dropped the first nuclear bomb at Hiroshima; they overflowed when the second one fell on Nagasaki and the guards told them they did not have to go to work that morning or any morning thereafter. It was August 15, 1945, and Japan had surrendered.

Pvt. Kenneth E. Cunningham, USMC (deceased)

In Japan cigarettes were practically impossible to get. We would trade anything we could obtain one way or another for them. After having worked with the Japanese for some years, we learned to jabber just like they did. It did not take long to make connections with the civilians to buy things through the black market. In those days in Japan, nearly all the civilians bought and sold things on the black market. After making a few contacts, we were able to do nearly the same thing.

The Jap black market was a hidden, shifty, undercover business. Every Jap was afraid of every other one, and they were all deathly afraid of the army. The army ruled Japan with an iron fist. They controlled all food rationing, all tobacco, and all businesses. The soldiers got the best of everything, and no one could dispute their rights, even if the civilians were starving. And the people were starving well before the end of the war. Regardless of that, the vicious handful of men who controlled Japan held a firm, tight rule.

One service they gave us, which they thought was a great privilege, was that of getting teeth pulled. I had a small cavity between two teeth, and it gave me some trouble. They took me to a Nip dentist. He looked me over and asked which one hurt. I showed him and he said OK, he would pull it. With no further comment, he picked up a pair of forceps, climbed up in the chair with me, and began to jerk and pull. When he had the tooth out, he gave me a small glass of water and then looked at the hole. After a few minutes of studying, he said, "Very sorry, must pull one more." One was not enough, so he went through the same process. Then he glared at me, gave me a glass of water and a small wad of rags, and said that was all, get out. I found out that it was not pleasant to have two jaw teeth pulled without any Novocain.

Another practice the Jap doctors did to get a person well was to give him a burn treatment. In this doctoring they took small wads of cotton soaked in alcohol and stuck them around your back with pins. Then they touched a match to them and let them burn up and burn off a little skin at the same time. This treatment caused several men to die and left all of those treated with bad scars. There were many men who were beaten and refused any kind of treatment because they said they would not be burned this way.

Somehow time passed and the months rolled on. In November 1944, those beautiful big silver B-29s started laying their eggs on the Matchbox City that was Tokyo. They used to come at night, in low at twelve thousand to fourteen thousand feet. There would be a lot of searchlights hitting them, but the AA fire was far above them. First came the high explosives and then the rain of incendiary bombs. Now the Japanese people could no longer believe the fantastic tales of the propaganda that the war ministry was handing them. They were getting a little of the medicine they had celebrated and laughed about over their bombing of Pearl Harbor. They were scared, and they hid in every small hole or shelter they could find every time they thought a plane was coming.

After two months of blowing up and burning Tokyo at night, the planes came in on daylight raids. Those big planes came over so high you could hardly see them, and they were impossible to reach with the Jap ack-ack fire. Seeing them up there made us feel pretty good. We couldn't show it. We knew that every time they came over, it put us just that much closer to getting out of there one way or another.

We never knew where those big bombs were going to fall, but we always figured they would not hit us, because those were our buddies up there dropping them. It was often said in prison camp that if they got me, they would get a thousand Japs, too.

The Army Air Force was brave in its missions. They would tell the Japanese people when and where they were going to bomb, and they always kept their word. On the night of March 3, 1945, the big planes came over Tokyo. They bombed and burned twenty square miles that night. We stayed in our barracks and watched them, and we knew that night that the summer would finish Japan. Then on March 23, they came again. Five hundred B-29s hit Kawasaki. The Japs all went into their holes. Thinking they couldn't leave us unguarded, they took us to a big tunnel under the railroad. We went down there at 11:00 P.M. and did not come out until 5:00 A.M. Soon after they started bombing, the power plants for the whole area were hit and the juice was shut off. We returned to camp the next morning and found it nearly destroyed by bombs, fire, and wind. We were sorry the whole camp didn't go up in smoke so we would have to move away from the steel mill. As it was, we patched things up and made the best of it. In that bombing they burned out about fifteen square miles, and most of it was residential districts. There were no people to run the mill and they had no power to operate it, so the mill was shut down.

We were in high spirits those days, and most of us felt a lot better. But the hotter things got for the Japs, the tougher they made it for us. Less food and more beatings came as regularly as the sunset. We POWs also became a little braver and told some of them what we thought of them and what was going to happen to Japan. We told them their wonderful rising sun was going down and before long it would be set and never rise again. Sometimes we got into trouble, but most of the Nips were too scared and distressed even to answer back. Being able to speak their language was a big help to us, because we could tell what they were talking about, while they could not understand what we said. We got news from all kinds of places, so we knew pretty much what was going on in other parts of the world.

It was this kind of news that kept us going through the last three months of the war.

After the mill closed, we did only salvage work where things had been burned. Then the camp broke up. Two hundred and fifteen men went to a mining camp in northern Japan and thirty-five of us went to Camp Omori in Tokyo Bay. In June 1945 Camp Omori was another hellhole for some six hundred POWs of several different nations. Holland, Norway, Java, Guam, China, England, and America all had men there. We were living, working, and starving to death together. Omori is an island about a mile and a quarter long and an eighth of a mile wide. The camp compound was 150 yards long and almost as wide as the island. It was enclosed by a fourteen-foot-high board fence with three strands of barbed wire on top. The buildings were long shedlike affairs that were dirty and drafty. They had an aisle down the center, which had a dirt floor and wooden platforms on either side, where we slept. They were just the same as all the rest of our quarters while in prison camp.

The POW complement of 616 men filled the camp. About 350 of those were Americans. There were 265 officers of the American services. We had a lot of pilots and submarine men. They had been shot down, or their subs had been sunk near Japan. They were made to do salvage work where the city had been bombed, and they were closely guarded and kept confined to their own barracks. They were classified as captives, not POWs. Their capture was never reported to the United States, so the Japs could do as they pleased with them. These men got only half as much to eat as we did, and we got only enough to keep us alive. They were subjected to continuous questioning and beatings, but there were not many who had their spirits broken.

Once in a while we got a chance to talk to some of those men, and they gave us some pretty recent news from home. I have seen the Japs beat some of those officers who had been reduced to no more than skin and bones, but they had more spirit than most people I have ever met. These men, continually beaten when they were more dead than alive, used to laugh at the Nips and say that they might never get back home, but Japan would belong to the United States some day. Then those of us who did get home would equalize things. Those officers were the real heroes of Camp Omori.

Camp routine there was a little different from Camp D-5. You were apt to have an inspection any day at almost any time, and if some small thing did not suit them, you were in for a lot of misery for a few days. This camp, however, was a little better than the former ones. We at least had a little more room, and it was cleaner and there was fresh air. The work was much heavier and it took quite a while to get used to it. We were working in a big railroad yard, where freight of nearly every kind came in to be moved on or to be stored and later distributed to the people. Our job was unloading the boxcars. We worked mostly with rice and soybeans.

All of this grain was in straw or burlap sacks. The soy bean sacks weighed two hundred pounds each, and carrying these all day was no fun, especially when someone was standing over you with a club and you knew you had to do it or else. There were 160 of us who worked there, and the rest worked in and around the camp. Those of us who went outside to work fared a little better than the ones who stayed in camp. We could always steal enough food to eat, and soon we worked out ingenious ways of cooking it. That way we could give the three regular meals we got in camp to one of our buddies who did not leave camp to work. Lots of them needed the extra food to keep them going. The ones who worked outside put on a little weight; our own bodies got hard and stronger. Then the work was not quite so difficult. We would walk about a mile across a bridge to the mainland, then get on a big semi truck and ride fifteen miles right into the heart of Tokyo, where we worked every day. Some of the bombing raids came close to us, but none of them ever hit the yards.

Fireman 2nd Class Dare Kibble, USN

While working in the steel mill at Kawasaki prison on the edge of Tokyo, I had a friend named Zeke. He was the bravest man I've ever known. One time when I was working in the steel mill, I dropped the *yaka* cart loaded with firebricks right on my ankle, causing me terrible pain. The civilian guard on our work detail was Sato, usually not too tough on us. But now I couldn't walk on my swollen ankle. Sato came up and started the old club work on my back to get me moving. That's when Zeke came running up, grabbed me, and put me on the *yaka*. Zeke started wheeling me toward the prison main gate with me riding in the *yaka*. He could easily have been killed for interfering with a guard and helping me.

When we arrived at the prison, Zeke helped me into the barracks. Kondo, our big-cheese guard, told Zeke to take me to the office. There Kondo grabbed my ailing foot and started twisting it at the ankle, with me yelling. Zeke reached over and stopped Kondo from hurting my ankle. He could have been shot dead on the spot for his bravery, but he bluffed out Kondo. I could never thank Zeke enough for what he did on that day so long ago. Zeke was six-feet-six inches tall, so you can imagine what poor health he was in with our limited diet. Also, Zeke was ten years older than me. If anyone deserved a medal for bravery in the whole Wake Island fracas, it is men like Zeke, and not the officers who were running the show.

Another story about the steel mill. I was assigned to the pipe operation with twenty POWs and thirty Korean women. We were to grind the burrs and impurities off the pipe ends before they went to an end use. The women worked at one end of the pipe operation and the POWs at the other. We were not to fraternize with the women. One particular Korean girl I noticed working the other end of the pipe looked about twenty; I was twenty-two at the time. Now and then she would smile at me, and I'd smile back or wink at her. She seemed to be really sweet. In a steel mill the noise is always deafening, so when I would knock on our pipe, she would feel the vibration and look at me. We would talk by hand signs, and several times she asked me if I was hungry. She would wrap a rice ball in some paper, then send it through the pipe to me by compressed air. We could pull the airhose off the portable grinder and blow things to each other through the pipes, which were about twenty feet long. We never did get any closer together than the length of those pipes; at break time the women went one way and we went the other. We were never caught by the guards practicing our innocent young romance. I have often wondered what happened to that young Korean girl.

Our health in all the prison camps was always a major concern. Everyone had dental problems. Our teeth would just rot away, and sometimes you could pull the roots out by hand. We all kept a chunk of roofing tar handy. When we started having a toothache, we put a slug of tar over it, and presto, the ache would subside, to some extent.

For dysentery, diarrhea, worms, and other ailments, we'd take plain black wood charcoal. Black charcoal was the only type of medication I saw in prison camp in my forty-four months. I developed stomach ulcers while a prisoner, and at times I felt as if my pain would cause me to commit suicide. Also, from the beatings, I began to have blackouts. Maybe the malnutrition caused them, I never knew. I had a touch of tuberculosis and a good case of malaria. After going to Kawasaki, I developed beriberi and my legs would swell to twice their normal size. We had one guy with beriberi whose waist went from twenty-six inches to eighty inches. He also went blind.

Sergeant Major Ewing E. Laporte, USMC (Ret.)
Hickory, North Carolina

On January 12, 1942, most of us were taken from Wake on a ship, stopping three days at Yokohama. Most of us were kept belowdecks in rusty holds. Then they shipped us to Shanghai, China. Most of the time in Shanghai we spent at hard labor, and the lack of food and medicine took a toll on our men. We had British prisoners from Hong Kong, Singapore, and ships. When B-29 bombers and P-51 fighter planes started raids around our area, the Japanese moved us. We had no doubt that they had something treacherous in mind, and it was a real ordeal they put us through. We left May 14, 1945.

We were moved by train, very much overcrowded, to the outskirts of Peking, China, for a few weeks. Then farther on, through Manchuria, and down through Korea to Pusan for a few weeks. Then we were moved again by ship, unmarked, through the straits of

Korea, on a very dangerous journey, through seas infested with American submarines. This is another case of the Japanese's total disregard for any humanitarian actions.

When we landed at Shimonoseki, Japan, we were loaded on boxcars. By this time American planes were bombing and strafing all trains and everything else; the B-29s had started intensive firebombing of Japanese cities, including Tokyo. The Japanese put blankets over the train windows, because they did not want us to see what was happening. As we progressed and moved through a city, we took chances by pulling back the blankets and looking. It was like opening a curtain to view the greatest show on earth. It was earth where once stood a city, now all ashes as far as you could see, each house having some type of vent pipe sticking up. The place looked like a pincushion. Inwardly, and when the Japanese weren't looking, we were laughing. This was payback, and we enjoyed it.

A lot of Japanese would line the tracks in some places. They were looking at us, but they were not smiling. Our trip was on to Osaka, Nagoya, Kobe, and Tokyo. The results of the firebombing were in evidence everywhere we went, and everywhere we went there were Japanese ready to beat on us or throw things. Some of our men were badly injured by bricks and rocks. They kept us in train stations when we stopped. This was the only time I was glad to know the guards were there to protect us.

At night we saw the entire sky light up red from the flames of the surrounding cities burning. When we entered Tokyo on July 4, 1945, the existing fireworks were very appropriate. From Tokyo we went on to Hokkaido Island, on July 8, where we were put to work coal mining. One day in August we were told there would be no more mine work, as there was typhus disease on the island. Very shortly we learned the war was over. The following day, after the emperor spoke, the Japanese guards and officers all left without our knowledge, and we were on our own. They were made to come back and surrender their weapons.

We were flown from Sapporo City in Hokkaido to a Japanese air base outside Tokyo, and then taken by bus to the docks to go aboard ship. The Japanese people were living underground and under lean-tos with corrugated roofing—a really terrible sight to see, especially to see the little kids there. We bore too much hatred to feel any remorse at the time. After a long leave, I was discharged.

I reentered the Marine Corps. I wanted to see those countries again. I went to Korea in 1953. I also went to Vietnam 1968 to 1969, with an infantry unit up at the demilitarized zone. When I flew out of Vietnam, we had a two-hour layover on Wake Island. I can't describe the eerie feeling I had to see some of the places where the worst fighting took place and also the change to the looks of Wake. As we flew out, I looked at the island below and thought, "I know my trouble started here and I'll leave it here."

I retired 1972 as a sergeant major, after thirty years of service.

If you ask us about the ending of the war, you will find most of us, at least, will say, "Thank God for the atomic bomb." We knew that the Japanese were killing our pilots, who had been shot down anywhere they found them. Fearing an invasion, they had moved us into a locality where thousands of prisoners were. Evidently they thought this might slow down an invasion. If you could have seen the women and children training in bayonet fighting, throwing grenades, and digging emplacements, you would realize they were ready for annihilation. So that was what was in store for us, too. The intelligence sections of the occupation forces had allegedly found orders to the effect that we prisoners were to be killed. The World War II Japanese were the most sadistic, cruel animals this world has ever seen.

Sgt. Max J. Dana, USMC

At the compound in Shanghai where all of the Japanese military equipment was repaired, we were allowed to choose the type of work we would perform. Not being a mechanic or welder, I chose the paint shop. They expected me to know something about it. My honcho soon found out I'd never had a paint gun in my hand before. I wasn't sure what trouble I was in. I lucked out. This honcho turned out to be a good egg. He just chuckled and scolded me for telling him I was a painter when I wasn't. He went on to teach me, and we got along great after that. Our work consisted mostly of scraping off old paint and sanding, then masking and spray painting the equipment. Some sabotage took place, but not to the extent that we got caught. My contribution to the mighty Imperial Japanese Army was a healthy piss call in the gas tank of each vehicle after we painted it up real pretty.

Where we worked we could see the B-29s flying overhead, way above the reach of enemy fire. They were returning to their base in Burma from their bombing raids over Japan. They always managed to have a few extra bombs to drop on the shipping yards in Shanghai. They would sink one boat in particular; after the Japanese would spend weeks of hard work raising it, the bombers would send it to the bottom again.

On a few occasions, P-51s would sweep in just over the rooftops and do what damage they could. It was a rare treat for the prisoners and sure helped our morale to see free Americans in action.

We were transported back and forth to work by bus. We had access to items of use if we could smuggle them into camp. We had to be careful, as we were searched on our return to camp. One method was to hide things under our hats. It was good until the Japanese got wise to it. Then we had to hold our hats in our hands while being searched, but we simply sewed a false lining in the cap and hid things under it.

The Japanese used straight grain alcohol for vehicle fuel. It was drinkable. One prisoner devised a system to get it into camp. He would cut and fill a small inner tube with alcohol and seal the ends. Then, he'd wrap it around his waist. With extra clothing it appeared quite natural. After overindulging one day, he was caught drunk. When sober enough to talk, he told the officials he needed the alcohol as medicine for his aches and pains and illness. They bought it and let him take a small portion of alcohol with him daily for his "treatment." He was a happy camper.

In May of 1945 they decided to move all POWs to Japan. Germany had surrendered. They knew a landing would be inevitable on the main island of Japan, and they would use us as hostages and shields. We went mostly by rail through China, up into Manchuria and down to Pusan, Korea. From there we went by boat to Japan, and then we were back on more trains. We wound up on the northern island of Hokkaido and worked in a coal mine.

Sergeant William F. Buehler, USMC

That last day of battle on Wake Island, December 23, I remember thinking what a beautiful, clear day it was. Then we got the word to surrender, and we knew the Japs didn't take prisoners. What a beautiful day it was to die, I remember thinking and hoping that my mother wouldn't take my death too hard. Then they changed the orders and let us live so we could work in their factories.

I spent most of my time in Shanghai, China, at the two camps there. Then in May of 1945 they shipped us up north in China and down to Pusan, Korea, by rail. We went by ship from there to Japan and then north again by railroad. We were in Tokyo on July fourth. The windows of the train cars were all shuttered, but we took some looks and saw the total destruction of Tokyo. We wound up in the northernmost island of Hokkaido, where we worked in a coal mine.

On August 15 I was on the afternoon shift and went to work in the mine at noon. Before then the Jap guards and all the camp people had a big meeting; a lot of the guards came out crying, and we knew something had happened. They told us we didn't have to go to work that day. After several days of better food and no work or guards, an army retrieval team arrived and told us to stay put, we'd be on our way home soon. I went by ship to Guam and then flew on to Oakland. I wound up at the Great Lakes Naval Hospital and took my discharge in February 1946.

I'm seventy-nine now, almost eighty. I still drive and get around pretty well. I figure that if you can live through what we did, you better just get on with your life and enjoy it.

Chief Warrant Officer Michael Benedetto, USMC (Ret.)

When I was a POW in China, they told a bunch of us to get ready to move. They took us to Neuetsu, Japan, where there was a foundry. The plant was on a twenty-four-hour routine and I worked mostly on the night shift. I got into the habit of picking up any spare keys that I saw. Then one day I happened to come into possession of a small file. With the file I could adjust the keys to fit different locks.

There was a warehouse near where we worked that was filled with hundred-pound sacks of rice. We were always hungry, so I thought this was my chance. I worked on the key and tested it and filed on it again. Then one night the key fit. We had lots of air raids about then, and when the sirens wailed, the prisoners were supposed to go from wherever they were working to concrete bunker air shelters. It gave us a few minutes of unsupervised time that we could wander around. This was when I tested the key. It worked, and I lugged a sack of rice up to the condensers in the foundry, which were used to melt down the scrap metal that was turned into the ingots of steel. Around the condensers were the same type of sacks the rice was in. They looked exactly the same, only the sacks around the condenser were filled with sand. I lugged the rice sack up on top of the others and hurried to the shelter. Soon I'd be eating all the rice I wanted every day.

Two days later, before I even had a chance to get to my stolen rice, the war ended and I didn't need the rice anymore. Maybe crime doesn't pay after all.

After the war I stayed in the Corps. I did my time in the Korean War and then retired in 1960 as a master sergeant after nineteen years. Back then nineteen was as good as twenty for retiring. After that I went to the Merchant Marine Academy in Kings Point, New York. I served there as a drill instructor and reached the rank of chief warrant officer before my second retirement.

Sgt. Max J. Dana, USMC

We awoke one morning and didn't have to go to the mines. There was a rumor that the shaft had caved in. The guards at Hokkaido wouldn't tell us anything, and the last thought we had was that the war was ending. We were afraid to get our hopes up. The third day that we didn't have to work, the guards disappeared and civilian police came in. A small group of Japanese officers accompanied by a Swiss consul told us that the war was over. "You will be free to go home to your loved ones, and we hope no hard feelings will linger," the Swiss diplomat said.

Needless to say, we rejoiced. It took a few days for this to soak in. We didn't know how to handle this freedom and had a lot of adjusting to do. But things happened fast. It wasn't long before bombers and fighter planes were parachuting food and supplies to us. All we had to do was make a large white cross where we wanted it dropped. We picked an open field nearby. Most of the packages were in fifty-gallon barrels and so heavy they broke from the parachutes and didn't quite land where they were supposed to. The fighter planes had auxiliary gas tanks full of food that they could swoop in and eject. The tanks slammed along the ground at high speed for quite a distance before stopping.

It was nearly a month of waiting for us. The military pulled out and a civilian patrol came in, but they had no arms. We roamed around freely. We enjoyed eating turkey and drank beer. I even ventured into a small town, where I had a shave. We were still jumpy and didn't know really what to do. It was like being in a fog. After several false alarms we finally got the official word to pack up. We had a short train ride to Sapporo, then flew to Tokyo. The crew was good to us, and as usual we could have anything we wanted. They had a small propane cooker aboard and plenty of canned food, so I warmed up something. The food was too rich for my small, hard stomach and didn't settle well. In Tokyo I threw up all over the place.

After the plane ride, we boarded a large transport vessel. Everywhere we went we had the best. We bunked in the sick bay, where we got firsthand medical attention. I even had a tooth pulled.

We traveled to Guam with a convoy of twenty ships. At Guam we were put in the hospital again. We had good food and lots of medical examinations and even a payday. It was beginning to soak in, what a great country we had fought for and all of the war machines and power we possessed. It was good to see our men instead of the enemy handling the guns. When it came time to ship out to the States, they took 400 men. I was number 401, and didn't get on board. I was dejected because there was no telling when the next ship would leave. But the next day a C-54 transport aircraft was to leave for the States with a group of officers. One of the men fell sick and couldn't make the flight. Since I was next on the shipping list, I got to join the officers' flight.

I landed in Oakland nearly two weeks ahead of my buddies on the ship. I was stationed at the Oak Knoll hospital for three months of convalescence, then had a thirty-day furlough to go home. After the hospital, I had orders to go to Treasure Island. There, eight months after the war ended, I received my back pay, a couple of promotions, and discharge papers on April 7, 1946.

Cpl. Martin Greska, USMC

My first prison camp was the big one near Shanghai, Woosung. Part of our work there was building a giant rifle range. We had to carry many buckets and baskets of dirt. The officers were kept separate from the men. Most of them had rooms to live in and they didn't have to work. Later I was taken to Japan, to Hokkaido, the northernmost Japanese island, where I worked far underground in the coal mine.

When the war was over, American planes came overhead and dropped boxes and barrels of food, clothes, candy, and all sorts of great stuff. Two barrels were tied together, and they slammed into a Japanese house, demolishing it. As soon as the prison guards found out the war was over, they simply vanished into the Japanese community. We never saw them again.

It was about a week before U.S. soldiers came and took us out of there. They put us on a special ship to take us home. Lots of doctors and nurses on board gave us physicals and good food and took care of us. We stopped at some islands and had liberty. The beer was terrible, we had to drink two of the bad beers before they gave us a good one.

We had liberty again in Hawaii and then made it to Oakland to a reception center. I was sent to Boston to a hospital since it was nearest my hometown of record. We got our back pay but no automatic promotions.

I got a thirty-day leave and then a ninety-day leave. When I reenlisted I got another ninety-day leave. I did some time as a recruiter and then worked with the Marine Corps Reserves.

I stayed in the Corps for thirty years and retired as a first sergeant. I've been living in this house in Oceanside now for over forty years.

Cpl. Dennis C. Connor, USMC

We were sent to Woosung Camp, near Shanghai. After a few months, they picked out seventy of us and shipped us to Kyushu, Japan. We did some wire splicing and blacksmithing and hauled ore off a ship. There was this one old Japanese man on the dock who yelled at us in English. He'd been a farmer in Colorado and went back to Japan for a visit. Then they wouldn't let him leave to go back to the States. He must have been in his seventies. We talked back and forth a little. He said he hated it there in Japan.

Three of us walked out of the camp after the war was over, and we hiked down to a big town where a lot of American troops landed. It was the 32nd Infantry Division. By the time we got there, we had picked up half a dozen more marines looking for the Americans. We met a private who took us to his captain, who was curious about where we had been. So we told him. The next morning we had bacon and powdered eggs. They sure were good. That same day a huge man who must have weighed three hundred pounds talked to us. He was a war correspondent, and he told us it had been a long, rough road for the country from Pearl Harbor to here. We just looked at him, us guys mostly skin and bones and him at three hundred pounds talking about a rough road.

That same day they flew us to Tokyo and, a day later, on to Okinawa and then down to Manila. A bus took us over to a replacement depot. We were the only ones in the navy side. They really gave us red-carpet treatment. Got us anything we wanted. We got all the beer we could drink. A colonel drove us in a command car to get our mail. We hadn't seen more than two letters in four years. I saw my sister in Manila. She was a first lieutenant in the WACs so we got the red-carpet treatment down there, too.

Then they flew us back to Cavite, the old navy base in the Philippines, before flying us to Saipan, where we stayed overnight. Then we flew to the Marshall Islands; we stayed there overnight in another Quonset hut. Next stop was Honolulu and the hospital. We got there about 3:00 A.M., and they cooked us up big steaks and let us have all the ice cream we could eat.

The next morning the nurses told us that Major Devereux was there and he wanted to see us. So they took us in a command car to a club, where we met the major along with Admiral William Halsey and a lot of other officers. The major said we would fly back to the States with him. Later that day we took off in a C-54 with Major Devereux and landed in Oakland and went to the navy hospital there. After our checkups we had open-gate liberty. I joined the Corps in December of 1939 and was discharged in June of 1946.

Cpl. Carroll Trego, USMC

The last months of the war about two hundred other prisoners and I spent our time in the farthest north island of Japan, Hokkaido. We were in a little mountain town called Tashimsi. Our job was to work deep underground in a previously abandoned coal mine. The war ended on August 15, but nobody bothered to tell us. Life went on the same for almost a month. Then, on September 5, a Korean slave labor man asked us why we were still working in the mine. He said the war was over. He convinced us, and all two hundred of us quit the mine and walked out and straight for the camp. When the Japanese guards saw us coming, they took off running.

We had no way to let the U.S. forces know where we were. We radio men constructed a small transmitter and broadcast our location. We connected with a squadron of torpedo bombers down near Tokyo. We gave them our position, and before we knew it they came flying over so low to the ground they almost hit it. They dropped rolled-up mattresses like torpedoes from eight or ten feet. Inside were cigarettes, food, candy, clothes, soap, everything we might want.

For a few days I simply roamed around the country. Freedom was something I wasn't used to. I met some of the native people. They are called Hairy Ainu. They are short and are matted with hair all over their entire bodies. They were friendly and I liked them. One day I saw a Japanese colonel walking along. I had appropriated a bicycle for my wanderings and I caught up with him easily. I yelled at him and ordered him to strip off his uniform and give me his sword. He did. I took them back to camp.

Major Devereux happened to see me come into camp, and he asked me where I got the uniform and sword. I told him. He said I wasn't allowed to do that and took the things away from me. I wonder what happened to them. That sword was a beauty.

Then we were contacted by some headquarters in Tokyo. They told us to paint a large white "X" on a hill and they'd drop more goods to us. We did. They did. They sent B-29s and they dropped fifty-five-gallon drums filled with anything we might want, from uniforms to canned food. They missed the mark with many of the drums, and the falling barrels killed several of our men. Here they had made it all the way through the fighting and prison camp and then got killed by a friendly barrel. That wasn't fair.

Part of the goods were brand new class-A uniforms. Major Devereux told us we had to wash, shave, get haircuts, and put on our new uniforms so we'd look good when we were rescued. We did. Soon trucks took us down to Sapporo Bay. Then we were taken to Tokyo. There a sergeant met us and told us we all had to be deloused. The major tried to intervene, but the sergeant was solid and sure. Every-one had to be deloused, and the clothes we wore had to be burned. Regulations for all POWs. So we did. Those brand new class-A greens went into the fire.

From there we went to a hospital ship in Tokyo Bay, where we were examined, fed well, and each given five hundred dollars in the form of five one-hundred-dollar bills. Nobody on the ship could break a one-hundred dollar bill. Then at Atsugi airport they paid us another five hundred dollars in five one-hundred dollar bills. Now each man had a thousand dollars he couldn't spend. They flew us to Guam, where we were given another five one-hundred-dollar bills. We needed shaving gear, toothpaste, combs, but the PX wouldn't touch our one-hundred-dollar bills. At last a bank in the area broke up our big ones into smaller bills so we could spend some. As we lined up at the PX at Guam, six black marines walked by. None of us had ever seen a black marine before. One of the guys noticed us and yelled, "Hey, marines, you don't have to worry. We've kept up your good name."

I was discharged on March 8, 1946, and went back to my civil-ian life as an accountant. Sometimes now I regret that I didn't stay in the Marine Corps.

Dr. Guy Kelnhofer Jr., Ph.D., USMC

From December 1941 to April 1942 I was listed as MIA, missing in action. From December 1941 to September 1945 I was listed as a POW. However, that was a misnomer, because I was not really a POW. That term connotes a certain legal status. We had no status, no rights, no privileges, and no protection of any kind. We lived at the whim of any Japanese military person who wished to do us harm. Wherever a Japanese commander chose to condone or encourage his troops to do so—and many did—we could be stabbed, shot, beheaded, starved, beaten, crucified, burned, disfigured, suffocated, frozen, drowned, electrocuted, hanged, buried alive, tortured, or eaten. The Japanese had been taught that we were their racial inferiors, that we were their enemies, and that we were keeping them from pursing their God-ordained destiny as rulers of Asia. In their view, we had disgraced our families, our country, and ourselves by surrendering. They could not understand such cowardice.

Only God knows how I survived. The statistics show that about 4 percent of those captured by the Germans in World War II perished in prison camps. This compares to a death rate of 33 percent in Japanese prison camps. I lived, where so many others died not because I was a better person, more deserving, smarter, or stronger. Luck played a major role in my case. Perhaps God had other plans for me that I still have not learned. My thick skull saved me a number of times when a thinner skull would have resulted in death. For some reason, I escaped malaria, pneumonia, TB, and dementia. Nor did any Allied submarine, ship, or airplane attack or sink any of the unmarked hell ships on which we were transported from Wake to China and from Korea to Japan. Neither did I happen to be standing under those portions of the coal mine roof that collapsed from time to time while I was an underground miner in Hokkaido, Japan.

When we were repatriated in the fall of 1945, we were told that after a good rest and after eating plenty of good cooking, we would be as good as new. However, on my repatriation leave, I found myself crying unexpectedly, suffering shaking hands, feeling estranged from family and friends, and being afraid to sleep because of terrifying nightmares. When I reported this to the doctors at the naval hospital, the Marine Corps told me that I was no longer fit for further military service, but they did not offer me a medical discharge. The Red Cross on its own initiative obtained for me a VA disability rating of 50 percent, which I retained for the most part until 1982. Then, because of beriberi contracted in China, I lost my hearing and I was frequently bedridden with severe vertigo. I was fortunate to be examined for three hours by a sympathetic VA psychiatrist. He was able to obtain for me a rating of 100 percent for post-traumatic stress disorder and other service-connected disabilities. Later one of the other presumptives caught up to me, ischemic heart disease, resulting in an angioplasty, a bypass, and two infarcts.

I coped with my history by repression and denial. That means I never discussed my prison camp experiences with anyone. I never associated with any military organizations. I never read any books or saw any movies that referred to the subject. Until 1974 I believed that I had put those experiences behind me. That year I was in Rome, where I met with a number of fellow United Nations personnel for lunch. A man of my age from Japan was seated next to me. He proved to be an engaging lunch companion, and we laughed and joked together. Then I noticed that my hand began to shake. Soon after that my whole body began to shake. I excused myself and returned to my hotel. There I told my wife what had happened. When I tried to tell her how the Japanese had treated us as prisoners, I broke down and wept, unable to continue.

After my 100 percent disability rating and my retirement, I decided that I would try to confront my past and try to associate with fellow ex-POWs. In 1985, in Seattle, I joined an ex-POW therapy group, which had been meeting at the VA hospital. Since then I have tried to continue as a member of these groups wherever I have lived. Through this uninhibited exchange of information and observations among my fellow ex-POWs, I have learned a great deal about myself. I tried to pass on what I had learned in a book entitled *Understanding the Former Prisoner of War: Life After Liberation*.

Reading has also had its rewards. For instance, in one novel about the Pacific War, a young marine confesses to an older man his shame about losing his temper in combat with the Japanese. The older man assures him that his actions were normal and reminds him that, after all, he is a human being, not some kind of fighting machine. It was then that I realized that I had been unwilling to admit my true feelings. Instead of the forgiving Christian gentleman I had been portraying to myself and the world at large, I was really and truly a very angry man, filled with hate and hungering for revenge. All of that terrible anger I had had to hide and repress in prison for self-protection had to go somewhere. It did not simply vanish and disappear just because I had to hide it then. I did see eventually how my life had been distorted by that tremendous store of hidden anger.

When I retired, I had time to reflect about my work history. It was difficult for me to rationalize away a pattern of job changes and relocations that had taken place every two or three years over the course of thirty years of work. What could have motivated me to move that frequently? The answer, I decided, was that I moved to avoid the prospect of confrontation with fellow employees, superiors or clients. Why was I so afraid of confrontations? I understood that if I ever lost control of my temper, if I ever let loose the anger I held inside me, it would be catastrophic for me and my family.

I am seventy-eight years old now. It is past time to forget the unforgettable and to forgive the unforgivable. If the Japanese would ever admit that they deliberately tortured and murdered us and now asked for our pardon, I could put down my burden of hatred and anger. There seems to be little prospect of that happening during my lifetime. Which means I will remain a prisoner until I die.

Fireman 2nd Class Dare Kibble, USN

In the spring of 1945 we began to see huge silver airplanes flying over Tokyo. They were B-29s, but we didn't know it, and the first ones were on recon. Then the number of big planes increased. After a few weeks they began bombing the greater Tokyo metropolitan area during the night. The Nips had no night-fighter aircraft. We would stop work at the sound of the air raid siren and go to a railroad underpass that was close to our work and our prison compound.

In May of 1945 we had a five-hundred-plane raid that scattered incendiary bombs on Tokyo like a farm gal feeding the chickens. These planes came in so low we could spot them in the light of the thousands of fires set by the gelatin bombs, which explode at a pre-set altitude and throw burning petroleum gel in all directions, the gel sticking to anything it touches and starting it on fire. At that time, 90 percent of Tokyo was built of paper and wood. Forty square miles of the city was on fire that one specific night.

The huge fire heated the atmosphere and caused a psuedocyclonic wind that tore and demolished the city's structures as if they were box matches and paper sacks. The raid must have lasted at least five hours. The fire departments and equipment were useless against such a wildfire. Our underpass bomb shelter started filling with water from broken fire mains. At one time during the night, we were certain the guards were going to leave us in the underpass and let us drown. Luckily, the water was cut off somewhere when it got to be three feet deep. One damn death-threatening episode after another. I thought, will death never come?

At the end of the raid we were marched back into the prison compound and told to stand at attention. We were to stand in this yard at attention for two days and two nights with no food or water as punishment for the damage the bombers had done to Tokyo.

After our stint at attention, we were divided into work parties and sent to the burned-out areas to start cleaning up the debris from the fire. A couple of our men were nearly beaten to death for writing "V for Victory" on the fire-blackened wall of a hospital where hundreds of patients had been burned to death. Thousands of Japanese were killed during the night raid. But we still say we are patriots and civilized humans.

After our stay at Kawasaki Camp, we were sent to a new prison at Niigata, on the China Sea side of the large Japanese island of Honshu. They marched us to the railroad and put 270 of us into regular train passenger cars with seats, windows, and Western-style toilets. We couldn't get over the toilets. I must have gone to the pot at least eight times during the eight-hour ride, just to enjoy the feeling. That afternoon they gave us box lunches. We had soy grasshoppers, white rice, pickled kelp, and a small portion of fish; it was marvelous. A typical Japanese meal. With this almost kind treatment we wondered if the war was over. The people on the train were as friendly as in any American society, and very courteous. But this would not last.

The Niigata Camp was seven miles east of the town. The countryside was beautiful, with some huge mountains on the east side of the valley, and Niigata has a natural seaport with a good estuary. There were now a thousand prisoners at the camp, where life was about the same as in Kawasaki, except the guards weren't quite as vicious. We walked six miles to work on the docks every day. We had a lot of POWs from the Bataan Death March and a lot of Canadian prisoners.

Four men were assigned to a work crew, which would load a forty-four-thousand-pound railroad freight car with coal from yeh-ho baskets. These were two baskets tied to a pole that you carried on your shoulders. Two men loaded the baskets on the ground, and the other two, with their full baskets, walked up a plank, to the top of the car, went down the length of the car on another plank and dumped the coal from the baskets. Then we walked down a third plank to the filling area and to get loaded up again with coal. Each basket held about 75 pounds of coal. So we had a lot of 110-pound men carrying a 150 pounds of coal. We would trade off on the carrying and the loading. We had to make a trip up the plank every five minutes in order to load a car in one workday, or else we didn't eat that night. We didn't know it then, but there were other POWs digging this same coal out of the mines and sending it to us.

Our guards at Niigata were military instead of the usual civilians, which made a difference in the treatment. One day they took us all down to the estuary and let us go for a swim. Man alive, but the swim was wonderful. While we were swimming, a ship blew up right in front of us from a proximity floating mine that had been dropped by an Army Air Force B-29. We soon realized that the B-29s were dropping a lot of these floating mines in the estuary and the harbor. Dozens of the ships that tried to come into the harbor blew up and sank.

During the latter part of July 1945, we noticed that the Nips had picked one of the sunken cargo ships to store barges of ordnance and ammunition on, thinking no one would attack a sunken ship listing to one side. Then one day, about noon, we heard the sweet sound of a multitude of American engines humming directly above us in the clouds. All at once, we could hear the engines starting to scream. Then they came down out of the clouds, one after another, all of them heading for designated targets. Four of the navy dive-bombers dove toward for the sunken ammo ship and hit it with bombs. From that day on for several days, the ship kept exploding.

When we began seeing navy planes flying from carriers, we knew the end of the war was in sight. However, we worried about the end, for the Nips continually told us that if the American troops landed on Honshu, they would kill all of us the way they did the ninety-eight civilians we had left behind on Wake Island.

Pvt. Kenneth E. Cunningham, USMC (deceased)

One day after we came back to Camp Omori after work, about 5:30, a big car drove in with a hundred Japanese troops guarding it. It was the great General [Hideki] Tojo himself. He had come in unexpectedly for an inspection. All the Japs were scraping and bowing and were so scared they were running around like crazy people. They were afraid that he would find something wrong and that some of them would lose their soft jobs and have to go to a fighting unit. By this time they were beginning to doubt the Japanese propaganda and starting to fear the thought of what the Americans were doing on the front. They were probably also afraid of what the Americans would do when they came to Japan. Most of the Japanese had begun to realize it would not be long before their homeland would be invaded.

Along about the first of August 1945, these fears and concerns grew so strong that the Japs started taking it a little easier on us and practically left us alone. All of us POWs knew it would be over soon and we would be home by Christmas if we didn't get blown up first. There were millions of Japs homeless and starving, and it was impossible for them to get through another winter. Besides their losses from bombings, there were thousands of Japanese dying every day from starvation and exposure. Our hopes were running pretty high.

We began making bets on dates all the way from August 5 to January for when the war would end. We knew about our air forces on the islands close in; we knew how our landing forces were getting ready to come and invade Japan. We also knew just about how big the U.S. fleet was that sat offshore. We figured most of the Japanese knew about the fleet as well, but we had better information than the Japanese people did.

We got two days off a month. August 15 happened to be my day off. At 11:30 practically every one of the POWs in camp knew the war was over, but we didn't dare rejoice or say anything. This knowledge was soon confirmed when Japan's surrender was announced over the radio to the Japanese public. We were then told by the prison officials that there would be no more work and we would only be held there until we could be sent home.

We were the happiest men alive that day. The thing we had waited on for over three years and eight months had finally happened. We were free, and we would soon be home to see those we had left so long before. We had been through hell, and it was quite a relief. Most of us were so happy we cried. We were really going home. Life as a POW was a lot better after the war was over. We took over the whole camp and ran things to suit ourselves. We ate all we that we could, we lay around and took things easy. We tore down the prison fence and lay on the hot sandy beach or went swimming. We got hundreds of letters that had been held back and hidden in a warehouse. The Japs didn't want us around and they didn't want to stay there, but they could not get away—although over the next few days quite a few of them did sneak off and disappear. Through our grapevine we heard that planes were coming to drop us supplies. On the night of August 21 we had a big typhoon that pretty well tore up the camp. Most of us got soaking wet, only we didn't care about that. All we wanted was to see those planes. The next day we got word that the planes had been held up for two days by the storm.

We didn't like it, but we managed to wait it out. On the morning of August 24, we were up early to wait for the boys to come flying in. About 9:00 A.M. a flight of F6F Grumman Hellcats zoomed over. They were followed shortly by a flight of F4U Chance Vought Corsairs. These were navy and marine carrier-based planes. We almost went crazy as they dived and barrel-rolled and buzzed the camp. Then they started dropping things from the ship's store: chewing gum, cigarettes, toilet articles, newspapers, and magazines. The pilots told us to write on the roofs what we wanted. We took white paint and wrote on the black roofs that we wanted food and indicated how many men there were in camp. We also printed a Marine Corps officer's name, Bayington, on the roof. Two hours later, part of the squadron of Grummans came in and really put on a show for us. It was the first time the outside world knew that Bayington was alive. They were around all day, and we went to bed that night a happy bunch of men.

The Jap civilians were all out on the tops of the buildings, waving and watching. They seemed nearly as happy to see the U.S. fighters as we were. Now they didn't have to be worried about being blown up, burned, or starved. They must have been glad the war was over, too. The next day there were more planes and more supplies were dropped. We talked to some of the planes by blinker light. That same day Grumman torpedo bombers came over with cases of food in their bomb bays. They were dropped just outside of camp on the soft sandy beach.

The big B-29s came over the next day. They were really loaded. They dropped tons and tons of food, clothes, cigarettes, and newspapers. The supplies came down on huge cargo parachutes, which broke, and the stuff got scattered all over the landscape when the heavy cases hit. We salvaged about half of what they dropped. There was enough clothing for two thousand men, and we were soon fixed up in new shoes and clean uniforms. The fighter planes had also dropped toiletries so we could have good baths and shaves. It made us feel like men again. We were a happy bunch of guys and so excited we hardly knew what we were doing.

The next day, amid the food bombing and excitement, some U.S. Navy warships pulled into Tokyo Bay about noon. They were almost two miles from our camp. When they arrived we forgot about the planes and watched the ships. For almost an hour nothing moved. By that time about twenty of us decided if they did not come in after us, we were going to go out that night. It would have been a long swim, but we would have made it. As things turned out, we didn't have to make the swim. About 3:30 P.M. three landing boats put off from the ships and they came right into camp. Seeing the Stars and Stripes flying from the stern of those boats made us feel great. Some of us swam out to meet the boats, and when they pulled us on deck we broke down and cried.

Fireman 2nd Class Dare Kibble, USN

On August 15 we hit the dirt floor of the barracks, ran out to the *benjo,* sounded off at roll call, and ate our cup of barley. Then the call came to fall out. We lined up to march the seven miles to work and waited. We stood in ranks for thirty minutes, wondering what was happening. Then the Nip interpreter came out and told us to go back to the barracks! But the only days we didn't work were Christmas and the emperor's birthday.

That's when it dawned on us. The Allies had landed on Honshu. This meant the Nips were going to keep their promise and slaughter us all if the Allied troops landed. We would be taken out into the fields to dig our own mass grave, they would line us up on the edge, and then the machine guns would open fire. *Oh, God, not after all we have been through during the last forty-four months, don't let this happen.*

You have never seen a bunch of men so nervous. Talk about scuttlebutt—it rolled out of the human mouths like oral diarrhea. Finally, all the guards were summoned to the camp commander's area for a briefing. Our most proficient interpreter was a French Canadian. And could that man speak Japanese. Later he assembled the prisoners, all one thousand of us, and told us we probably would not believe the message he was about to relay to us.

He said the emperor of Japan had accepted an unconditional surrender of the armed forces of Japan to the Allies, and in two days Allied planes would be coming over with food and clothing for us. We were to build a huge PW sign on the hill above the prison compound. Make it a hundred feet tall, he said, so the planes could find us. General MacArthur also told the Nips that prisoners were not to be molested by Nip troops or civilians or there would be hell to pay. The Nips had a great deal of respect for MacArthur and took him at his word. The interpreter also told us we would be leaving the island of Honshu as soon as the arrangements could be made.

The day after the big news we were in the compound, patiently waiting for something to happen, when about twenty-five dive-bombers and Grumman fighters flew over. We looked almost naked to them, so they stripped off pants and shirts and threw them out their bomb bays for us along with any cigarettes they had.

The next day they came back and flew low and slow and dropped seabags filled with everything imaginable. You could tell the men aboard ship had tried to guess what they would like to have provided to them had they gone through our experiences. They had scrounged through the ship for cigarettes, candy bars, underwear, pants, shoes, and editions of *Time* magazine. From *Time* we learned about the atomic bombs, although we didn't realize the deadly impact they had on human life in those cities.

On the fifth day of our freedom B-29s flew over our area, dropping supplies of food, clothing, and medicines. They had their bomb-bay doors open, and we could see the pallets upon which the goods were strapped. The pallets were rigged to huge parachutes, which let the supplies float down to a drop area. They dropped everything to satisfy our needs. Even fresh milk came down in gas tank containers.

I was extremely proud of a new pair of GI shoes and khaki pants and shirt. I even had a pair of new socks to wear, even though my feet were covered with open sores. And soap, oh, the lovely soap with which to bathe. How wonderful it was. I carried a bar of soap around in my pocket for some weeks after that, just in case the war broke again. I also took some clothes and hid them in the compound in case of an emergency.

A few days after the Nip surrender, I thought I'd go nuts sitting in the compound waiting for the arrival of somebody from the Allies. Another guy and I went for a walk. We hiked a couple of miles north-east, up toward the mountains. We came to a small village, and the people came out to greet us. We knew a little of the language by then and managed to tell them about the end of the war. They had heard it on their radios.

One elderly man invited us to lunch with his family. We went to his small straw-and-paper house with a thatch roof, took off our shoes, and entered. The man had a wife and two daughters. The man and my buddy and I sat down on our haunches before a small table, while the wife and daughters sat at another table. I remember thinking the daughters were extremely pretty.

The Nip told us he had three sons in the war and he knew one had been killed. He didn't know where the other two were, but he presumed they were alive. His wife soon started cooking food for us— a stew of fish and some veggies accompanied by the ever-present rice. Also, they served us some saki, which was delicious. What astonished me was the complete absence of animosity in their attitude. It seemed they were more or less relieved to see the end of the war.

I expected my shoes to be missing when I stepped outside on the threshold, but the Nip assured me you could leave your shoes there to the end of time and no one would touch them. Stealing was a serious criminal offense in Japan. We thanked the family profusely and returned to the compound.

Pvt. Kenneth E. Cunningham, USMC

When the Allied landing craft came to Camp Omori in Tokyo Bay the commanding officer of the party gave us a speech. He was a commodore, and his landing party was heavily armed and had a short-wave radio and three navy corpsmen. He told us that we all would be off the island and on board the ship that night. This kind of rescue surprised us, but nothing could have suited us better. The sailors who came ashore wanted souvenirs, so we all started to hunt. We took all the Jap rifles, bayonets, and swords we could find. Some of the Japs protested, but a few waves with a submachine gun at them changed their minds. The old Jap colonel who was POW commander of all prison camps made Omori his home. He said he had received no orders from the emperor; and until he did, the POWs must stay there. The commodore said that was too bad, because he had orders from his admiral, who made the emperor look like a buck private—and anyway, who was going to stop him? Amid insults and jeers yelled out in Japanese by us POWs, the old colonel got out of there as quickly as possible.

After we found the souvenirs, we were divided into groups and sent in the landing craft out to a huge hospital ship. As we pulled away from that island, we knew we were free men at last. We were going away from that hell that wouldn't stop and out into a new, clean life. It was just like being born all over again. We would be able to enjoy life again. We knew that a real tough time was now over. It brought tears to our eyes when we stopped to realize just what lay ahead of us. It was a quiet ride from shore to ship. Every man was thinking a lot. We were happy, and no words could express it.

When we arrived at the hospital ship, we were immediately assigned to bunks. Then we were given instructions by pretty nurses as to what to do. We received physicals and new outfits of clothes. We were interviewed and sent to supper. It was my first meal under the Stars and Stripes for three years and eight months—ham and eggs and ice cream—and I ate so much I was afraid I was going to be sick. I just couldn't get enough of them. Right after eating we were split up; a few of us boarded a destroyer that lay alongside. Here we were given bunks and treated like a bunch of kings.

The next day we wrote home, and the rest of the time we ate and talked with the crew members. For the next five days all we did was eat and sleep and ride ten miles up and back on Tokyo Bay in the destroyer. On September 4 we were classified, and the sailors and marines were put in one group. We left the destroyer that afternoon for a big transport. Here we were treated with even more respect than on the smaller ship. She was the USS *Ozark*, and had been built in Portland, Oregon. That was near my hometown. A lot of Portland boys on her knew where I lived. I even knew some of them, and it was good to talk about home.

On the night of September 5, about 8:30, a yeoman came down to our compartment. He read off a long list of names, some from our camp and some from other camps. My name was on the list. He said the ones named were to leave at 5:00 A.M. to go to an airport in East Tokyo, where we would board planes and fly to Guam. No one slept much that night, and we were all on deck at 4:45 A.M. with our luggage. There were ninety-six of us; we'd make up three planeloads. We left the ship at 5:00 A.M. and took landing craft across the bay to the bomb- and shell-torn airfield in East Tokyo. When we arrived at the airport, five big C-54s, navy transports, were waiting for us. At 8:30 we climbed on board—thirty-two ex-POWs on each of three planes—and lifted off at 9:00 A.M. sharp, headed for Guam.

The skipper of our four-engine plane climbed up to ten thousand feet and leveled off, then banked over to the right and made two big circles of Tokyo and Yokohama. It was then that we first saw what had been done to the once-enormous cities of Japan. We had seen it all from the ground a little at a time over a period of months, but now we saw it all at once. Yokohama was gone, just a lot of ashes and wreckage. Tokyo had only four or five square blocks of her downtown business district left standing. The great industrial center of Kawasaki had been entirely wiped out. Those once-huge factories and mills were now only twisted, melted wreckage. After the second circle we headed out over Mount Fujiyama. That snow- capped peak sticking up above the clouds was the prettiest thing I saw in Japan. As I saw it fade away in the distance, I knew that I had seen the last of Japan.

A few minutes later the plane's navigator came back to tell us that soon we would see Uncle Sam's Pacific Fleet. When we saw it out the windows, I realized that despite all of the stories I had heard, it was still beyond all of my expectations. It stretched out for miles and miles. Just seeing it made me proud.

We had a good, smooth trip all the way to Guam. We were there for two nights and one day. In that time some of us made a trip around the island and tried to look up some old buddies. I found one man I knew. He had been a warrant officer before the war and at one time my battery commander. He came down to the naval air station barracks to see me. He was a colonel by then and just as big and rough as ever. He told me about some of the boys in our old outfit.

On September 8, 1945, we left Guam and flew to Kwajalein for a fuel stop, then on to Johnson Island for more fuel. We ate there and then flew on to Pearl Harbor. We landed at the naval air station, and as I stepped out of the plane, the commanding officer of my old battalion was there to meet me. I got in his car and we followed the buses up to the naval hospital. We talked over old times before the war and about some of the boys I did duty with. He was eager to hear how some of the Wake Island POWs had fared.

We left Pearl the next day for a long flight to San Francisco. The good old United States at last was only a few hours away. It was foggy over San Francisco, but we could land. We were back on the good old U.S.A. at last. Some of the boys kissed the pavement of the runway and some stamped their feet on it. All of us swore we would not leave her again for a long time. We were home! It was hard to believe it after what we had gone through in the past forty-four months. Some of us laughed, some cried, some shouted for joy. That night, four days after waving goodbye to Mount Fuji, we were home. We went to the big navy hospital up on the hill, where we had physical exams for the next four days. The first day back I made a phone call to my folks in Forest Grove, Oregon. I passed my physical easily, and the evening of September 14, 1945, I was given my traveling orders and my temporary health record.

At 8:00 P.M. I boarded a Western Airlines plane for my last ride home. At 12:30 A.M. on September 15, I called Forest Grove from the Portland airport, woke up my parents, and asked them to come and get me. They did.

For the first time in nearly five years I was home.

END
NOTE

Slave Labor . . . No Pay to the Prisoners

In *Unjust Enrichment,* published by Stackpole Books in 2001, Linda Goetz Holmes declared the use of Allied prisoners of war for slave labor by Japanese companies one of the great unresolved crimes of World War II. As many as one hundred Allied POWs died every day on Japanese industrial and business property between 1942 and 1945—most of them as a result of overwork, brutal beatings, untreated diseases, and starvation. Records show further that nine out of every ten POWs who died in World War II met their end while under Japanese prison camp control.

This exploitation of our POWs was an integral part of the Japanese government's regulations and policy. Organizations in Britain, the Netherlands, and the United States desperately tried to get relief to these prisoners, but the Japanese government systematically blocked all humanitarian efforts except for a minute amount from the International Red Cross.

Some claim that the Japanese companies—more than forty of them—asked the army for the use of POWs as slave laborers; that the idea did not originate with the army. Nonetheless, the army complied, and also demanded of the companies a fee for each day they used each prisoner. The companies paid two yen per man per day, which was a fair wage back in 1942, to lease the POWs from the army. The Japanese government, however, told the companies that they also had to pay the prisoners the same wages that Japanese soldiers earned, according to the rank of the POW. The companies did in fact make monthly reports that show they were paying the POWs, or so it would appear. The Japanese government records show, too, that the men were being paid regularly. In reality, though, the POWs were not paid a red cent.

A new legal claim has been filed by some POWs against the Japanese companies. The POWs assert that the Japanese firms were directed by their government to pay the prisoners. As the companies failed to do so, they now owe the prisoners for money earned, and with interest. Japanese government records also show that the companies were ordered to provide adequate housing, food, sanitation, and heat for the workers. Instead, the men were worked long hours, were often starved, bore extreme cold, and died of exhaustion and diseases that could easily have been treated and cured by regular Japanese medical personnel.

Japanese factories, shipyards, and mines were the biggest offenders of the slave labor crimes. Many of those same firms are today's huge conglomerates in Japan. Many say these companies got their start and a big boost by using slave labor during the war. That slave labor force comprised more than twenty-five thousand American POWs.

APPENDIX

Detailed here are the complete rosters of the men in the military service who fought on Wake Island during World War II. Included are all the marine, navy, and army personnel. They are listed alphabetically regardless of the service; initials in quotation marks were assigned by the military and do not stand for a given name. This list includes both those who lived through the fight on Wake Island and those who gave their lives on the atolls.

Ackley, Edwin M.
Adams, "E" "O" S.
Adams, Richard P.
Agar, Paul R.
Allen, Jack "V"
Anderson, John B. L.
Andrews, Arthur D.
Andrews, Thomas J., Jr.
Arthur, Robert O.

Atwood, Laurence M.
Austin, Rufus B.
Baker, "S" "L"
Balhorn, Marvin W.
Bamvord, Roger D.
Barger, Lester L.
Barnes, Earl H.
Barnes, James E.
Barninger, Clarence A., Jr.

Bastien, James S.
Batelme, Herbert E.
Beaver, Darnell L.
Beck, William D.
Bedell, Henry A.
Beese, Fred A.
Bendenski, Joseph B.
Benedetto, Michael A.
Benjamin, Armand E.
Bennett, Arthur K.
Bentley, Joseph M.
Berkery, James J., Jr.
Bertels, Alton J.
Besancon, Victor C.
Bird, Edwin A.
Blandy, John F.
Bogdonovitch, Edward M.
Boley, Kenneth C.
Borchers, Orville N.
Borne, Joseph E.
Borth, Harold C.
Boscarino, James F.
Bosher, Raymond R.
Bostick, William F.
Bourquin, Robert E., Jr.
Bowsher, Walter A., Jr.
Box, Robert S., Jr.
Boyd, Berdyne
Boyle, Hugh L.
Bragg, Lorel J.
Breckenridge, Albert H.
Brewer, Artie T.
Brown, Buell S.
Brown, Gene E.
Brown, James R.

Brown, Kenneth LeR.
Brown, Robert L.
Brown, Robert McC.
Browning, James S.
Broyles, Earl M., Jr.
Bryan, Pershing "B"
Buchanan, Gerald E.
Buckie, William B., Jr.
Buehler, William F.
Bumgarner, Alvin A.
Burford, Phillip L.
Busse, Wilbur J.
Byard, Lester C.
Byer, Lawrence M.
Byrd, Harry J.
Byrne, Herbert R.
Cain, Orville J.
Calanchini, Arthur J.
Caldwell, Richard R.
Caldwell, Robert E.
Camp, Charles H.
Carr, Gerald J.
Cemeris, John
Cessna, Harry J.
Chambliss, Jessee R.
Chapman, Henry H. W.
Chew, Hoyle "E"
Christenson, Alfred B.
Chudzik, Joseph T.
Clark, Emery T.
Comfort, Floyd H.
Comin, Howard D.
Commers, Joseph F.
Conderman, Robert J.
Condra, Charley H.

Conner, Warren D.

Connor, Dennis C.

Cook, Hal, Jr.

Cook, Jack B.

Cook, Walter J.

Cooley, Delmer E.

Cooper, Clarence S., Jr.

Cooper, Paul C.

Cooper, Robert E.

Cornett, John

Couch, Claude C.

Couch, Winslow

Coulson, Raymond L.

Covert, Phillip G.

Cox, James H.

Cox, Roy T.

Crouch, James A.

Culp, Joseph C.

Cunningham, Kenneth E.

Cunningham, Winfield S.

Curlee, Albert C.

Curry, Robert E.

Dale, John R.

Dana, Max J.

Darden, James B.

Davidson, Carl R.

Davis, Eschol E.

Davis, Floyd H.

Davis, Jack E.

Davis, James J., Jr.

Dawson, Harvey L.

Deeds, Robert L.

DeLoach, Emett D.

Descaps, Clarence C.

DeSparr, Marshall E.

Devereux, James P. S.

Dilks, Carl W.

Dimento, Frank

Dodge, Bernard A.

Doke, Cecil E.

Domingue, Alton J.

Dorman, Roger

Double, John F.

Drake, Elmer S., Jr.

Dunham, Estille G.

Durrwachter, Henry L., Jr.

Eaton, Edward F.

Economou, Michael N.

Edwards, Robert P.

Elliott, Norman D.

Elrod, Henry T.

Emerick, Billie E.

Enyart, Clinton H.

Everist, Joseph L.

Farrar, Herbert D.

Fields, Marshall E.

Finley, Lloyd B.

Fish, Cyrus D.

Fitzpatrick, James A.

Fleener, Gene A.

Fleming, Manton L.

Fortuna, Stephen

Frandsen, Andrew J.

Franklin, Theodore Douglas

Fraser, Harry S.

Freuler, Herbert C.

Frey, Robert L.

Frost, Lynn W.

Fuller, Andrew A.

Futtrip, Paul F.

Gardner, Douglas D.

Gardner, Glen G.

Garr, Robert F., Jr.

Garrison, Everett

Gatewood, Martin A.

George, John "F"

George, Joseph E., Jr.

Gerberding, Oliver L., Jr.

Giddens, George G.

Gilbert, Richard C.

Gilley, Ernest N., Jr.

Gleichauf, William A.

Godbold, Bryghte D.

Godwin, William F.

Gonzales, Roy Jr.

Gordon, William

Gragg, Raymon

Grant, Everard M.

Graves, George A.

Graves, Leon A.

Gray, Robert L. J.

Greeley, Robert W.

Greey, Elmer B.

Gregouire, Sylvester

Greska, Martin A.

Gross, Franklin D.

Grubb, Glenn E.

Gruber, Walter J.

Guilbeaux, Stanley P.

Guthrie, Frank "A"

Hagerty, Oliver P., Jr.

Haggard, Fred D.

Haidinger, Robert F.

Hair, Steven Y.

Haley, Gifford LaF.

Hall, James W.

Halstead, William C.

Hamas, John

Hamel, Fred M.

Hamilton, William J.

Hanna, Robert M.

Hannah, Clyde W.

Hannum, Earl R.

Harper, Joel E.

Harringer, Ewalk

Harrison, Charles L.

Hartung, Arvel N.

Hassig, Edwin F.

Haugen, Henry

Hearn, Jack D.

Hemmelgarn, Paul F.

Hendrickson, Russell W.

Henshaw, George H.

Hesson, James F.

Hicks, Albert, Jr.

Hill, Charles C.

Himelrick, John R.

Hodgkins, Ray K., Jr.

Holden, Frank J.

Holewinski, Ralph J.

Hollbrooks, Benjamin

Holmes, Charles A.

Holt, Johnson P.

Horstman, Herbert J.

Hoskison, Larence D.

Hotchkiss, Clifford E.

Hotchkiss, Richard L

Houde, Severe R.

Houschildt, Frank H.

Howard, John R.

Hubley, George G.

Huffman, Forest

Hughes, "A" "R," Jr.

Hundley, Robert T.

Hunt, Quince A.

Hyder, Luther "E"

Hyzer, Morris F.

Ickett, Ralph H.

Jackson, Sammy C.

Jamerson, Joseph P.

Jenkins, Haley "B"

Johnson, Edward E.

Johnson, George LeR.

Johnson, Harland R.

Johnson, John S., Jr.

Johnson, Phillip W.

Johnson, Ralph E.

Johnson, Solon L.

Johnson, Thomas W., Jr.

Johnston, Lillard L., Jr.

Jones, Otis T.

Joyner, Paul C.

June, Randolph M.

Kahn, Gustav M.

Katchak, John

Kaz-Fritzshall, Norman N.

Keene, Campbell

Kelnhofer, Guy J., Jr.

Kennedy, Walter T.

Kessler, Woodrow M.

Ketner, Bernard O.

Kibble, Dare K.

Kidd, Franklin B.

Kidd, Walter

Kilcoyne, Thomas P.

King, Curtis P.

King, Kirby K.

King, James O.

Kinney, John F.

Kleponis, Vincent

Kirk, John T.

Klein, Arthur A.

Kliewer, David D.

Kohlin, Alfred T.

Koontz, Benjamin D.

Krawie, John W.

Krenistki, William

Kroptavich, James S.

Kruczek, Walter J.

Krueger, Darius C.

LaFleur, Albert H.

Lambert. John W.

Lane, Lloyd G.

Langley, Edgar N.

Lanning, John R.

LaPorte, Ewing E.

Larson, William C.

Latham, Joe T.

Lauff, Bernard J.

Laursen, Norman J.

Lechler, William R.

Lee, Robert E.

Lepore, Anthony

Lewis, Clifton H.

Lewis, George H.

Lewis, William W.

Lillard, George E.

Lindsay, Wilford J.

Locklin, Eugene D.

Lorenz, Henry D.

Ludwich, Kirby, Jr.
Lutz, Eugene J.
Madere, Joseph A.
Mackie, Robert J.
Malleck, Donald R.
Malone, Thomas J., Jr.
Manning, Bernard H.
Manning, William H., Jr.
Marlow, Clovis R.
Marshall, Gordon L.
Martin, Gerald J.
Martin, Virgil E.
Marvin, Kenneth L.
Mathis, Charles L.
Mayhew, Richard C.
McAlister, John A.
McAmis, Terrance T.
McAnally, Winford J.
McBride, James E.
McCage, Malrvey E.
McCall, James F.
McCalla, Marvin P.
McCaulley, Wade "B"
McClanahan, Wilbur C.
McCoy, William H.
McDaniel, George W.
McFall, William E.
McGee, Robert H.
McKinstry, Clarence B.
McWiggins, James C.
McQuilling, Robert E.
McReynolds, Wendel
Melton, Kenneth L.
Mercer, Harris L.
Mergenthaler, John J.

Mettscher, Leonard G.
Milbourn, Ival D.
Miller, Hershal L.
Miller, Howard
Mitchell, James P.
Mitwalski, Robert W.
Moore, Carl, Jr.
Moore, John P.
Morgan, "R" "C"
Moritz, LeRoy G.
Mosley, Harvey L.
Mullins James M., Jr.
Murphy, LeRoy G.
Murphy, Robert B.
Nanninga, Henry D.
Nevenzel, Jay
Nowlin, Jesse E.
O'Connell, John J.
Oelberg, Christian, Jr.
Olcott, Chester W.
Olenowski, Michael
Owen, Lester C.
Page, Robert E. L.
Painter, John S.
Parks, Lawrence "A"
Paszkiewicz, Andrew J.
Patterson, Billy LeR.
Paul, Archie "T"
Pearce, Herbert N.
Pearsall, John E.
Pechacek, Thomas J.
Pellegrini, Alfred F.
Percy, "R" "C"
Petrick, Edward N.
Phipps, Ralph E.

Pippi, Louis
Pistole, Erwin "D"
Pickering, George F.
Plate, William O.
Platt, Wesley McC.
Plecker, Mcpherson
Poindexter, Arthur R.
Polousky, Anthony
Potter, George H., Jr.
Pratt, Robert M.
Prochaska, Albert J.
Puckett, Ray V.
Purvis, Gordon W.
Putnam, Paul A.
Qubre, Tony T.
Quinn, Fenton "R"
Rasor, Herman L.
Ray, Sanford K.
Raymond, Samuel W.
Reed, Clifford M.
Reed, Dick L.
Reed, Alvey A.
Reeves, Joe M.
Regg, Norman M.
Renner, Francis J.
Rex, James B.
Richardson, Bernard E.
Richey, Lewis H.
Richter, Eugene V.
Rickert, Albert P.
Rietzler, Junior H.
Roberson, Ted "J" "D"
Robinson, George LeR.
Robinson, James G.
Rogers, Charles G.

Rogers, Ernest G.
Roman, Oldrich B.
Rook, Edward B.
Rozycki, Stanley J.
Rush, Dave J.
Ryan, Eugene R.
Sado, John E.
Sanders, Clifton C.
Sanders, Jacob R.
Sandvold, Julian K.
Sapp, Charles W.
Sargent, Charles A.
Schneider, LeRoy N.
Schulz, Glenn R.
Schulze, Carl H.
Schumacker, William T.
Shellhorn, Melvin W.
Shelton, Clifford E.
Shores, Robert
Short, Ernest E.
Shugart, Eugene W.
Shumard, Gene D.
Sickels, Percy H.
Sieger, Norman P.
Silverlieb, Irving B.
Simon, Adolph
Skaggs, Jack R.
Skaggs, Viktor V.
Slezak, Rudolph M.
Sloman, Wiley W.
Smith, Cassius D.
Smith, Dempsey
Smith, Elwood M.
Smith, Gordon L.
Smith, John C.

Smith, Robert N.
Sorrell, Jesse D.
Stafford, Virgil D.
Stahl, Rudolph W., Jr.
Stegmaier, Carl E., Jr.
Stevens, Robert L.
Stewart, Jesse L.
Stocks, Artie J.
Stockton, Maurice E.
Stowe, Joe M.
Stringfield, George W.
Sturgeon, Edward V.
Sutton, Mack P.
Swartz, Merle E.
Switzer, Raymond C.
Tallentire, Gilson A.
Tate, Willis
Taylor, Dale K.
Taylor, Rudolph J.
Terfansky, Joseph E.
Terry, Arthur F.
Terry, Mabry A.
Thaire, Grover E.
Tharin, Frank C.
Thompson, Harold Ray
Thorsen, John Thomas
Tipton, Wiley E.
Todd, Herman A.
Tokryman, Paul
Tompkins, Raymond M.
Tramposh, Charles E.
Trego, Carroll E.
Tripp, Glenn Eugene
Troney, Morris Henry
Tuck, Erville R.

Tucker, William M.
Tusa, Joe M.
Unger, John I.
Vaale, Ernest Christian
Vardell, Virgie P.
Vaughn, James
Vega, Vincent H.
Venable, Alexander G., Jr.
Venable, James C.
Wade, "Q" "T"
Walish, Robert C.
Wallace, Verne L.
Waronker, Alvin J.
Warren, Howard E.
Warsing, John W., Jr.
Webb, Henry G.
Webster, Guy
Weimer, Jacob G.
Wheeler, Mackie L.
White, Clyde
Williams, Bermont M.
Williams, Harold Raymond
Wilson, Franklin Marquette
Williams, Henry, Jr.
Williams, Luther
Williamson, Jack R.
Wilsford, Clyde D.
Wilson, Henry Stanley
Winslow, Robert E.
Wiskochil, Robert I.
Wolfe, Clarence Eugene
Wolney, George James
Wood, Ivan S.
Woods, Chester J.
Woodward, Theodore H.

Wright, Johnalson E.
Wynne, Marion L.
Zarlenga, Joseph D.

Zellay, George P.
Zivko, Stephen M.
Zurchauer, Robert Jr.

BIBLIOGRAPHY

Abraham, Theodore A., Jr. *Do You Understand, Huh? A POW's Lament,
    1941–1945.* Manhattan, KS: Sunflower University Press, 1992.
Alexander, Colonel Joseph. *The Battle History of the U.S. Marines: A Fellowship
    of Valor.* New York: Harper Perennial. The History Channel, 1999.
American Ex-POW Inc. *The Japanese Story.* Marshfield, WI: National Medical
    Research Committee, 1980.
Astarita, Joseph. *Sketches of POW Life.* Brooklyn, NY: Rollo Press, 1947.
Bayler, L. J. *Last Man off Wake Island.* New York: Bobbs Merrill, 1943.
Cohen, Stan. *Enemy on Island—Issue in Doubt: The Capture of Wake Island,
    December 1941.* Missoula, MT: Pictorial Histories Publishing, 1983.
Condon, Don. *Combat World War II: Pacific Theater of Operations.* New York:
    Arbor House, 1983.
Cressman, Robert J. *A Magnificent Fight: The Battle for Wake Island.* Annapolis,
    MD: Naval Institute Press, 1995.
———. *The Official Chronology of the U.S. Navy in World War II.* Annapolis,
    MD: Naval Institute Press, 2000.
Cunningham, Winfield Scott. *Wake Island Command.* Boston: Little, Brown,
    1961.
Darden, James B. III. *Guests of the Emperor: The Story of Dick Darden.*
    Clinton, NC: Greenhouse Press, 1990.

Daws, Gavan. *Prisoners of the Japanese: POWs of World War II in the Pacific.* New York: William Morrow and Company, 1944.

Devereux, Colonel James P. S. *The Story of Wake Island.* New York: J. P. Lippincott Company, 1947.

Graybar, Lloyd. "American Pacific Strategy After Pearl Harbor: The Relief of Wake Island." *Prologue,* 12 (fall 1980), 56–72.

Heinl, Robert D. *The Defense of Wake.* Washington, DC: U.S. Marine Corps Historical Section, 1947.

Hill, Richard Vernon. *My War with Imperial Japan: Escape and Evasion.* New York: Vantage Press, 1990.

Holmes, Linda Goetz. *Unjust Enrichment: How Japan's Companies Built Postwar Fortresses Using American POWs.* Mechanicsburg, PA: Stackpole Books, 2001.

Kessler, Woodrow M. *To Wake Island and Beyond: Reminiscences.* Washington, DC: U.S. Marine Corps History Division, 1988.

Kinney, Brigadier General John F., USMC, retired. *Wake Island Pilot: A World War II Memoir.* Dulles, VA: Brassey's, 1995.

Landreth, Don Tomas. *Avail the Time: Prison Tales 1941–1945.* Calgary, Alberta: Thief Zone Publishing, 2000.

Lord Russell of Liverpool. *Knights of Bushido: The Shocking History of Japanese War Atrocities.* New York: E. P. Dutton, 1958.

Mace, Frank. "The Story of Wake Island: Before, During and After Life as a Prisoner of War of the Japanese." Pamphlet, 1981.

McBrayer, James D., Jr. *Escape: Memoir of a World War II Marine Who Broke out of a Japanese POW Camp and Linked up with Chinese Communist Guerrillas.* Jefferson, NC: McFarland Publishing, 1994.

Miller, Nathal. *War At Sea: A Naval History of World War II.* New York: Scribner, 1995.

Mulkins, Wayman. *The 1942 Issue in Doubt.* Austin, TX: Eakin Press, 1944. *The Pacific Campaign.* New York: Time-Life Books, 1977.

Perrett, Byran. "Last Stand! Famous Battles Against the Odds." *Arms and Armour,* 1991.

Price, M. R. "The Race For Wake Island." *U.S. Army Military Review,* May–June 2000.

Reynolds, Quentin. *Officially Dead: The Story of Commander C. D. Smith, U.S.N.* New York: Random House, 1945.

Schultz, Duane. *Wake Island: The Heroic Gallant Fight.* New York: St. Martin's Press, 1978.

Smith, S. E. *The U.S. Navy in WW II.* New York: William Morrow, 1966.

Sommers, Stan. *The Japanese Story.* Marshfield, WI: American Ex-POW Inc.,
    National Medical Research Committee, 1980.
Spennemann, H. R. *To Hell and Back: Wake Island During and After WW II.*
Urwin, Gregory. *A Siege of Wake Island: Facing Fearful Odds.* Lincoln, NE:
    University of Nebraska Press, 1997.
Werstein, Irving. *Wake: The Story of a Battle.* New York: Thomas Y. Crowell
    Company, 1964.
Wheeler, Richard. *A Special Valor: The U.S. Marines and the Pacific War.* New
    York: Harper and Row, 1983.
Wake Island Wig Wag. Newsletter. Independence, MO: Defenders of Wake
    Island Association, 2002.
Young, Donald J. *First 24 Hours of War in the Pacific.* Shippensburg, PA: Burd
    Street Press. 1998.

INDEX